中国古典文学英译丛书

咏情言志

历代著名诗词曲赋英译鉴赏

卓振英 编著

Songs of Weal and Woe

Annotated Chinese Poetry Oft-Quoted through the Ages

创于1897　The Commercial Press

图书在版编目(CIP)数据

咏情言志:历代著名诗词曲赋英译鉴赏:汉、英/
卓振英编著.—北京:商务印书馆,2023
(中国古典文学英译丛书)
ISBN 978-7-100-21941-9

Ⅰ.①咏… Ⅱ.①卓… Ⅲ.①汉语—英语—对照
读物 ②古典诗歌—诗歌欣赏—中国 Ⅳ.①H319.4:
I207.227.2

中国版本图书馆 CIP 数据核字(2022)第 255982 号

中国古典文学英译丛书
咏情言志
历代著名诗词曲赋英译鉴赏
卓振英 编著

商 务 印 书 馆 出 版
(北京王府井大街36号 邮政编码100710)
商 务 印 书 馆 发 行
北京市十月印刷有限公司印刷
ISBN 978-7-100-21941-9

2023 年 4 月第 1 版 开本 880×1240 1/32
2023 年 4 月北京第 1 次印刷 印张 20⅝

定价:138.00 元

Dedicated to the Sacred Cause of World Peace

About the Author

Zhuo Zhenying is the chief professor of the Research Centre for the Studies on Classics Translation at Home and Abroad, Zhejiang Normal University. As a leading figure in the field of studies on the translation of classics, he has initiated the establishment of the National Association of Classics Translation Studies, developed the theory of the poetic paradigm governing the related area, and published some books and research papers. Positions he has  held include Director of Research Centre for the Translation of Classics, Shantou University (STU), member of the STU Academic Committee, Vice-chairman of the National Association of Studies on Classics Translation, member of the Standing Council of China Association for the Comparative Studies of English and Chinese (CACSEC), Co-chairman of CACSEC Disciplinary Committee of Classics Translation, Honorary Member of CACSEC Executive Council, and Adviser to the CACSEC Sub-committee of Classics Translation.

目　录
Contents

Songs of Weal and Woe

Chapter Two　Poetry of the Han Dynasty

咏情言志

2

Chapter Three　Poetry of the Three Kingdoms, the Jin Dynasty and the Southern and Northern Dynasties

Chapter Four　Poetry of the Sui and the Tang Dynasties

5

Songs of Weal and Woe

Chapter Five　Poetry of the Song Dynasty

Songs of Weal and Woe

咏情言志

10

11

Songs of Weal and Woe

咏
情
言
志

12

13

Songs of Weal and Woe

Chapter Six   Poetry of the Liao, the Jin and the Yuan Dynasties

Chapter Seven   Poetry of the Ming Dynasty

Chapter Eight　　Poetry of the Qing Dynasty

17

Songs of Weal and Woe

A Poem Composed on Board the Ship　Qiu Jin

咏情言志

18

Preface

"Poetry is the expression of the inner self," says The *Book of Antiquity*(《尚书》). It may evoke feelings, inspire ideas, reflect the reality, cultivate fellowship or to slash on the wrong and the vicious, as is furthered by Confucius (551 BC−479 BC) in *The Analects*. Capable of sublimating the soul, it may facilitate the ascent to "the zenith of benevolence," an ideological realm likened to water which "purports to favour all life without vying for any self-interest" (Laocius, c.571 BC−c.471 BC). On a keynote similar to that idea H.W. Longfellow (1807 AD−1882 AD) chants beyond the Pacific:

> "God sent his Singers upon earth
> With songs of sadness and of mirth,
> That they might touch the hearts of men,
> And bring them back to heaven again." (The Singers)

We may still venture to add that, psychically speaking, poetry helps to maintain mental sanity, etc. As sure as fate, poetry is multifunctional.

As a great cultural heritage of all mankind, the poetry left behind by the oriental muses reflect the values, sentiments and, in the final analysis, the national character of the Chinese. It is national, in which lies what's universal.

It's a pity that the absorption of the nutritious Chinese poetry is hindered by language and cultural barriers on the part of non-Chinese-speaking people, and the translation of Chinese verse is a real challenge. Notwithstanding that, Chinese and foreign scholars have made laudable efforts since the eighteenth century, though there is still much to be desired in the translations by and large.

Perhaps the imagery of Chinese poetry can be reconstructed in English without diminishing the wonderful aesthetics of the original? Perhaps something more can be perceived and achieved by standing on the shoulders of the giants before us? The answers could be in the affirmative, provided that we make assiduous attempts.

The present booklet is supposed to be one of such attempts. It includes around 200 pieces of poetry through the ages (1100 BC–1910 AD), which have been established as classics. The ancient-style poems, metrical poems, *ci*-poems, *fu*-poems, dramatic songs, song-poems and folk songs fall into eight chronologically-arranged chapters, each chapter (or part) opening with Introductory Remarks about the historical background, the schools of poetry, the artistic features, the philosophy, the customs and the cultural drifts in question, etc. The English version of each poem is preceded by the original and followed by the Notes and Commentary, which give prominence to the analyses and appreciation of the sentiments and thoughts expressed therein. As an earnest practice of the theory of the poetic paradigm majorly developed in *A Theoretical Outline of Chinese Verse Translation*, the booklet purports to obtain the maximum approximation of the emotional, ideological and stylistic beauty in the originals.

The Tower of Babel can be constructed only when men, who are scattered all over the world, have built up a perfect understanding among themselves. May this booklet offer itself as a little and yet useful brick for the construction of the Babel.

Zhuo Zhenying

College of Foreign Languages,

Zhejiang Normal University

March 12, 2020

3

Songs of Weal and Woe

Chapter One   Pre-Qin Poetry

Part I *The Book of Poetry*

Introductory Remarks

Humanism, from which have branched out such concepts as of charity, fraternity, filial piety, benevolent governance, harmonious co-existence with nature, etc., is deep-rooted in Chinese philosophy. As early as around 1100 BC, Yu Xiong (鬻熊), known as the earliest Daoist, had preached that "It is concordant to the Ultimate Truth if policies and laws are promulgated for the welfare and livelihood of the populace." (ref. Zhuo Zhenying, An Anthology of Yue Songs Ancient and Modern, 2018: 4) And we can find records of laws and regulations about ecosystem protection in *History as a Mirror for Governance* (《资治通鉴》) and other classics.

The Western Zhou period (1100 BC−771 BC) of the Zhou Dynasty (1100 BC−221 BC) saw the prime of the serf system in China. The system in lieu of slavery had readjusted the class relations, and the idea that government of Zhou was the "Mandate of Heaven" had been inductive, on the part of the rulers, to exacting obedience from the subjects. Territory was vast, land was fertile, and the Nine-Square System of land ownership had, to a great extent, stimulated agricultural productivity. Prompted by the new technology of bronze manufacture, handicraft had gathered momentum. In terms of culture, Chinese characters, which facilitated writing, had reached maturity. All these factors combined were bound to call forth monumental works.

The Book of Poetry, for one, bespeaks the splendour of literature. As a rule, professionals were regularly dispatched by the royal court to collect grass roots' opinions expressed in the folk songs, which were studied and taken for reference in the formulation or adjustment of policies. When he was appointed Grand Master (who was in charge of music and poetry) of the dynasty, Yin Jifu (尹吉甫，852 BC–775 BC) began to champion the compilation of poems. Later on Confucius brought out his own edition of *The Book of Poetry*, which consists of 305 poems (excluding 6 ones without extant texts). The poems fall into three categories: 160 folk songs of fifteen states, 105 poems set to refined (or: orthodox) music, and 40 hymns dedicated to the ancestors.

Those poems, mostly rhymed and of tetrasyllabic lines, give a panorama of Chinese society between 1100 BC and 600 BC by means of narration, repetition, associative opening and figures of speech:

In the ever-changing pageant of such crops as wheat, rice, millet, soya beans, jute and sorghum, the haggard slaves are singing the eternal theme of sorrow over their sufferings and hatred against "the giant rats" (硕鼠) — the lords who have deprived them of their freedom and fruit of labor. Somewhere a maiden is singing a song of sincere love to the soul of her heart in spite of the shackles on the freedom of marriage; In the air is resounding the song of friendship, advocating the concept of "huge reward in return for tiny kindness"; Driven to the battle-field to meet the invading nomads, a man with a weather-beaten face begins to hum a low-keyed tune to express his deep concern for his aged parents at home, only to find a ready echo among his fellow soldiers.

Life of the idle aristocrats constitutes a poignant contrast to the wretchedness of the slaves. At one of the magnificent temples located in the capital Hao, the royalty are offering sacrifices. Chanting and dancing to the resounding music they pray for stability, prosperity and what not, and cherish the memory of their ancestors, among whom are Qi — the god of agriculture, and King Wu, who had overthrown the Shang Dynasty and founded the Zhou Dynasty; For pleasure as well as for political coalition the powerful lords go on sprees; Far into the night, a grand banquet is still going on at the hall of a magnificent mansion. Some sober guests are chatting, picking at the delicacies or sipping at their cups of jade, whereas others are at war with the plates or dancing girls; The dissipated Duke Ling of Chen is seen riding in a carriage and four to meet the wife of one of his senior officials.

The lower stratum of the aristocracy, however, are indignant and sarcastic. They lament the injustice, protest against invented charges, appeal for justice, denounce the tyrannies and express their sympathy for the slaves, who live under inhuman treatment.

The Book of Poetry is one of the most important sources of Chinese culture. For approximately 3,000 years it has been quoted and re-quoted to educate the ignorant, to convince the dubious, to console the unfortunate, to expose the evil and to eulogize the virtuous, or to imply ideas on diplomatic occasions, etc. Many ideas embodied in it — for instance, honesty, fidelity, filial piety and love of peace — have become accepted values. It has had a tremendous impact on the Chinese language and on the development of Chinese literature. It has also reflected the social life and natural phenomena of the period in question. With its unfathomable cultural and artistic values *The Book of Poetry* will forever shine.

1. 关雎

无名氏

关关雎鸠，
在河之洲。
窈窕淑女，
君子好逑。

参差荇菜，
左右流之。
窈窕淑女，
寤寐求之。
求之不得，
寤寐思服。
悠哉悠哉，
辗转反侧。

参差荇菜，
左右采之。
窈窕淑女，
琴瑟友之。
参差荇菜，

The Ospreys in Tune[1]

Anonymous

Coo![2] Coo! One osprey calls[3], the other does reply
On the islet in the river pleasant to th' eye.
The maiden nice and fair will evidently knit
With th' man of virtue an ideal conjugal tie.

Being dredged up, now from the right, now from the left,
Are the floating hearts[4] varied in length in the stream.
I love, nay, I adore the maiden fair and deft,
Be I sober-minded or at night in a dream.
My affections so far being without return,
This earnest heart of mine with keen longing does burn.
Love-sickness lingering in the mind in the course
Of long long nights, I lie awake and toss and turn!

Being gathered, now from the left, now from the right,
Are the floating hearts varied in length in the stream.
Let the *qin*[5] be played and th' *se*[6] be plucked so as
To befriend the maiden who's worthy of esteem!
The floating hearts, varied in length, are being chosen

左右芼之。
窈窕淑女，
钟鼓乐之。

Intensively now from the left, now from the right.

Let the drum be beaten and let the bell be chimed

So that the maiden virtuous I may delight.

2. 伐檀

无名氏

坎坎伐檀兮，
寘之河之干兮，
河水清且涟猗。
不稼不穑，
胡取禾三百廛兮？
不狩不猎，
胡瞻尔庭有县貆兮？
彼君子兮，
不素餐兮！

坎坎伐辐兮，
寘之河之侧兮，
河水清且直猗。
不稼不穑，
胡取禾三百亿兮？
不狩不猎，
胡瞻尔庭有县特兮？
彼君子兮，
不素食兮！

Felling Sandalwood Trees[1]

Anonymous

Thud[2], thud! Sandalwood trees we fell

And to th' riverside we propel.[3]

Th' river with ripples is clear, ho![4]

He ne'er reaped, never did he sow,

Why does he own three hundred[5] bunches of crop, though?

He never trapped, ne'er did he hunt,

Why at his courtyard are seen many badgers hung?

Lo, a "descent noble" is he,

And plunderer he might not be!

Thud, thud! For spokes lumber we cut[6],

Which then to th' river's bank we tug.

The river with waves is limpid!

Sowing and reaping he ne'er did,

Why does he take bundles of crop by the hundred?

No trapper and hunter he's been,

Why then in his courtyard lots of big game are seen?

Lo, a "descent noble" is he,

And parasite he might not be!

坎坎伐轮兮,
寘之河之漘兮,
河水清且沦猗。
不稼不穑,
胡取禾三百囷兮?
不狩不猎,
胡瞻尔庭有县鹑兮?
彼君子兮,
不素飧兮!

Thud, thud! We fell trees to wheels make,

Which then to th' river-mouth we'll take.

Th' river with whirlpools is so clean!

Sowing and reaping he's ne'er seen,

In hold of countless bales of crop why has he been?

Of game he's never gone on th' trail,

Why in his courtyard are hanging so many quail?

Lo, a "descent noble" is he,

And exploiter he might not be!

3. 伐木（节选）

无名氏

伐木丁丁，
鸟鸣嘤嘤。
出自幽谷，
迁于乔木。
嘤其鸣矣，
求其友声。
相彼鸟矣，
犹求友声。
矧伊人矣，
不求友生？
神之听之，
终和且平。

Cutting Wood (an excerpt) [1]

Anonymous

Thud, thud! The sound of cutting wood is heard;

Tweet, tweet! Much alarmed is many a bird,

Which together from the deep deep dale flee

To perch on a lofty and secure tree.

The birds chirp and sing with a purpose clear:

To cultivate a fellowship sincere.

Lo, e'en the little birds earnestly seek

Goodwill, whose value itself does bespeak[2],

Let alone we humans, whose life depends,

To a great extent, on the help of friends.

It is to the good intent that we cling;

Peace and order to us may our gods[3] bring.

4.采薇（节选）

无名氏

昔我往矣，
杨柳依依。
今我来思，
雨雪霏霏。
行道迟迟，
载渴载饥。
我心伤悲，
莫知我哀。

咏情言志

20

Gathering Ferns (an excerpt) [1]

Anonymous

My native willows green and gay

Did wave me farewell in the past;

Now that I'm on my home-bound way,

The sleet is falling thick and fast.

Stricken with both hunger and thirst,

I'm staggering at a pace slow;

And worst of all, my heart does burst

With such sorrow as none could know![2]

5. 小旻（节选）

无名氏

不敢暴虎，
不敢冯河。
人知其一，
莫知其他。
战战兢兢，
如临深渊，
如履薄冰。

Petty Heaven (an excerpt) [1]

Anonymous

Without adequate means nobody dare

Attempt a beast or a stream, for life's dear. [2]

Of obvious dangers men are aware,

But 'bout the latent perils few are clear, [3]

Which strike into your honest heart such fear

That of facing an abyss you'll feel th' dread,

Or as if th' ice would crack under your tread. [4]

Part II *Folk Songs*

Introductory Remarks

Thousands of years ago, there lived in the vast areas south to the Qinling Mountains and the Huai River a multitude of tribes, which are termed "Multitude of Yues" (百越). In the course of cultural exchanges and historical developments, the Yue culture has converged with the Central Plain culture (中原文化), the Jing-Chu culture (荆楚文化), the Dongyi culture (东夷文化) and the Northern culture (北方文化).

The heroic and industrious people of the south, from the great sages and philosophers to the rank and file, have lent incomparable charm and glory to the profound and magnificent Chinese culture. As the cultural heritage of all the mankind, the vivacious songs of Yue, passed on from generation to generation, reflect the customs, beliefs, philosophy, literature, social reality and cultural drifts of the south.

The Yue songs boast of their own glamour and characteristics: the employment of supplementary words and clauses; freedom in form and sentence patterns in spite of the metrical regulations; natural ease and primitive simplicity in style. Included in this part are just a few flowers from the garden of Yue songs.

6. 弹歌

无名氏

断竹，
续竹；
飞土，
逐宾。

Song of the Catapult[1]

Anonymous

Bend a measure of trim bamboo,

And fasten its ends with a string;

You'll get game for a roast or stew[2]

If a stone at the chase you sling.

7. 禹上会稽

姒禹（大禹）

呜呼，洪水滔天，
下民愁悲，
上帝愈咨！
三过吾门不入，
父子道衰。
嗟嗟，不欲烦下民！

A Song Chanted Atop Mount Kuaiji[1]

Si Yu (Yu the Great) [2]

Alas, th' devouring floods are surging up to th' skies,

Driving the rank and file to absolute despair!

More wrathful than e'er, Heaven seems deaf to their cries!

Not that about family duty I don't care —

Oh, I've thrice passed by home without entering it —

But that with th' folk weal and woe I resolve to share![3]

8. 越人歌

无名氏

咏情言志

30

今夕何夕兮，
搴舟中流；
今日何日兮，
得与王子同舟！
蒙羞被好兮，
不訾诟耻，
心几烦而不绝兮，
得知王子！
山有木兮木有枝，
心悦君兮君不知。

The Yue's Song[1]

Anonymous

Oh, what a special night tonight,

Which witnesses this midstream float!

Oh, what a special date today,

When I'm graced to share with th' prince th' same boat! [2]

Shy as I am, I'd boldly admit my love!

And what if people should snort and sneer?

Ah, affections wells up in my heart,

Affections which are keen and sincere!

Oh, th' tree clings to th' mount, and th' branch embraces the
   tree;[3]

I love Your Highness, but Your Highness o'erlook me!

31

9. 越人土风歌

无名氏

其山崔巍以嵯峨，
其水溢溷而扬波，
其人仚砢而英多！

The Yues' Song of Their Own Mores[1]

Anonymous

Our mounts soar up from th' ground;

Our rivers surge along and pound!

Men are sturdy, and th' wise abound!

Part III *The Verse of Chu*

Introductory Remarks

The Spring-and-Autumn (770 BC−476 BC) and Warring States (475 BC−221 BC) periods, the infancy of feudalism, or the Axial Age in the words of Karl Jaspers (1883 AD−1969 AD), had witnessed the boost of productivity owing to the popularization of ironware and cattle in tillage, the prosperity of science and technology (e.g. astronomy, medicine, mathematics, the technology of iron smelting, etc.), the political and economic reforms in various states and the warfare for predominance among the states, and the unprecedented cultural prosperity prompted by the ideological contention, which had involved 189 schools of thought (the Daoist, Confucianist, Mozist and Legalist schools being the prominent ones) and produced 4,324 works according to "Records of Literature and Art" in *The Chronicles Compiled in the Han Dynasty* (《汉书·艺文志》).

In literature, *The Verse of Chu* has broadened the poetic spectrum. Like *The Book of Poetry*, it is one of the sources of Chinese poetry and, in a broad sense, of Chinese culture. The sixteen-volume edition compiled by Liu Xiang of the Western Han Dynasty, which had included not only the poems composed by Qu Yuan and Song Yu, but also those written by Jia Yi, Dongfang Shuo, Wang Bao and others of the Han Dynasty, has already been lost. The earliest edition extant today is *The Verse of Chu* with Notes and Commentary compiled by Wang Yi of the Eastern Han Dynasty, which supplies us with information about the sixteen-volume edition and rather detailed textual interpretations. In the

Southern Song Dynasty, Hong Xingzu compiled *The Verse of Chu* with supplementary Notes and Commentary on the basis of *The Verse of Chu* with Notes and Commentary, and Zhu Xi put out his *Variorum of the Verse of Chu*. In the Qing Dynasty, Wang Fuzhi and Jiang Ji respectively published *The Verse of Chu with Verified Explanations* and *the Shandai Pavillion Edition of the Verse of Chu*. Besides, modern and contemporary scholars have also published valuable works on *The Verse of Chu*.

The works of the representative Qu Yuan are imbued with the spirit of active romanticism. The poet subtly merges the pursuit of the ideal with artistic imagination and mystical conception. For example, "Tales of Woe" describes how he, having talked to Chonghua, rides on the gale and seek for the Beauty (which embodies the genuine, benevolent and beautiful) up hill and down dale, during which he meets with not a few frustrations and disappointments (e.g. his encounter with Fufei the Nymph, who turns out to be slick) ; "The Voyage" narrates how he ascends Mount Kunlun, dines on jasper, and tour the Jade Garden with Chonghua. Besides, he employs mythology and legends as subject matter in the composition of such poems as "The Nine Hymns", "Inquiries into the Universe" , "The Pilgrimage" and "Making Choices through Divination" , etc. His soaring imagination is unique in history.

Qu Yuan's works are eloquent and rich in local color. In form, they are full of variety, for the poet writes with a easy and free style; and in language, they exude with literary grace, as they are tinctured with the refined vernacular expressions of Chu. In a succinct style Qu Yuan takes advantage of figures of speech to express his sentiments. He uses the Beauty and the Flowers to symbolize "Good Government" and people of moral integrity while likening the crafty and evil to the thorny shrubs and harmful weeds, thus making a sharp contrast between the true, good, beautiful and the sham, evil and hideous.

The Verse of Chu, having broken through the forms of expression of *The Book of Poetry,* has enhanced the expressiveness of poetry and produced a great impact on the formation of *fu*-poetry (a literary form of descriptive prose interspersed with verse) of the Han Dynasty, and has opened up a new horizon for the development of Chinese poetry. No wonder that *The Verse of Chu* has enjoyed an increasing popularity in the world.

10. 橘颂

屈原

后皇嘉树，
橘徕服兮。
受命不迁，
生南国兮。
深固难徙，
更壹志兮。
绿叶素荣，
纷其可喜兮。
曾枝剡棘，
圆果抟兮。
青黄杂糅，
文章烂兮。
精色内白，
类任道兮。
纷缊宜修，
姱而不丑兮。

嗟尔幼志，
有以异兮。
独立不迁，

Ode to the Orange Tree[1]

Qu Yuan[2]

Oh, under th' sky and on the earth

Your solemn existence you claim.

You live in th' south with joy and mirth,

Adhering firmly to your aim.

Deep-rooted and distraction-tight,

You defy attempts to you sway.

What with leaves green and flowers white,

You're gloriously lush and gay.

Oh, your branches dotted with many a prick,

What golden fruits you bear!

Having as a foil the leaves thick,

You present a splendid charm to share.

The outside pure and th' inside white,

Justice you signal to embrace.

Luxuriant and shaped right,

You brim with unusual grace.

Hail orange! Though young you aim high;

Distinctive are your features fine.

You're firm and on yourself rely,

岂不可喜兮？
深固难徙，
廓其无求兮。
苏世独立，
横而不流兮。
闭心自慎，
终不失过兮。
秉德无私，
参天地兮。
愿岁并谢，
与长友兮。
淑离不淫，
梗其有理兮。
年岁虽少，
可师长兮。
行比伯夷，
置以为像兮。

Showing such qualities as shine!

Deep-rooted and distraction-proof,

You have a broad mind from vice free.

Sane and from worldly thoughts aloof,

You never drift with th' tide in th' sea.

Prudently yourself you restrain,

And to avoid mistakes your best you try.

Detached from private loss or gain,

You're as noble as the Earth and the Sky.

I wish to be your life-long friend,

And stay with you each night and day.

Unwavering despite the trend,

You stand upright in fine array.

Oh, though you are tender in age,

A worthy tutor you can be.

As virtuous as Boyi[3] th' sage,

You're the right paragon to me!

11. 离骚（节选）

屈原

驷玉虬以乘鹥兮，
溘埃风余上征。
朝发轫于苍梧兮，
夕余至乎县圃。
欲少留此灵琐兮，
日忽忽其将暮。
吾令羲和弭节兮，
望崦嵫而勿迫。
路曼曼其修远兮，
吾将上下而求索。

Tales of Woe (an excerpt)[1]

Qu Yuan

Towards the sky, riding on a dust-raising gale,

My phoenix carriage[2] and four draught dragons does sail!

The brake was taken off at dawn in Mount Cangwu[3],

And I arrive in the evening at Mount Xuanpu[4].

Around the holy gate I wish awhile to stay,

But lo, the sun's to end his journey of the day!

With Yanzi in sight, the sun may as well his time take;

And thus I motion Xi He[5] to ride on the brake.

Long long is th' way, but my efforts nothing'll arrest;

Up hill and down dale for the Beauty I shall quest![6]

12. 涉江

屈原

余幼好此奇服兮，
年既老而不衰。
带长铗之陆离兮，
冠切云之崔嵬，
被明月兮佩宝璐。
世混浊而莫余知兮，
吾方高驰而不顾。
驾青虬兮骖白螭，
吾与重华游兮瑶之圃。
登昆仑兮食玉英，
与天地兮同寿，
与日月兮同光。
哀南夷之莫吾知兮，
旦余济乎江湘。

The Voyage[1]

Qu Yuan

Canto I

For this unique attire my love's been keen and strong,

Which still remains unchanged e'en when I am now old.

The sheath to my endeared saber is mottled and long;

My Cloud-Touching Hat bears a grandeur that's untold.

For a perfect entity Moon Pearls brightly glow,

And my jadeite pendant is pleasant to the eye.

The confounded world, however, does not me know,

And hence without regret I shall go far and high!

Th' dragons green and white escort me to Mount Kunlun[2], where

I join Chonghua in the tour of the Jade Garden. We dine

Upon the ruby flowers, thus eternity we share

With Earth and Heaven, and like th' stars we shine!

O'er th' fact that I'm not understood in th' nescient south I

mourn,

Thus I'll start my voyage along th' Yangtze and th' Xiang at

dawn!

Songs of Weal and Woe

乘鄂渚而反顾兮,
欸秋冬之绪风。
步余马兮山皋,
邸余车兮方林。
乘舲船余上沅兮,
齐吴榜以击汰。
船容与而不进兮,
淹回水而疑滞。
朝发枉渚兮,
夕宿辰阳。
苟余心其端直兮,
虽僻远之何伤。

入溆浦余儃徊兮,
迷不知吾所如。
深林杳以冥冥兮,
猿狖之所居。
山峻高以蔽日兮,
下幽晦以多雨。

Canto II

Ashore on th' Ezhu Isle[3] I look back at th' endear'd place,

And sigh over receding winter's biting blast.

My horses at the foot of th' hill walk at a sluggish pace,

My carriage, howe'er, arrives at Fanglin[4] at last.

Against the surges of the Yuan River I sail upstream,

The oars of Wu applied in chorus so as th' waves to cleave;

Howe'er reluctant to advance my windowed boat does seem,

And 'midst the whirling pools little headway does it achieve.

At dawn my embarkation Wangzhu does see,

In th' eve I reach Chenyang, where I spend the night.

So long as I uphold my morality, nothing to me

Matters — e'en banishment that's reduced me to such a plight!

Canto III

I enter Xupu, where I wander 'bout,

Bewildered as to where I ought to go.

The deep and gloomy woods can be made out

To be the homes of apes, as the signs show.

Th' sun is hidden by many a perilous peak,

The sky's o'ercast with dark clouds which are hanging low.

Songs of Weal and Woe

霰雪纷其无垠兮，
云霏霏而承宇。
哀吾生之无乐兮，
幽独处乎山中。
吾不能变心而从俗兮，
固将愁苦而终穷。

接舆髡首兮，
桑扈裸行。
忠不必用兮，
贤不必以。
伍子逢殃兮，
比干菹醢。
与前世而皆然兮，
吾又何怨乎今之人！
余将董道而不豫兮，
固将重昏而终身！

乱曰：
鸾鸟凤皇，
日以远兮。
燕雀乌鹊，

The weather rainy, the place is awfully bleak,

And at times the world is permeated with snow.

Oh, what a life denied of happiness!

Solitude in deep mounts I'm now to know.[5]

Unwilling to conform to worldliness,

I'm bound to suffer lifelong plight and woe.

Canto IV

Jieyu protested with his head shaved, [6] and sure

Enough Sanghu[7] had stridden about nakedly.

Appointments loyalty can never ensure,

And for promotion wisdom is no warranty.

Wu Zixu[8] shed his blood, and Bi Gan[9] was slain.

Such cases are not rare in history.

About today's pretty state of affairs

What's the need for me to complain?

I shall uphold the truth resolutely,

Though doomed to face a life of endless cares.

Finale

The phoenixes are flying farther day by day,

While crows and sparrows in th' court and hall do stay.

The Winter Daphne and Lily Magnolias die

巢堂坛兮。
露申辛夷，
死林薄兮。
腥臊并御，
芳不得薄兮。
阴阳易位，
时不当兮。
怀信佗傺，
忽乎吾将行兮！

咏情言志

50

Where weeds and thorny plants are growing thick and high.

When what is smelly is regarded as so dear,

How can the fragrant be permitted to come near?

The positive and the negative have been reversed,

And absurd are the times, which deserves being cursed.

When loyalty has brought blight, what have I to say?

The soonest I shall go, and go far far away!

13. 国殇

屈原

操吴戈兮披犀甲,
车错毂兮短兵接。
旌蔽日兮敌若云,
矢交坠兮士争先。
凌余阵兮躐余行,
左骖殪兮右刃伤。
霾两轮兮絷四马,
援玉枹兮击鸣鼓。
天时怼兮威灵怒,
严杀尽兮弃原野。
出不入兮往不反,
平原忽兮路超远。
带长剑兮挟秦弓,
首身离兮心不惩。

咏情言志

52

Eulogy on the Martyrs of the State[1]

Qu Yuan

(Sing in Chorus the Soldiers Incarnate:) [2]

Clad in rhino armor, dagger-axes we wield;

Th' chariots clashing, at the foes we bravely tear.

Th' banners hiding th' sun, the foes surge like clouds in th' field,

Yet we charge ahead despite flitting arrows in th' air.

(Sing the Warrior Incarnate:)

Our lines broken through, our ranks are in disarray;

My left-side steed's killed, and th' right side one's crippled become.

The reins are entangled, and bogged down two wheels stay;

I raise high the stick of jade, though, and beat the signal drum.

Fierce battles over, littered with corpses is now the plain;

It seems that Heaven were falling because of wrath and pain,

(Sing the Warrior and the Soldiers Incarnate:)

We set out resolved not to return but die

A heroic death in the remote battle field.

Our heads chopped off, without the least regret we lie.

Th' Qin bows[3] are clenched tight, and th' sabers we still seem to wield!

诚既勇兮又以武，
终刚强兮不可凌。
身既死兮神以灵，
魂魄毅兮为鬼雄。

礼魂

成礼兮会鼓，
传芭兮代舞；
姱女倡兮容与。
春兰兮秋菊，
长无绝兮终古。

(Sing the Populace Incarnate:)

Oh, devoted and valiant souls of the state,

Indomitable, a lofty realm you attain!

Your are slain, but with glory will shine your deeds great,

And souls of all souls you shall forever remain!

Epilogue *(Sing the Populace Incarnate:)*

Th' rites performed, majestic th' drums sound

And melodious th' belles chant. To pay

Homage we dance in turn and pass round

The posy. Orchids in spring we'll lay

And mums in fall for e'er and aye.[4]

55

Songs of Weal and Woe

14. 渔父

屈原

屈原既放，游於江潭，行吟泽畔；
颜色憔悴，形容枯槁。
渔父见而问之曰："子非三闾大夫与？
何故至於斯！"屈原曰："举世皆浊我独清，
众人皆醉我独醒，是以见放！"
渔父曰："圣人不凝滞於物，而能与世推移。
世人皆浊，何不淈其泥而扬其波？
众人皆醉，何不餔其糟而歠其醨？
何故深思高举，自令放为？"
屈原曰："吾闻之，新沐者必弹冠，
新浴者必振衣；
安能以身之察察，受物之汶汶者乎！
宁赴湘流，葬於江鱼之腹中。
安能以皓皓之白，而蒙世俗之尘埃乎！"

A Dialogue with the Fisherman[1]

Qu Yuan

Qu Yuan strolls along the riverside, humming a tale

Of woe. Being in exile he looks haggard and pale.

"Could you be the Lord of the Three Clans, sir? "[2] at his sight

A fisherman asks, "What's reduced you to such a plight?"

Qu Yuan replies: "I'm banished 'cause into vice th' world's sunk

While I am pure, and I'm sober when th' public is drunk."

The fisherman remarks: "A wise man is not confined

To concepts, and to adapt to the times he's inclined.

Since the whole world is, as you say, filthy out and out,

Wherefore don't you in the mire splash and wallow and rout?

Now that people around are already mellow with drink,

Why then from wine and the distiller's grains do you shrink?

And to profound thoughts and lofty ideals why have you stuck,

which has consequently incurred so tough a luck?"

"As the saying goes," Qu Yuan retorts, "One shakes his clothes

And dusts his cap after bath to rid the dirt he loathes.

How can I, honest and pure and from corruption free,

Allow the external world to contaminate me?

The filth of th' corrupt world beyond what I can endure,

In the Xiang River I might as well drown this self pure."

57

Songs of Weal and Woe

渔父莞尔而笑，鼓枻而去，
乃歌曰：

　"沧浪之水清兮，可以濯吾缨。

　沧浪之水浊兮，可以濯吾足。"

遂去，不复与言。

The fisherman, with a faint smile, paddles away,

Humming a ballad to express what he has to say:

  "When the Canglang River is clear,

  I can wash my tassels and gear;

  Even when turbid the stream grows,

  I can yet rinse my feet and toes." [3]

注释　Notes and Commentary

1. 关雎　The Ospreys in Tune

1 "The Ospreys in Tune" — a love song which relates a young man's ardent admiration for a fair and virtuous maiden, is the first poem in *The Book of Poetry*. The opening stanza associates the harmonious cooing of a pair of ospreys to the man's affection for the maiden, whom he deems an ideal life-partner-to-be. The second and third stanzas narrate how he yearns for her love day and night and, when his love is yet unrequited, how he suffers insomnia. The last two stanzas tell how he is determined to approach her and win her love by means of fine music.

　　The first two lines of the second stanza, which narrate the collection of the floating hearts, are repeated with a change in the use of verbs (all being monosyllabic in the original) in the fourth and fifth stanzas. This may serve to convey a manifold connotation — the connotation that the water plant is symbolic of love, that the man's pursuit of the maiden is seriously sincere and that the maiden is industrious. Confucius points out that this poem is decently pleasant, i.e. joyous without the slightest obscenity. Other critics remark that this poem touches the fundamental issue of ethics — the relation between man and woman. These comments at least partly explain why this poem has enjoyed extensive popularity.

2 Coo! — This is a case of onomatopoeia denoting the utterance of ospreys.

3 One osprey calls — the osprey is believed to be a bird of fidelity, which will voluntarily starve to death when his/her mate dies.

　　The image of the osprey is seemingly irrelevant to, but actually suggestive of, the central subject. Associative opening — the technique of starting verse composition by evoking such images — is commonly employed in *The Book of Poetry*.

4 the floating hearts — a water plant with heart-shape leaves, the tender ones of which are edible.

5 the *qin* — a flat musical instrument with five or seven strings.

6 the *se* — a flat musical instrument with twenty-five strings.

2. 伐檀　Felling Sandalwood Trees

1 "Felling Sandalwood Trees" — This is one of the folk songs of the State of Wei. It reflects the stern reality and sharp class contradiction of the

time, and expresses the slaves' hatred against, and contempt for, the idle nobles who live off the fat of the land.

Many folk songs and poems set to refined music overflow with righteous indignation and feature a bold and unrestrained style. Of all the devices employed in this poem two are especially worthy of our notice:

a) The device of rhetoric question: there are two rhetoric questions in each stanza, which convey the meaning that the slave-owners can by no means justify their exploitation. These questions heighten the militant effect of the poem and demonstrate the class consciousness of the slaves.

b) The device of irony: the last two lines of each stanza (possibly sung in chorus) contains a case of irony, and thus can be paraphrased as follows:

Though outwardly refined in manners, he (the lord) is actually a plunderer (parasite / exploiter).

However, the original, which inflicts a poignant satire on the "descent noble," can better express the strong emotion of the slaves.

2　Thud — a case of onomatopoeia.

3　And to ... propel. — Then timber is tugged to the river (for transportation).

4　Th' river ..., ho! — Here the technique of description is involved.

5　three hundred — In the Chinese language, such numerals as three, six and nine are sometimes used to denote "a large number," "a great deal" or "incalculable" instead of specifying an exact number.

6　For spokes lumber we cut — We make lumber to produce spokes for carts (or carriages). The invention of carts and carriages is generally attributed to Emperor Huang, one of the earliest Chinese ancestors who lived about 4,700 years ago.

3. 伐木（节选）　Cutting Wood (an excerpt)

1　"Cutting Wood" — one of the Refined-Music lyrics, deals with the importance of building up and maintaining friendship and good relations. It consists of three stanzas, of which the present excerpt is the first.

This excerpt, which reflects the sense of community, brings forward the central theme by means of associative opening, onomatopoeia and analogy.

2　whose value itself does bespeak — which bespeaks its own value.

3　our gods — The ancient Chinese, like the ancient Greeks, were in general polytheists. Among the gods they worshiped were the God of

Agriculture, the Sun God, the Moon Goddess, Fate the Minor, and Nuwa — the goddess who had created the human race and repaired the heavens with molten rock, and others.

Chinese religions are tinctured with humanism — the gods and ancestors whom people worship are supposed to bring blessings to man.

4. 采薇（节选） Gathering Ferns (an excerpt)

1 "Gathering Ferns" — one of the poems set to refined music, is composed in the tone of a soldier garrisoning the frontiers. It consists of six stanzas, of which the present excerpt is the last.

The first expression in the opening line — "Gathering Ferns" is used as the title, as is the case with many other poems in *The Book of Poetry*. It is relevant to but does not embody the central subject that the invasion of the northern nomads has caused great misfortune and hardship to the soldier.

In this excerpt, the poet's feeling is manifested by way of the following techniques:

a) Contrast: when the soldier left home for the front, the willows were lovely and green — how could he bear to part? But when he returns from the front, things are even worse — the sleet is permeating the universe, how wretched he should feel! Here the depiction of and contrast in scenery serve as a conveyance of feelings.

b) Creation of vivid images: the word picture of green willows, falling sleet and the hunger-stricken soldier is so vividly created that it seems alive in the reader's mind.

2 And worst of all, ... /... none could know! — The last two lines only tell us that the soldier's heart bursts "With such sorrow as none could know," but the impact produced is immense. They leave the reader an aftertaste and set them thinking: what sorrow could it be? The sorrow over his lost youth, the sorrow over social disturbance, or that caused by his deep concern about his family, whose survival is uncertain? We can well imagine what woeful physical and psychological effects war has exercised upon the soldier.

5. 小旻（节选） Petty Heaven (an excerpt)

1 "Petty Heaven" — a satirical poem of six stanzas, of which this excerpt is the last. The anonymous poet is believed to be a senior official in the

reign of King You of Zhou. There are different explanations as to why the poem is entitled "Petty Heaven" — a question not to be delved into here.

The poet exposes the fatuousness of the king, analyses the political quality and mental attitude of the vicious officials whom the king trusts, and sheds light on the danger of relying on those politicians in formulating policies and exercising power.

Apart from narration, simile and metaphor are ingeniously employed to illustrate ideas and express feelings. Some expressions from the original have become popular Chinese idioms, e.g. "of facing an abyss you'll feel th' dread," "as if th' ice would crack under your tread," etc.

2 Without ... life's dear. — If not properly armed, one will not fight a wild beast at the risk of his life; and without a boat or a bridge one will not venture to cross a river.

3 Of ... few are clear. — Such dangers as are mentioned in the first two lines can be easily seen, but few are aware of the latent perils which those politicians, towards whom the king shows great favor, can inflict upon honest people and the country at large.

4 Which ... under you tread. — The latent perils incurred by the sinister officials strike terror into the hearts of the innocent people, who easily fall a victim to the intrigues. Who can tell that the poet himself will not become a target of attack some day? It is then quite natural that he should feel as if he were put on the very edge of a deep abyss or were treading on a thin layer of ice!

6. 弹歌　Song of the Catapult

1 "Song of the Catapult" — According to Zhai Ye's *History of the States of Wu and Yue* (《吴越春秋》), when Goujian (勾践 , 520 BC-465 BC), King of the State of Yue, asked him about the development of the bow and the crossbow, Chen Yin (陈音 , a famous archer of the State of Chu) replied by citing the ancient song as an explanation of the making and functioning of a catapult, from which the two kinds of weapons were developed.

The song features a style of natural ease and simplicity, and its language is succinct. In just eight characters it vividly and explicitly narrates how the catapult is made and how it works.

2 You'll get ... or stew — You'll enjoy the meat of the game in a way you like.

63

Songs of Weal and Woe

7. 禹上会稽　A Song Chanted Atop Mount Kuaiji

1　"A Song Chanted Atop Mount Kuaiji" (《禹上会稽》) — improvised by Yu. In his *Records of Music — Ancient and Modern* (《古今乐录》, written in 568 AD), the author (the Buddhist Zhijiang, 释智匠) says: "In the course of taming the floods, Yu ascended Mount Kuaiji. At the sight of the rampant flood he composed the present song."

　　The legend goes that in ancient times floods had often devastated the reaches of the Yellow River, and that to protect agriculture Emperor Yao (尧帝) had appointed Gun (鲧) to tame the floods, who adopted the guideline of checking the floods with dams, and consequently was banished to Mount Yushan (羽山) for his failure. Later Shun (舜), who had succeeded to the throne, entrusted the mission to Gun's son Yu (禹). Yu wholeheartedly devoted himself to the cause. He dredged the streams by splitting the Dragon Gate and clearing a passage through Yique (the gate of the Yi River) with his magic ax, invented some prospecting devices and successfully accomplished the task by taking the strategy of dredging the streams.

　　The first two lines "Alas, th' devouring floods surging up to th' skies, / Driving the rank and file to absolute despair!" is an exclamation, in which the rhetorical device exaggeration is involved. In the line "More wrathful than e'er, / Heaven seems deaf to their cries!" personification is employed to picture natural forces. The language is plain and the style easy.

2　Si Yu (?–?), posthumously known as Yu the Great (大禹), had contributed tremendously to the taming of the serious floods, demarcated the Nine Domains and laid the foundation for the establishment of the Xia Dynasty. He came to the throne abdicated by Shun in around 2029 BC.

3　It is said that Yu had been preoccupied with taming floods for thirteen years, that for three times he had passed by his own home without entering it, and that he could not even afford to spare a little time to show care and love for his baby son. As a proof of his exertion to the mission all the hair on his legs had been worn off.

8. 越人歌　The Yue's Song

1　"The Yue's Song" — This song，which expresses the Yue's love for the Prince of E and demonstrates her courageous pursuit in spite of the fetters of social ethics and rites, is an excerpt from the 11th volume of

Garden of Doctrines and Theories (《说苑》), a book written by Liu Xiang (appr. 77 BC–6 BC) of the Han Dynasty, which comprises introductions and annotations to the classics that the author had collated. Part of the story about the Prince of E (named Zixi, the prime minister of the State of Chu) and the Yue boatwoman goes as follows:

In the year 528 AD, the Prince of E held a grand ceremony, at which a Yue boatwoman sang him a song. As the song was sung in the boatwoman's own language, the prince didn't understand it. When it was rendered impromptu into the official language of Chu, the prince, deeply touched, stepped forward to the boatwoman, draped her with his embroidered cloak, and embraced her.

2 Oh, what a special night tonight, / Which witnesses this midstream float! / Oh, what a special date today, / When I'm graced to share with th' prince th' same boat! —These lines, which consist of two exclamations, lively convey the Yue's great delight in the event, which brings her and the prince together.

3 Oh, th' tree clings to... the tree; —This line presents a hint, foreshadowing the idea to be expressed in the next line. The tree and its branches symbolize the close interrelation of two young people in love.

9. 越人士风歌 The Yues' Song of Their Own Mores

1 "The Yues' Song of Their Own Mores" — The earliest versions of *The Yues' Song of Their Own Mores* appeared in print successively in *Chronicals of the Three Qins* (《三秦记》, written by a scholar of the Jin Dynasty, whose surname is Xin) and *Anthology of Anecdotes and Stories* (《语林》) written by He Liangjun (何良俊 , 1506–1573). Du Wenlan (杜文澜 , 1815–1881) of the Qing Dynasty gave it the title in light of *Comments on and Criticisms of Classics* (《说文长笺》) by Zhao Huanguang (赵宦光 , 1559–1625).

This song, by glorifying the mounts and rills in the regions of Yue and eulogizing the natives' talent, expresses the pride of the Yue people.

10. 橘颂 Ode to the Orange Tree

1 "Ode to the Orange Tree" — This ode, honored as the trail-blazing piece of object-chanting poetry, eulogizes the fine qualities of the orange tree by means of personification, symbolism and other rhetorical devices. The "tree" is not only endowed with excellent looks, but "he" also

Songs of Weal and Woe

shines with such wonderful qualities as altruism, dauntlessness, noble-mindedness, etc. No wonder the poet expresses his determination to follow the fine example set by the tree.

2   Qu Yuan (c.340 BC−c.278 BC), alias Qu Ping, was born during the Warring States Period in Dangyang (the now Zigui of Hubei). He was a distinguished statesman and the earliest great poet in the history of China. Astute and eloquent, he advocated the reliance with the State of Qi in resistance against the aggression of Qin and helped King Huai of Chu in the reforms for the strengthening of Chu when he was in the positions of Lord of the Three Clans and Senior Councilor of Statutes. As a result, Chu became so powerful that it became the mainstay of the Vertical Reliance against Qin.

As he was in acute conflict with the decadent aristocratic clique, Qu Yuan was calumniated and supplanted by Zilan, the Minister of Personnel, and was consequently estranged by the king. In 304 BC (the 15th year of King Huai's Reign), Zhang Yi, who came to Chu from Qin, bribed Jin Shang, Zilan and Zheng Xiu (the king's concubine) into treason and, with the "territories of Shang and Yu" as a lure, induced Chu to break ties with Qi. Aware of the deception, the humiliated King of Chu flew into a rage and launched two campaigns against Qin, only to be fatally defeated. In such circumstances Qu Yuan was sent as the state's envoy to Qi to restore friendly relations. At this critical moment, however, Zhang Yi came to Chu once more to disintegrate the alliance between Qi and Chu. In 295 BC (the 24th year of King Huai's Reign), Qin and Chu signed the Treaty of Alliance at Huangji, which marked the submission of Chu to Qin. As a result, Qu Yuan was deported from the capital Ying and exiled to the north of the Han River.

In 299 BC (the 30th year of King Huai's Reign), regardless of the warning of Qu Yuan, who had return from exile, King Huai went to the Wuguan Pass to meet the king of Qin, only to be detained by Qin. When he ascended the throne, King Qingxiang continued the policy of capitulation. Qu Yuan was once again deported from Ying and exiled to the south, wandering about between the Yuan and the Xiang Rivers. In 278 BC (the 21th year of King Qingxiang's Reign), the Qin forces under the command of Bai Qi captured the capital Ying. In his great sorrow and indignation Qu Yuan drowned himself in the River of Miluo.

Qu Yuan's works include "Tales of Woe," "Nine Lyrics," "Eleven

Elegies and Epics," and "Inquiries into the Universe," etc. In his immortal works, Qu Yuan attacks the corrupted ruling clique of Chu, manifests his progressive political ideal and fervent love for his people and country, and expresses his deep sorrow over the failure of the reforms. He also demonstrates his boldness to pursue truth and challenge accepted ideas, as well as his originality in thinking in such works as "Inquiries into the Universe," in which more than one hundred and seventy questions are raised concerning the formation of the universe, doubts or appraisals of historical characters, events and what not.

The glory of the lofty personality of Qu Yuan, as Sima Qian (145 BC?-?) says, can be compared to the sun and the moon. Every year the Chinese people observe the Dragon Festival as a rule to pay homage to the great poet. In 1953, Qu Yuan was acknowledged as one of the Four Most Renowned Cultural Figures in the World.

3   Boyi — Boyi of the Shang Dynasty had been generally regarded as a righteous man of backbone.

11. 离骚（节选） Tales of Woe (an excerpt)

1   "Tales of Woe" is a lyrical-cum-narrative poem of 373 lines. After recounting his good descent and noble aspirations, the poet narrates how he, unyielding in face of fierce opposition, gives vent to his sentiments before the presence of the ancient sage Chonghua, and how he decides to stay in his beloved country instead of going far and high when returning from his unsuccessful pilgrimage to Heaven in quest of God's judgment on his thoughts and conduct.

This poem, in which mythology and reality merge into a perfect entity and rhetorical devices (e.g. figures of speech and symbolism) are ingeniously employed, demonstrates the poet's ardent patriotism, lofty moral character and unyielding integrity.

The present excerpt is taken from the poem.

2   phoenix carriage — carriage decorated with the image of the phoenix (a mythical bird).

3   Mount Cangwu — the mountain where the wise ancient king Chonghua died in light of Chinese legend.

4   Mount Xuanpu — a mythical mountaintop midst the Kunlun Mountains said to be inhabited by immortals.

5   Xi He — a petty god in Chinese mythology who pilots the carriage for

the Sun God.

6   Long ...; / ... quest! — The Beauty is a case of metonymy referring to the poet's political ideal. These two lines are often quoted to show someone's determination to pursue truth or knowledge in spite of hardships and perils.

12. 涉江　The Voyage

1   This is one of "The Nine Songs".

Canto I narrates the contradiction between the poet's lofty ideal and the grim reality, stating why the poet is compelled to go far and high. The depiction of the unique attire is suggestive of noble ideas and unusual talent, and the narration of the tour with the wise king Chonghua in the fairyland serves to set off the reality by contrast.

Canto II tells of the hardships the poet undergoes on the voyage and expresses the poet's indomitable will to maintain his moral integrity. The boat is personified and the narration of struggling with the raging waves is vivid.

Canto III describes the wretchedness the poet encounters upon entering Xupu and tells that the poet would rather die in poverty than drift with the current. In this canto the unpropitious environment serves as a foil to the poet's firm integrity.

In Canto IV, by recounting historical personages who had been unjustly persecuted, the poet satirizes the exciting state of affairs and once again expresses his determination to uphold truth. The poet's technique of "satirizing the present by relating historical events" had been inspiring and enlightening to writers of future generations.

The Finale, with a series of extending metaphor, lays bare the perverseness of the ruling clique. Here the phoenix, the winter Daphne, the lily magnolia and the fragrant are used to signify talented people of moral integrity, who suffer estrangement and unjust treatment; while crows, sparrows, weeds, thorny plants and what is smelly symbolize crafty officials who are mentally and intelligently mean and low but have managed to find favor in the king's eyes.

If the reader takes the fact into account that one of the poet's ideas was to "recommend and appoint the worthy and talented", he might understand the poet's bitter indignation better.

2   Mount Kunlun — a mountain similar to the Greek Olympus, which is

believed to have been inhabited by immortals.

3   th' Ezhu Isle — an isle in the Yangtze River within the realm of the now
    Hubei Province.

4   Fanglin, Wangzhu, Chenyang, Xupu are places in the now Hu'nan
    Province.

5   ... I'm now to know . — ... I'm now to face and experience.

6   Jieyu protested with his head shaved — The ancients as a rule wore long
    hair, and a shaved head was a sign of penalty. However, Jieyu, a hermit
    in the State of Chu, offered an exception: he did so of his own accord, for
    he refused to conform to the convention.

7   Sanghu — an ancient sage who, like the Greek Diogenes, found an
    expression of his philosophy and attitude in remaining naked.

8   Wu Zixu — a senior official of the State of Wu, who was compelled to
    commit suicide by the king for his frank admonishment.

9   Bi Gan — prime minister of the last king of the Shang Dynasty, who was
    put to death for admonishing the king against misconduct.

13. 国殇   Eulogy on the Martyrs of the State

1   In the mind's eye of the ancients, martyrs ranked high among the deities.
    The present piece is one of "The Nine Songs", which are recreated
    on the basis of a group of legendary songs of antiquity intended for
    entertaining such deities as the Sun God, the Fate the Great and others.
    It eulogize the souls who have dedicated their lives to the security of
    the state and the populace, and expresses people's love and gratitude
    for the martyrs. The performances of singing and dancing were usually
    conducted by Wu (In history "巫" had once been versatile professionals
    specializing in worship, medicine, astrology, history, etc.), each playing
    his / her own role. The style is vigorous and fervent.

2   Bracketed in the English version are something like play instruction,
    which is added by the translator.

3   The bows made in the State of Qin were known for their strength.

4   Orchids... / ... for e'er and aye. — We will pay homage to you by offering
    you orchids in spring and asters in fall (as floral tribute). Here " for e'er
    and aye" is an emphatic expression.

14. 渔父   A Dialogue with the Fisherman

1   This verse, in the form of a dialogue, lays bare the poet's inner conflict.

On the one hand, he might abandon his outlook on life and yield to the filthy world so as to drag out an ignoble existence; on the other he might persevere in his principle of justice at the risk of loosing his position, status or even life. In face of the alternatives the undaunted poet embraces the latter.

2　The questions show the fisherman's surprise at the sight of the sorry state of the high-ranking poet.

3　This ballad, which is mentioned in the works of both Confucius and Mencius, had circulated as early as in the Spring and Autumn Period. The fisherman might hint that one should adapt himself to the circumstances.

Chapter Two   Poetry of the Han Dynasty

Introductory Remarks

The warfare among the states ended in the founding of the first feudal empire — the Empire of Qin (221 BC−206 BC), whose high-handed policies incurred the Uprising of Chen Sheng and Wu Guang. Liu Bang, who had risen in response to the uprising in question, ascended the throne as founder of the Han Dynasty (206 BC−220 AD).

The early Han rulers proved to be much wiser than the rulers of Qin, had enforced a series of policies to centralize state power, to strengthen the multinational country and to spur the development of economy and culture. As a result, relative stability and periodic prosperity had been attained. It was not by mere chance that the seismograph and the technology of paper-making were respectively invented and perfected in the Han Dynasty.

At first, Daoism was embraced as the mainstream ideology, but was later on replaced by Confucianism.

In the realm of poetry, the Institute of Music, of which the duty was to collect folk songs and sponsor the composition of music and words, had played an important role. It has left behind a legacy of folk songs, which are generally referred to as Music-Institute poems. These poems, mostly composed during the Eastern Han period (25 AD−220 AD), reflect the bitter life and grievances of the common people. In those poems, which are characteristics of succinct language, singular imagination and a rich colouring of romanticism, diction and action are ingeniously employed as techniques of characterization.

The evolution of language gave rise poems of five-character lines, which began to take shape in Western Han (206 BC−25

Songs of Weal and Woe

AD) ballads and enjoyed popularity with the Eastern Han Music-Institute songs. The new form also inspired men of letters, whose representative works are "Nineteen Ancient Poems." Those poems, as it were, are deep moans of intellectuals of the lower stratum, who had been caught in the predicament of dark and chaotic society during the decline of the Han Empire. They are marked by the implicit style and the euphonious, picturesque and figurative language.

15. 大风歌

刘邦

大风起兮云飞扬，
威加海内兮归故乡，
安得猛士兮守四方！

Ode to the Wind Mighty and Stern[1]

Liu Bang[2]

Clouds dispersing, oh, rising is th' wind strong and stern!

The land brought under command, I now home return.

Where are brave men for th' bounds[3]? That's my deepest

    concern!

16. 十五从军征

无名氏

十五从军征，
八十始得归。
道逢乡里人：
"家中有阿谁？"
"遥看是君家，
松柏冢累累。"
兔从狗窦入，
雉从梁上飞。

中庭生旅谷，
井上生旅葵。
舂谷持作饭，
采葵持作羹。
羹饭一时熟，
不知贻阿谁！
出门东向看，
泪落沾我衣。

咏情言志

78

Conscripted at the Age of Fifteen[1]

Anonymous

Conscripted at th' age of fifteen, I had not yet retired

From the military service until eighty years old.

Coming home I met a fellow-villager and inquired:

"What kinsfolk of mine at home do I still have ?" and was told:

" Clusters of pines grow and many a tomb lie over there,

And amid those your sorry cottage is dimly in sight." [2]

Alarmed by my arrival through the dog's hole fled the hare,

And from the beams and ridge-poles pheasants took a hasty

  flight.

In the courtyard wild millet multiplied well and good,

While an edible wild herb grew at the well mouth hither.[3]

I picked and pounded millet by pestling for staple food,

And for soup such herbs as marshmallows I did then gather.

Very soon the soup was ready and the food was prepared,

But then with whom could this solitary soul have them

  shared?[4]

Staggering to the doorway into the east did I peer,

And my garment's front was wet with sad and sorrowful tear.

17. 上邪

无名氏

上邪！
我欲与君相知，
长命无绝衰。
山无陵，
江水为竭，
冬雷震震，
夏雨雪，
天地合，
乃敢与君绝。

Oh Providence[1]

Anonymous

Oh Providence! With my lover

I resolve to be closely bound,

Our affections shall wane never!

Unless mounts collapse to the ground,

Unless all the river go dry,

Unless thunders in winter pound;

Unless snow falls from the summer sky,

Unless the Earth merges with Heavens,

Ne'er shall we break our silken tie[2]!

18. 陌上桑

无名氏

日出东南隅，
照我秦氏楼。
秦氏有好女，
自名为罗敷。
罗敷善蚕桑，
采桑城南隅。
青丝为笼系，
桂枝为笼钩。

头上倭堕髻，
耳中明月珠；
缃绮为下裙，
紫绮为上襦。

行者见罗敷，
下担捋髭须。
少年见罗敷，
脱帽著帩头。

Mulberry on the Roadside[1]

Anonymous

Canto I

Behold, the morning sun in th' east does rise

And on th' Qins' storey building shed its light.

The Qins' daughter Luofu[2] is, as implies

Her name[3], a worthy girl who's fair and bright.

Collecting mulberry leaves Luofu's oft seen

For silkworm breeding, at which she is good, [4]

With a basket whose ties are silk cords green

And whose handle's made of cassia wood.

Her raven hair's worn in a tilted bun,

Her ear drops are splendorous pearls of th' moon;

Of yellow patterned silk her skirt is done,

Her violet blouse invites a feeling boon.

At sight of Luofu, people passing by

Will stroke their beards, leaving their loads aside;

And youngsters will attempt to catch her eye

By lifting hats to get their hair retied;

耕者忘其犁，
锄者忘其锄；
来归相怨怒，
但坐观罗敷。

使君从南来，
五马立踟蹰。
使君遣吏往，
问是谁家姝。

"秦氏有好女，
自名为罗敷。"
"罗敷年几何？"
"二十尚不足，
十五颇有余。"
使君谢罗敷，
"宁可共载不？"
罗敷前致词：

"使君一何愚！
使君自有妇，
罗敷自有夫。"

The tiller will forget about his plough,

And farming will pass out of th' hoer's mind.

When reaching home they'll get into a row —

To feast their eyes they've left their work behind.[5]

Canto II

The prefect, coming from the south, takes fire;[6]

Halting his carriage and five[7] suddenly,

He sends an official o'er to inquire

About the pretty girl's identity.

"She's designated by the name of [8] Luofu,

And she's the worthy daughter of the Qins."

"Impart to me: what's the age of Luofu?"

"She's 'tween fifteen and twenty ," the man grins.

The prefect brightens up, and his eyes shine.

He asks in person: "Why not come away

With me and get on this carriage of mine?"

Luofu, taking a step forward, does say:

"From what you have just said, my lord, Luofu

Have realized how thick-headed you can be.

Just as you're married on the part of you,

So I have an ideal husband to me."

"东方千余骑，
夫婿居上头。
何用识夫婿？
白马从骊驹，

青丝系马尾，
黄金络马头；
腰中鹿卢剑，
可值千万余，

十五府小吏，
二十朝大夫，
三十侍中郎，
四十专城居。

为人洁白皙，
鬑鬑颇有须；
盈盈公府步，
冉冉府中趋。
坐中数千人，
皆言夫婿殊。"

Canto III

"My man and his thousand riders in th' east

Oft form a procession that's grand indeed.

To tell who's my man needs ado the least:[9]

His aide's black horse follows close his white steed.

"A ribbon green does tie up his steed's tail,

And of golden stuff is its bridle made.

The sword he wears is worth many a tael

Of gold, its handle being set with jade.

"He was courtier at twenty, but a page

To th' prefect when he was only fifteen.

He was titled — at thirty years of age—

Shizhong[10]; and now forty, prefect he's been.

"He has a complexion that's fair and clear;

Somewhat light his beard and moustache appear.

It is with graceful yet majestic stalks

That to meet his subordinates he walks.

The comments of thousands come into line

Upon their head—my darling, who does shine!"

19. 长歌行

无名氏

青青园中葵,
朝露待日晞。
阳春布德泽,
万物生光辉。
常恐秋节至,
焜黄华叶衰。
百川东到海,
何时复西归?
少壮不努力,
老大徒伤悲。

A Long Song[1]

Anonymous

Green are the garden's sunflowers wet with dew,

Awaiting the sun who's to rise anew.

The spring benign is lavishing her favour

On all plants, which are glowing with splendour.

In their lush growth there's still the fear

That they will wither when autumn comes near.[2]

All the rivers eastwards to the sea flow,

When have the waters returned, though?[3]

One who in his youth does not take great pains,

When old, will but moan and regret in vain.[4]

20. 枯鱼过河泣

无名氏

枯鱼过河泣，
何时悔复及。
作书与鲂鱮，
相教慎出入。

A Landed Fish Is Sobbing When Sent
Across th' Stream[1]

Anonymous

A landed fish[2] is sobbing when sent along th' stream;

"It is too late to regret!" sadly blubbers he.

Hence he writes a message to the carp and the bream,

Reminding his friends that too careful one can't be.[3]

21. 京都童谣

无名氏

直如弦，
死道边。
曲如钩，
反封侯。

Children's Rhyme Circulated in the Capital[1]

Anonymous

Men straight like the string of a bow[2]

Are condemned to a life of woe;

Whereas those as sly as a crook

Should have managed high ranks to hook![3]

注释　Notes and Commentary

15. 大风歌　Ode to the Wind Mighty and Stern

1　In 195 BC, Liu Bang returned from his triumphant expedition against Ying Bu's rebellion via Pei Country — his hometown, where he held a banquet in honour of his native folks. At the banquet he sang out this song impromptu to express his aspirations to maintain the unity of the empire.

　　Here the poet follows the tradition of starting a poem by evoking images seemingly irrelevant to but actually suggestive of the central subject. The clouds and the mighty wind metaphorically denote the remnants of turbulent elements and the powerful army under the poet's command.

　　The present tercet conveys a mixed feeling: on the one hand, the poet is filled with the two-fold joy brought by his great success and happy return; on the other, he is very much concerned about the fate of the nation, which might fall apart if not properly guarded and governed. According to the records of *The Book of Han*, Liu Bang shed rows of tears when he finished singing the song.

2　Liu Bang (256 BC–195 BC), a famous statesman and strategist, was the founding emperor of the Han Dynasty. He had made great contributions to the unification of the nation as well as to the development of culture.

3　for th' bounds — for safeguarding national security.

16. 十五从军征　Conscripted at the Age of Fifteen

1　This poem tells the woeful story of a veteran, who returns home after sixty-five years' service only to find his home in ruins. It denounces the cruel enslavement of feudal society and reflects the catastrophe inflicted upon the populace by war.

　　"Song of a Veteran" might be a better title for this poem, but the first line is adopted in stead, as is the same case with some other poems.

2　"Clusters of pines..., / ... dimly in sight." — What used to be your home is amid the graves in the distance.

　　What the veteran hears about home is rendered in the form of direct speech, which is apt to create a vivid effect of sound. The sad news is the first shock the poet receives.

3   Alarmed... hither. — These four lines describe, by creating vivid images, the desolation the poet is confronted with, which gives him a second shock. Those images produce a visual effect.

4   I picked ... have them shared? — These few lines may secure a psychological effect. The food, which deals a third shock at the poet, further arouses his emotions: before he was conscripted, he could happily share food with the other members of the family, now that he has been rendered homeless, he'll have to eat a lone meal and live a forlorn life henceforth. What heart-breaking pathos!

17. 上邪　**Oh Providence**

1   This is one of the Music-Institute folk songs. It expresses, in the form of an oath, a lady's passionate love for and unswerving faithfulness to her lover.

The lady's determination solemnly expressed in the first stanza is reinforced in following stanzas by means of the enumeration of impossibilities, which are put in five clauses introduced by "unless" to build up to a climax (a rhetorical device).

In feudal China, where the freedom of love and marriage was unthinkable, this poem might have been a crashing thunder in the smothering air.

2   silken tie — cordial relationship between lovers.

18. 陌上桑　**Mulberry on the Roadside**

1   "Mulberry on the Roadside" , one of the Music-Institute songs, is a masterpiece of narrative poetry.

Canto I plays up Luofu's attractiveness by merely elaborating her attire and other people's reactions to her looks, which are designed as a foil to set off Luofu's beauty. The narration, tinged with exaggeration and humour, is lively and vivid.

Words, in the form of direct speech, are employed in character portrayal in Canto II, which narrates the impudent prefect's flirtation and displays Luofu's daring spirit in standing on her dignity.

Canto III, rendered in the form of a monologue, demonstrates how Luofu, standing on her dignity with grave composure, resourcefully invents a husband, who is handsome and prominent in position and in talent, to outshine the prefect, thus maneuvering herself out of the awkward position.

   In light of tradition, beauty without virtue, like talent devoid of morals, is hatefully contemptible. As the image of the girl created in this poem tallies with the Chinese aesthetic standards, it touches the average heart.

2 Luofu — The Qins' daughter is named after Luofu, a great beauty of the State of Zhao (404 BC−221 BC).

3 as implies / Her name — as her name implies.

4 Collecting ... / ... is good, — From this we can see that Luofu is able and industrious.

5 When ...— /... their work behind. — When they get home, they'll blame each other for having left their work undone owing to the fact that they had spent the time feasting their eyes on Luofu's beauty.

6 To take fire (of somebody) means to nurture love (for somebody).

   In the Han Dynasty, a prefect was to make an inspection tour of the subordinate counties in spring so as to "acquaint himself with the local custom" and to "encourage farming." However, some prefects (like the one in this poem) took advantage of the opportunity to pursue their own interests. To take fire means to nurture a sense of love (for somebody).

7 carriage and five — carriage pulled by five horses. In ancient times, the number of draught beasts was taken as a token of social position.

8 She's designated by the name of .... — She's called ....

9 ... needs ado the least — ... needs the least ado, i.e. is the easiest thing to do.

10 Shizhong — official title of the imperial guard.

19. 长歌行   A Long Song

1 "A Long Song" originally name of the music, is used as the title of this Music-Institute song, which admonishes people against whiling away their youth by means of analogy.

2 In their lush growth ... / ... autumn comes near. — This constitutes an analogy, which carries with it the figurative meaning that people in their buoyant youth should be aware that old age creeps on without being noticed.

3 All the rivers ..., / ... though? — This is another analogy, which implies that time lost cannot be regained.

4 These two lines, which make up the conclusion, are often quoted to stimulate young people into striving for knowledge, truth and success.

20. 枯鱼过河泣　A Landed Fish Is Sobbing When Sent Across th' Stream

1   This Music-Institute song is a parable. By telling how the fish caught weeps over his ill luck and exhorts his fellow fishes to take care, it reflects the stern reality in which people live in constant fear of being ensnared.

    In this poem, a serious socio-political problem is treated in a jocular way, but the burlesque cannot hide the bitter tears of the fish personified, who still hopes that his fellows will not meet with the same ill fate as he did.

    This poem, which demonstrates the poet's peculiar imagination and optimistic attitude, bespeaks the function of poetry as a social corrective.

2   Just as some other scholars do ("晒干的鱼", ref.: https://baike.so.com/doc/5809428-6022229.html), I formerly took it for granted that "枯鱼" should be "a dried fish". On the reasoning that "枯鱼" is ambiguous (a dried fish or a landed fish), and that it would be ridiculous to fancy a dried (dead and dehydrated) fish shedding tears, taking a move or uttering a sound, I've redressed my translation.

3   Hence ..., /...can't be. — Hence the landed fish writes to remind his fellows that one can't be too careful. Though he himself has fallen a victim to the perilous environment, he does not forget to give a warning to his fellows. How touching and admirable his altruism is! The humour in this poem is comparable with the black (or sick) humour of the 1960's, isn't it?

21. 京都童谣　Children's Rhyme Circulated in the Capital

1   Lucidity, brevity, sprightly rhythm and concurrence with the event, these are the basic requirements for a children's rhyme, which is usually meant as a mass medium. The present piece meets all those requirements.

    In the Eastern Han Dynasty, Liang Ji, a powerful relative of the royal family's, murdered Emperor Zhi and crowned Marquis of Liwu, who was to be known as Emperor Huan. In the first year of the Reign of Jianhe, Li Gu, the ex-Minister of War who had opposed himself to Liang's tyranny, was imprisoned and then killed. This perverse act had roused great indignation among the citizens of Luoyang, who spread the rhyme.

    Folk rhyme, more often than not, are transient. This one is perhaps an exception, for it reflects an issue of universality, the issue that honest people are, as a rule, cold-shouldered and even persecuted by the despotic and sinister.

2   This line contains a case of simile, in which upright and honest are likened to a bow.

3   Whereas ... /... to hook! — And yet those who are crafty should have managed to snatch high ranks by hook or by crook!

Chapter Three   Poetry of the Three Kingdoms, the Jin Dynasty and the Southern and Northern Dynasties

Introductory Remarks

At the close of the Han Dynasty, the land split into the Three Kingdoms of Wei (220 AD−265 AD), Shu (221 AD−265 AD) and Wu (222 AD−280 AD). Reunification was achieved in the Jin Dynasty, but was in turn followed by the confrontation of the Northern and Southern Dynasties (382 AD−589 AD). The history of approximately 360 years after the Han Dynasty was, so to speak, a woeful tale of wars and feudal separations.

Notwithstanding that, people had not forgotten about discovery and creation. In mathematics, Liu Hui of the Three Kingdoms period approximated π (the ratio of the circumference of a circle to its diameter) at 3.1416, and Zu Chongzhi of the Southern Dynasties accurately calculated it to seven places of decimals. In philosophy, Fan Zhen of the Southern Dynasties published his *On Atheism*. In agronomy, Jia Sixie of the Northern Dynasties published his *Strategies of Governance* — the most encyclopedic work of agronomy published so far. The Yungang Grottoes and the Longmen Grottoes are treasure houses of sculpture bequeathed by people of the Northern Dynasties. In the field of poetry, each of the ages boasts of a legacy of its own.

In the Reign of Jian'an in the late Eastern Han Dynasty, such poets as Cao Cao, Cao Zhi and Wang Can versified their ideals, aspirations and anxieties concerning the turmoil caused by the warlords in a vehement and pathetic way, which is known as the Vigour of Jian'an Style. To those poets we owe the formation of the poems with five-character lines.

From the turn of the Kingdom of Wei and the Western Jin Dynasty down to the Eastern Jin period, Confucianism gave way

Songs of Weal and Woe

to Buddhism and Daoism, and poets of the Metaphysical School sought refuge from the political complication in their dull and transcendental discussions. However, the great artistic attainments of Ruan Ji, Zuo Si and Tao Yuanming may tell us how misleading generalization could be.

The Music-Institute folk songs of the Northern and Southern Dynasties differ in content and style. Those of the former cover a wider range of subjects and are of a simple and bold style, while those of the latter mainly deal with the theme of love in a fresh and flowery fashion. What with the rise of phonology and what with the influence of folk songs, New Verse of strict rules began to take shape. Important poets of this era are Bao Zhao (414 AD−466 AD), Xie Lingyun (385 AD−433 AD), Xie Tiao (464 AD−499 AD), Yu Xin (513 AD−581 AD) and Shen Yue (441 AD−513 AD).

22. 短歌行

曹操

对酒当歌，
人生几何！
譬如朝露，
去日苦多。
慨当以慷，
忧思难忘。
何以解忧？
唯有杜康。
青青子衿，
悠悠我心。
但为君故，
沉吟至今。
呦呦鹿鸣，
食野之苹。
我有嘉宾，
鼓瑟吹笙。
明明如月，
何时可掇？
忧从中来，
不可断绝。

A Short Song

Cao Cao[1]

I wonder, o'er the cup and in the song,

Whether the human life is short or long?

Perchance it is just like the morning dew, [2]

Of whose limited time much is found gone.

Though a mellow quality the songs impart,

Th' pent-up thought[3] in me refuses to part.

It is only Du Kang[4] that can appease

This anxiety-laden secret heart.

Oh, talent of th' land, whose robes are deep green,

How my yearning for your presence is keen![5]

'Tis your arrival that I'm expecting

With a heart as sincere as it's e'er been.

The deer squeal invitingly in high glee

As soon as the green mug-wort they see.

I'll with delight have the *se* and *sheng* played

When distinguished visitors come to me.[6]

My earnest heart is just like the moon bright,

Which ne'er ceases to shed its immense light;

Out of the bosom of mine is bursting

A boundless longing that will never blight.

越陌度阡，
枉用相存。
契阔谈宴，
心念旧恩。
月明星稀，
乌鹊南飞。
绕树三匝，
何枝可依？
山不厌高，
海不厌深。
周公吐哺，
天下归心。

Oh, would you please kindly deign me a call

Despite th' barriers of distance and all?

To enjoy our happy reunion,

Feasts we shall make and friendship we'll recall.

The moon outshining the stars in the sky,

Crows and sparrows are seen to southward fly;

Hovering 'bout the woods they cannot find

A single branch on which they can rely.[7]

For their love of earth mounts attain their height;

Th' seas deep and vast ne'er of water make light.[8]

For one like th' Duke of Zhou[9], who broke off thrice

A meal[10], mass support is th' keenest delight!

23. 七步诗

曹植

煮豆燃豆萁，
豆在釜中泣：
本是同根生，
相煎何太急！

A Seven-Pace Poem

Cao Zhi[1]

Th' bean stalk spitefully burns with flames which leap,

And th' beans in the cauldron with pain do weep:

"After all we are growths from the same roots,

Whereat[2] should you bear us a hate so deep?"

24.咏怀
（其三十八）

阮籍

炎光延万里，
洪川荡湍濑。
弯弓挂扶桑，
长剑倚天外。
泰山成砥砺，
黄河为裳带。
视彼庄周子，
荣枯何足赖。
捐身弃中野，
乌鸢作患害。
岂若雄杰士，
功名从此大。

Intonation of My Sentiments (No. 38)

Ruan Ji[1]

With impetus the torrents onward flow,

And th' sun brightens a myriad *li* of land.

Behold the giant, the weight of whose great bow

Only th' enormous Fusang Tree[2] can stand,

And whose long sword outstretches to the sky:

The Yellow River serves him as a belt,

For grinding weapons he employs Mount Tai.

Beside Zhuang Zhou[3], to whom "decline" had spelt

The same as "thrive" , and "honour" as "disgrace," [4]

And whose posthumous body[5] lay exposed

To hawks and crows, th' giant, who does embrace

Sublime aspirations, stands out and glows

With meritorious and immortal fame,

Putting the poor philosopher to shame.

25. 咏史

左思

郁郁涧底松，
离离山上苗。
以彼径寸茎，
荫此百尺条。
世胄蹑高位，
英俊沉下僚。
地势使之然，
由来非一朝。
金张藉旧业，
七叶珥汉貂。
冯公岂不伟，
白首不见招。

咏情言志

112

Reflections on History

Zuo Si[1]

On bottom of the dale stand the gigantic pines,

While tiny bushes occupy the mountain peak.[2]

And thus those, vainly gifted with pillar-like spines,

Are dominated by these — whose small stems are weak.

Possessing vital posts are men of high descent;

Reduced to subordination are fertile brains.

The situation has reigned to th' sorry extent

That everything's been predetermined by "terrains."[3]

The Jins and Zhangs[4], with status their ancestors gained,

For seven generations marten tails[5] have worn;

And yet the white-haired Feng Tang had never been deigned

An interview, although a genius he was born.[6]

Songs of Weal and Woe

26. 归园田居

陶渊明

少无适俗韵，
性本爱丘山。
误落尘网中，
一去三十年。
羁鸟恋旧林，
池鱼思故渊；
开荒南野际，
守拙归田园。
方宅十余亩，
草屋八九间；
榆柳荫后檐，
桃李罗堂前。
暧暧远人村，
依依墟里烟；
狗吠深巷中，
鸡鸣桑树颠。
户庭无尘杂，
虚室有余闲；
久在樊笼里，
复得返自然。

Return to Country Life

Tao Yuanming[1]

Of conformist qualities I have derived naught

From birth; while by nature my love for mounts is keen[2].

Since in the net of worldly affairs[3] I got caught,

Alas, a good thirty years it's already been!

As a fish in the pool recalls his days in the lake,

So yearning for his woods is the bird that is caged.[4]

Having retired to farming for character's sake,

In reclamation of th' southern wastes I'm engaged.

Around my thatched house of nine rooms lies a track

Of land, which measures below twenty *mu* in all.

The elms and willows shade my house's eaves at th' back,

While peach and plum trees grow nicely in front of th' hall.

A village is located some distance away,

Above whose chimneys wisps of smoke are hanging low.

At times from the deep lanes the dogs will bark and bay,

And roosters atop mulberry trees will proudly crow.

My court's devoid of th' dust of secular concerns;

My plainly-furnished home signifies ease and peace.

Eventually to nature I've now returned,

Like a pent-up animal that obtains release![5]

Songs of Weal and Woe

27. 折杨柳歌辞
（其五）

无名氏

健儿须快马，
快马须健儿。
跸跋黄尘下，
然后别雄雌。

Snapping the Willow Twig
(No. 5) [1]

Anonymous

A gallant rider fails without a steed,

Which likewise does a worthy rider need.[2]

To see whoever gets the upper hand, [3]

Let's just go at a gallop on th' vast land!

28. 木兰诗

无名氏

唧唧复唧唧，
木兰当户织。
不闻机杼声，
惟闻女叹息。
问女何所思，
问女何所忆。
女亦无所思，
女亦无所忆。
昨夜见军帖，
可汗大点兵。
军书十二卷，
卷卷有爷名。
阿爷无大儿，
木兰无长兄。
愿为市鞍马，
从此替爷征。

Song of Mulan[1]

Anonymous

Canto I

Chug, chug![2] In the front of the room

Mulan is working at the loom.

Suddenly she ceases to weave

And repeated sighs she does heave.

"Do you think of one you expect

Or anything in retrospect?"

"I have no mood for things of the kind,[3]

But one thing is weighing on my mind;

Last eve I read the notice all,

The Khan's issued the battle call.

The muster-rolls do bear Dad's name,

Twelve volumes of them all the same.

Dad has no sons older than I,

That's the reason why I sigh.

I'll get a horse and bridle fine,

And in Dad's place go to th' front line."

东市买骏马，
西市买鞍鞯，
南市买辔头，
北市买长鞭。
旦辞爷娘去，
暮宿黄河边。
不闻爷娘唤女声，
但闻黄河流水鸣溅溅。
旦辞黄河去，
暮至黑山头。
不闻爷娘唤女声，
但闻燕山胡骑鸣啾啾。
万里赴戎机，
关山度若飞。
朔气传金柝，
寒光照铁衣。
将军百战死，
壮士十年归。
归来见天子，
天子坐明堂。
策勋十二转，
赏赐百千强。
可汗问所欲，

Canto II

At the eastern market she gets a steed,

At the west a saddle she does prepare;

At th' south she buys the bridle nice indeed,

She purchases a whip at th' northern fair.[4]

At dawn with her dad and mom she does part,

To reach the Yellow River in the gloom.

She hears no more of her parents' calling near to her heart,

Meeting her ear are but th' Yellow River's babble and boom.

When it dawns she takes leave of th' river's shore,

And gets to Mount Black in the close of day,

Where th' intimate calling of her parents she hears no more

And where she hears but th' Tartar horses in Range Yanshan neigh.[5]

To seize the opportunity to fight,

To be flying o'er the barriers they seem!

The watchman's gong bewails the cold of night,

The soldiers' armor catches th' chilly moon's gleam.

In action some generals lost their lives,

And most warriors return in ten years.

Mulan, who fortunately th' war survives,

In the palace before the throne appears.

By the Son of Heaven, who does court hold,

Rewards are granted and titles bestowed

To th' warriors who've proved resourceful and bold

Songs of Weal and Woe

"木兰不用尚书郎，
愿驰千里足，
送儿还故乡。"

爷娘闻女来，
出郭相扶将；
阿姊闻妹来，
当户理红妆；
小弟闻姊来，
磨刀霍霍向猪羊。
开我东阁门，
坐我西阁床，
脱我战时袍，
著我旧时裳。
当窗理云鬓，
对镜贴花黄。
出门看伙伴，
伙伴皆惊忙：
同行十二年，
不知木兰是女郎。
雄兔脚扑朔，

And whose loyalty the ordeal has showed.

When asked what she will of the Khan request,

"I want no titles," Mulan tells the crown.

"A camel would meet my wish th' very best

Of returning to my long-missed hometown."

Canto III

Hearing that she's stepped on her native land,

Th' old folks go out of town and clasp her by the hand;

Hearing that towards home she does progress,

Her sister, waiting at the gate, tidies her dress;

Hearing that she will very soon arrive,

To kill livestock her brother does sharpen his knife.[6]

In through the east door of their house she goes,

On bed in th' west room she sits in repose.

After that she takes off her wartime plumes[7]

And her girlhood attire she then resumes.

Ere the window she combs her raven hair,

In th' mirror she adorns her brow with care.

When she reappears out of her house gate,

Her battle companions' surprise is great:

"Together for twelve years we've marched and fought,

That Mulan is a girl has been utterly beyond thought."

"A buck will usually briskness show,

雌兔眼迷离;
双兔傍地走,
安能辨我是雄雌?

While shyness marks the nature of a doe.

But when both are running at utmost speed,

'Tis hard to distinguish 'tween them indeed!" [8]

29. 敕勒歌

无名氏

敕勒川，阴山下。
天似穹庐，
笼盖四野。
天苍苍，野茫茫，
风吹草低见牛羊。

126

Song of the Chile[1]

Anonymous

At th' foot of Mount Yinshan th' Chile Plain lies;

Shielding th' world is th' enormous yurt-like[2] skies.

On the prairie so vast, under the azure[3] clear,

Whenever flavourable winds sweep past,

Th' grass stoops low and herds of cattle appear.

30. 拟行路难
（其六）

鲍照

对案不能食，
拔剑击柱长叹息。
丈夫生世会几时？
安能蹀躞垂羽翼！
弃置罢官去，
还家自休息。
朝出与亲辞，
暮还在亲侧。
弄儿床前戏，
看妇机中织。
自古圣贤尽贫贱，
何况我辈孤且直！

Poems in the Form of
"Life's Journey Is Perilous" (No. 6)

Bao Zhao[1]

At table there's no mood for food, as I'm ridden with grief;

Striking the pillar with my sword, long sighs I heave!

How can a manly man in his brief life-time droop

His wings[2]? How can he walk at a slow pace and stoop?[3]

This position I shall soon abdicate;

About going home I'll not hesitate —

Where at dawn of my family I take leave,

But I can still return to them in the eve;

I'll play before the bed with my small boy,

And my wife's deft hands at th' loom I'll enjoy.

From of old sages have been reduced to an adverse fate,

Not to speak of us, who are solitary and so straight[4]!

注释　Notes and Commentary

22. 短歌行　A Short Song

1　Cao Cao (155 AD−220 AD), a great statesman, strategist, writer and King of Wei, was from the Qiao County of Peiguo — the now Bozhou of Anhui. His verse, mostly of four-character lines, bears a rich political colouring and is brimming over with power and enterprise. He and two of his sons (Cao Pi and Cao Zhi), being outstanding representatives of the Jian'an Literary School, are termed the Three Cao's in the history of Chinese poetry. While carrying forward the tradition of realism of the Han Music-Institute songs and of *The Nineteen Ancient Poems*, they had absorbed the good qualities of folk songs in their verse composition and had spurred the development of the poetic form of five-character lines.

咏
情
言
志

130

　　In this song, which is believed to have been composed at a banquet, the poet expresses his ambition to unify the nation and his sincere yearning for talent by employing such artistic techniques as simile, metaphor, metonymy and allusion.

2　This is a simile illustrating the transience of life.

　　If life is short, what then should one do? Different kinds of people have different answers to this simple question. Hedonists believe they should seize the moment to seek pleasures, whereas those with a sense of mission in life hold that they should lose no time to pursue their goals, be they selfish or altruistic. Cao Cao, who had adopted unification-oriented policies and unified the north of China, certainly belonged to the latter kind.

3　Th' pent-up thought — This refers to the ambition to unify the nation, which is seething in the poet's mind.

4　Du Kang — This is a case of metonymy denoting wine. Du Kang, according to a Chinese legend, was the first person who brewed wine.

5　Oh, talent ..., /... is keen! — These two lines are aptly quoted from *The Book of Poetry* to express the poet's admiration for talented people.

6　The deer squeal ... /... visitors come to me. — These four lines are a quotation from *The Book of Poetry*, meaning: Just as the deer are delighted at the sight of green mug-wort, so I'll be overjoyed with the arrival of talented people.

　　The *se* and the *sheng* are Chinese musical instruments.

7   The moon outshining ... /... on which they can rely. — These four lines, by metaphorically referring the Kingdom of Wei to the bright moon and the Kingdoms of Wu and Shu to the bedimmed stars, crows and sparrows, constitute a contrast between the Wei and the other kingdoms, hinting that talented people can find a bright future only in the former rather than the latter, which have been cornered to the south.

     Some scholars hold that the poet likens the crows and magpies to the talented people who have dispersed to the south and have found nobody to turn to. I disagree on the reasons that crows and sparrows are not proper images for good people in the history of Chinese literature, and that the presumption of talented people have dispersed from the north to the south is not true of the then situation.

8   For their love...; /... of water make light. — These two lines, also a case of metaphor, imply that there can never be too much earth for high mountains and too much water for deep seas and that, likewise, there can never be too many talented people for a broad-minded person (like the poet).

9   ... th' Duke of Zhou   — This is a case of allusion. The Duke of Zhou, wise and meritorious regent in the reign of King Cheng, was reputed for his respect for learned and talented people.

     This allusion suggests that the poet will follow the example set up by the Duke of Zhou.

10   It was said that the Duke of Zhou would stop what he was doing in order not to keep visitors waiting and that there were occasions on which he broke off his meal or bath several times to usher in and interview his guests.

23. 七步诗   A Seven-Pace Poem

1   Cao Zhi (192 AD−232 AD), important poet of the Jian'an School, cherished a high aspiration for national unification when young. Since his elder brother Cao Pi mounted the throne, he had lived under house arrest. His poetry reflects the chaos caused by war, the internecine strife of the ruling class and the people's bitter sufferings.

     Cao Pi once challenged Cao Zhi to improvise a poem within seven paces, hence this parable. In this parable, the beans being cooked are activated by the poet's brilliant imagination and encouraged to condemn the persecution of kinsfolk of consanguinity and, in a broader sense, of countrymen.

2 Whereat — Why

24. 咏怀（其三十八） Intonation of My Sentiments (No. 38)

1 Ruan Ji (210 AD−263 AD) was from Chenliu — the now He'nan Province. He had nourished a high ambition when young. Resentful of the Sima clique, who had usurped the state power of the Kingdom of Wei, he became an ardent advocate of the doctrines of Laozi (604 BC?− 531 BC?) and Zhuangzi (369 BC?−286 BC), assuming an unrestrained manner, which was an expression of his frustrated personality. His poetry, with its pessimistic colouring and oblique style, reflects the dark reality, expresses his inner conflicts and in some way criticizes the hypocritical feudal ethics. He had played an important role in the development of the poetic form of five-character lines.

In this poem, however, he eulogizes the lofty aspiration of heroes by creating a series of great images and by criticizing Zhuangzi's philosophy, which is regarded by him as nihilistic.

Is he possibly a rebel under the mask of eccentricity?

2 The Fusang Tree is a huge mythological tree which grows, it is said, where the sun rises.

3 Zhuang Zhou — philosopher of the Spring and Autumn period, who further developed and expounded Laozi's Daoism.

4 … to whom "decline" … as "disgrace" — to whom declination and prosperity made no difference and honour meant the same as disgrace

5 … whose posthumous body … — Before his death, Zhuangzi, who thought that the sky and the earth would sufficiently serve as his shrouds and resting place, forbade his students to bury him in the conventional way, hence the allusion.

25. 咏史 Reflections on History

1 Zuo Si (250 AD?−305 AD?) was from Linzi of the now Shandong Province. His poetry, allegoric and vigorous, is filled with a strong indignation at the family caste system of the Jin Dynasty.

In this poem, he expresses his resentment at the privilege of distinguished families by employing the techniques of contrast, metaphor and allusion.

2 The "gigantic pines" metaphorically refer to talented people of low social strata, while tiny bushes to people of reputable families who,

though weak in moral and intellect, occupy dominant positions. Here the bushes are brought in contrast with the pines.

3   "terrains" — birth or descent

4   The Jins and Zhangs — This is a case of allusion. Since the reign of Emperor Wu of the Han Dynasty, Jin Midi, Zhang Anshi and their descendants had retained vital positions for generations.

5   marten tails — This is an allusion to the official system of the Han Dynasty, in light of which the hats of certain senior officials (i.e. Shizhong and Zhongchangshi) were decorated with marten tails.

6   Feng Tang of the Han Dynasty was known for his exceptional merits and talent, but he had never been entrusted with any important task.

26. 归园田居   Return to Country Life

1   Tao Yuanming (365 AD − 427 AD) was from Xunyang, the now Jiujiang of Jiangxi Province. At the age of forty-one, he abdicated his position as county magistrate only eighty days after the appointment and lived in seclusion ever since. He was indignant at and in some way critical of the family caste system. On the other hand, however, he tended to escape reality.

As one of the earliest pastoral poets, Tao has made a far-reaching impact on poets of later generations. In his poem, he recreates the beauty of nature and of simplicity in a fresh, simple and natural style. He is also known for his essay on the Chinese "Utopia" — "The Peach Blossom Health" .

The present poem relates why the poet has retired to farming, describes the tranquility of country life and expresses the poet's happy feelings over his return to nature. In it is embodied the Chinese concept of the harmonious unity of man and nature.

2   while by nature my love for mounts is keen — "Just as the wise love water, so the humane adore mountains" — this Chinese saying may throw light on the implication of this clause, which reveals the poet's temperament.

3   the net of worldly affairs — To the poet, fame, promotion and material gains are but nuisance, hence the metaphor.

4   As a fish ..., / ... is caged. — These two lines metaphorically express the poet's love for freedom.

5   Eventually to nature ..., / ... obtains release! — The two final lines, which contain a simile, express the poet's great rejoice over his return to nature.

27. 折杨柳歌辞（其五） Snapping the Willow Twig (No. 5)

1　This is one of the five folk songs under the title of "Snapping the Willow Twig", which have been passed on from the Northern Dynasties. In the form of an invitation to a race, it demonstrates the pride, vigour and unconstrained mentality of the northerners.

　　Included in The Music-Institute Songs are not a few songs of the ethnic communities, which were translated into the Han language owing to the compatibility of Chinese culture.

2　which likewise does a worthy rider need — which likewise needs a worthy rider.

3　To see ... upper hand, — To see who is the best in horsemanship.

28. 木兰诗 Song of Mulan

1　"Song of Mulan" is the longest folk song of the Northern Dynasties. By narrating how Mulan, in lieu of her father, enlists for military service in man's disguise, it eulogizes the noble character of the heroine, who fights bravely in defence of her homeland without seeking personal fame or gain.

　　Canto I relates that, as her father is old and she has no elder brothers, Mulan makes up her mind to go to the front in her father's place. Canto II narrates how the heroine has braved hardships and dangers in the war and how she declines the Khan's offer of titles when she has returned in triumph. Canto III tells of her happy reunion with her kinsfolk and of her battle companions' great surprise at finding out her true identity.

　　On the one hand, this song has fit in with the traditional standards of filial piety (to one's parents) and loyalty (to one's country and/or monarch); on the other hand, it has been a direct challenge to the feudal concepts that women should confine themselves to household activities and that inability is a feminine virtue.

　　"I want no titles ... hometown." — Why does Mulan ask for a camel to send her home rather than an official position? The reason may be manifold. In the first place, her sex constitutes an insuperable barrier to assuming any title or position; in the next, she may think that, she has done nothing more than a citizen's duty in face of foreign aggression; in the third place, she may value a life of peace and love more than anything else.

This poem is of great artistic attainment: the portrayal of the image of Mulan is successful, and the use of artistic devices (e.g. metaphor, parallelism, repetition, onomatopoeia, dialogue, etc.) ingeniously effective.

2　chug — a case of onomatopoeia

3　"Do you think of ... ?" " ... of the kind," — This is a dialogue between the father and the daughter, which helps to bring out the reason why Mulan feels upset and why she makes up her mind to go to the front in her father's place.

4　At the eastern market ... at th' northern fair. — The detailed narration of these four lines is conductive to heightening the lively atmosphere.

　　It could have been more concise to say "She buys a horse and bridle", but in that case the effect of urgency would have been lost.

5　Where ... / ...Yanshan neigh. — Tartar was one of the nomadic groups living to the north of ancient China. The Tartar horses refer to the invading cavalry from the north. These two lines bring the heroine closer to the battlefield — there must be a change in Mulan's mood.

6　Hearing that she's stepped ... /... knife. — These six lines give a vivid and detailed narration of the reaction of Mulan's kinsfolk, playing up the atmosphere of warmth.

7　wartime plumes — military uniform

8　"A buck ... 'tween them indeed!" — Mulan's reply (the last four lines) metaphorically suggests that women can compete with men in strength and ability in spite of natural differences. It sounds somewhat feminist, doesn't it?

29. 敕勒歌　Song of the Chile

1　This folk song of the Chile ethnic community, overflowing with zeal and bearing a rich flavour of pastoral life, creates a word picture of the peculiar landscape of the grassland: under the blue sky which is like an enormous yurt, the prairie stretches far into the distance; here and there flocks and herds can be seen amid the luxurious ant grass when the wind sweeps past.

　　The language is brief and vivid for the use of simile (yurt-like), metaphor (shielding) and parallel structures (on the prairie so vast, under the azure clear).

2　yurt-like — that which is like a yurt.

3　the azure — the sky

Songs of Weal and Woe

30. 拟行路难（其六） Poems in the Form of "Life's Journey Is Perilous" (No. 6)

1   Bao Zhao (412 AD? — 446 AD) was from Donghai, the now Northern Lianshui of Jiangsu Province. He was one of the most important poets of the Southern Dynasties and had made contributions to the development of poetry with seven-character-lines.

"Poems in the Form of 'Life's Journey Is Perilous'" consists of eighteen pieces, this being the sixth. In this poem, as in many of his other poems, he expresses, in a direct and vigorous style, his burning indignation at the family caste system and his great sorrow over the impossibility of realizing his aspirations in the grim reality.

2   droop his wings — be in a depressed state of mind (a case of metaphor)

3   How can a manly man ... / ... a stoop? — These two rhetorical questions figuratively mean that, as a man of moral integrity and lofty aspirations, one just can't endure a submissive life.

4   In this line "solitary" and "straight" respectively mean "without companions or influential social connections" and "honest; upright".

The poet was of obscure birth, and thus he was belittled by, and could hope for no support from, the ruling few. Note the cynic tone of the poet in the last two lines.

136

Chapter Four   Poetry of the Sui and the Tang Dynasties

Introductory Remarks

Short-lived as it was, the Sui Dynasty (581 AD−618 AD) is remembered for the national unification after around 300 years of social upheavals, the establishment of the Civil Examination System, the political and economic reforms, and the accomplishment of the Great Canal.

It's true that some poems of the dynasty, such as those composed by Lu Sidao (535 AD−586 AD), Xue Daoheng (540 AD−609 AD) and Yang Su (?−606 AD), had shown signs of vigour and freshness, but by the large the poetic circle hadn't been able to rid itself of the shackles of the Courtly Style — a style passed down from the Liang Dynasty (502 AD−557 AD) and the Chen Dynasty (557 AD−589 AD). To cleanse the poetic world of that vulgar, feeble and formalist style it was a task which fell to the lot of later poets to perform.

The founding of the Tang Dynasty (618 AD−907 AD) opened up vast vistas for the development of poetry. It was in the dynasty that Chinese verse reached the zenith of its glory.

Of course, Rome was not built in a day.

The Early Tang period (618 AD−712 AD) witnessed the Four Distinguished Poets (namely Wang Bo, Yang Jiong, Lu Zhaolin, and Luo Binwang) and Chen Zi'ang rising against the convention, the former by widening the range of subjects and making a style of their own, and the latter by infusing into verse such vigour and vehemence as are characteristics of the Han and the Wei poetry. They had inherited and perfected the forms of the metrical verse of five-character and of seven-character lines, which had begun to take shape in the Southern Dynasties (420 AD−589 AD), and paved the way for the further development of Tang poetry.

The High Tang period (712 AD–761 AD), in which the flowers of verse bloomed in a blaze of colour, marked the prime of Tang poetry. The pastoral poets (such as Wang Wei and Meng Haoran), as if standing aloof from worldly affairs, represented the beauty of nature and the tranquility of country life with an irresistible artistic charm, whereas the frontier poets (such as Gao Shi, Cen Shen, Wang Changling and Cui Hao), inspired by an active and enterprising spirit, pictured the hardships of frontier life and the images of gallant frontier guards in a vigorous style. Atop the peak of Romanticism, Li Bai extolled the good and lashed out at the evil while revealing the inner world of an honest man caught in the contradictions between ideal and reality, between the spirit of enterprise and the sense of justice, etc.; on the summit of realism, Du Fu offered a most complete picture of High Tang society by exposing the evils of the corrupt, fatuous and predatory few and by reflecting the sufferings of the many in light of humanism.

The Middle Tang period (762 AD–826 AD) saw poetry climbing from the depression caused by the An-Shi Turmoil to the miraculous revival, which rose to a climax in the Reign of Yuanhe (806 AD–820 AD). Headed by Bai Juyi and Yuan Zhen, the poets of the New-Music-Institute School (such as Zhang Ji, Li Shen and Wang Jian) followed the realistic tradition pioneered by Du Fu to decry the perverse acts of the ruling class and reflect the adversities of the people. On the other hand, the poets of the Han Yu -Meng Jiao School (such as Jia Dao and Li He) carried on Du Fu's creative and pioneering spirit to blaze new trails through the presentation of the beauty of the wild, the sombre and the absurd. Also among the prominent poets of this period were Liu Zongyuan and Liu Yuxi. The former offered fresh and succinct word-paintings which embody the dauntless spirit and lofty aspirations of a reformist, while the latter made rapier thrusts at the social evils.

Bringing up the rear of the gigantic procession of muses were Du Mu, who was honoured as Du the Junior, Li Shangyin, who was posthumously revered as Li the Junior, Wen Tingyun, whose light and luscious style exerted a rather extensive influence on Late Tang poetry, and the social critics such as Cao Ye, Luo Yin, Lu Guimeng and Du Xunhe. Those poets of the Late Tang period (827 AD–907 AD) had played an indispensable role in the creation of a poetic splendor so far unrivalled.

The development of Tang poetry was by no means a fortuitous phenomenon. The dynasty gave rise to the fusion of Daoism, Confucianism and Buddhism, as well as to the Buddhist Chan Sect. The comparatively healthy economy, the colourful social life enriched by the merging and unity of the many nationalities as well as by the active cultural intercourse with foreign countries, the rather lenient policies towards different ideas, ethnics and religions, the importance of versification accentuated by the Official Examination System, the artistic heritage handed down from the previous dynasties, and the expressiveness of the Chinese language, etc.— all those factors had contributed handsomely to the full flourish of Chinese poetry in the dynasty.

31. 人日思归

薛道衡

入春才七日，
离家已二年。
人归落雁后，
思发在花前。

Homesickness on Man's Day[1]

Xue Daoheng[2]

Alas, it's now Man's Day, which marks spring's seventh day,

Thus two years have passed since from home I was away.

My return will be later than that of th' wild geese[3],

But homesickness buds earlier than the floral trees!

32. 无向辽东
浪死歌

王薄

长白山前知世郎，
纯着红罗绵背裆。
长槊侵天半，
轮刀耀日光。
上山吃獐鹿，
下山吃牛羊。
忽闻官军至，
提刀向前荡。
譬如辽东死，
斩头何所伤！

Don't Go East to Liao and Die for Nothing in a Strange Land[1]

Wang Bo

In red robes of silk and red waistcoat of brocade

The seer is operating in Mount Ever White.

His lance, held sideways, hides half the sky in the shade;

His sword, when wielded, forms a sun-like sphere of light.[2]

On mountains deep he feeds on wild game — bucks and deer;

Downhill he is provided with goats and cattle.

He'll swoops ahead on the Royal Troops, sword in hand,

Once they dare to come near.

He'd rather die a hero in the battle

Than perish east to Liao in a strange land!

145

33. 咏鹅

骆宾王

鹅，鹅，鹅，
曲项向天歌。
白毛浮绿水，
红掌拨清波。

The Goose[1]

Luo Binwang[2]

Gaggle, gaggle, gaggle![3]

Stretching her neck skyward the goose bursts into song.

Her whitish plumes gliding o'er the limpidity,

With her pinkish feet she's proudly paddling along.

Songs of Weal and Woe

34. 送杜少府之任蜀州

王勃

城阙辅三秦，
风烟望五津。
与君离别意，
同是宦游人。
海内存知己，
天涯若比邻。
无为在歧路，
儿女共沾巾。

Farewell to Du[1]

Wang Bo[2]

From th' capital[3] shielded by the Three Qins[4] I gaze

Into the Five Ferries dimly veiled in the haze.[5]

At a time when for a position you'll forth fare,

As roamers of th' same career[6] th' same feelings we share:

So long as you have a friend devoted and dear,

E'en if he's far away you'll e'er feel he's near.

Why then, at the crossroad, where company we'll part,

Should we shed womanly tears[7] with a saddened heart?

Songs of Weal and Woe

35.滕王阁诗

王勃

滕王高阁临江渚，
佩玉鸣鸾罢歌舞。
画栋朝飞南浦云，
珠帘暮卷西山雨。
闲云潭影日悠悠，
物换星移几度秋。
阁中帝子今何在？
槛外长江空自流。

The Tower of Prince Teng[1]

Wang Bo

Gone are th' pendant wearers[2] in carriages with phoenix bells
to th' thill;

Void of song and dance the Tower of Prince Teng on th' river
stands still.

Its painted ridge-beams are fondling morning haze from South
River-mouth,

Its beaded curtains flirting with the evening rains brewed in
West Hill.[3]

Day in and day out their shadows on the pool the idle clouds
cast;

In th' endless pageant of events and seasons many years have
passed.

At the tower not even a trace of the prince can now be found,

Out of the banisters th' ignored river's flowing, now slow, now
fast.[4]

Songs of Weal and Woe

36. 登幽州台歌

陈子昂

前不见古人，
后不见来者。
念天地之悠悠，
独怆然而涕下！

Ascent of the Youzhou Tower

Chen Zi'ang[1]

The ancients[2] cannot be revived and seen;

Moderns of the type[3] are not to be found!

Lo, infinite is th' universe, as it's e'er been;

Forlorn, I weep tears of sorrow, which knows no bound.

153

37. 回乡偶书

贺知章

少小离家老大回，
乡音无改鬓毛衰。
儿童相见不相识，
笑问客从何处来。

Random Lines on My Return to Hometown

He Zhizhang[1]

Away at a tender age I'm back when decayed.[2]

Although my accent's unchanged, [3] my hair has been grayed.

Th' native kids, in whose eyes I'm a stranger entire,

Friendly smile to me. "Where are you from?" they inquire.[4]

38. 春江花月夜

张若虚

春江潮水连海平，
海上明月共潮生。
滟滟随波千万里，
何处春江无月明！
江流宛转绕芳甸，
月照花林皆似霰；
空里流霜不觉飞，
汀上白沙看不见。
江天一色无纤尘，
皎皎空中孤月轮。
江畔何人初见月？
江月何年初照人？
人生代代无穷已，
江月年年只相似。
不知江月待何人，
但见长江送流水。
白云一片去悠悠，
青枫浦上不胜愁。
谁家今夜扁舟子？

The Flower-Fringed River in a Moonlit Night[1]

Zhang Ruoxu[2]

In spring the brimming river melts into the sea,

O'er which the moon serene arises with the tide.

The river does undulate a myriad *li*,

And th' moon, chasing th' waves, reveals a world vast and
  wide.

The river meanders in th' landscape nice and fair,

While th' trees and flowers look nebulous in th' moon's glow,

As if an invisible frost were filling th' air

And bedimming the sand-bar in its peaceful flow.

The dustless air and th' river harmonize in hue,

The wheel-like lonely moon above is hanging bright.

What was the man who happened first the moon to view?

When did the moon begin to cast on men its light?

In its endless line eternity men obtains,

And year after year just the same the moon remains.

For whom the moon's been waiting? There's no way to know,

'Tis only clear the river's surging onward, though.

The cloud having floated away, a sadness keen

Now hovers o'er the riverside with maples green.

P'rhaps others are sailing too tonight? But then where

何处相思明月楼？
可怜楼上月徘徊，
应照离人妆镜台。
玉户帘中卷不去，
捣衣砧上拂还来。
此时相望不相闻，
愿逐月华流照君。
鸿雁长飞光不度，
鱼龙潜跃水成文。
昨夜闲潭梦落花，
可怜春半不还家。
江水流春去欲尽，
江潭落月复西斜。
斜月沉沉藏海雾，
碣石潇湘无限路。
不知乘月几人归，
落月摇情满江树。

Are their sweets who should find their yearning hard to bear?

The elfish moon o'er the storey-house 'tis sad to see,

Which lays bare the dressing table of th' absentee.[3]

Th' fluttering screens try to dispel its light in vain;

After whisking it comes to th' washing block again!

We yearn for each other, but can't each other hear.

I wish I could, riding on light, fly to my dear!

Th' swans seem aimless, and no conveyance does light make;

The fishes swim and dive, but just ripples appear.[4]

Th' dream of fallen flowers[5] on th' pool disturbed my rest

Last night — at th' long absence of my love I'm distressed.

Oh, washing down the river, spring is nearly o'er,

And lo, the moon is sinking o'er the pool in the west!

Th' distance 'tween Jieshi and Xiaoxiang[6] seems to increase;

May there be men who've reached home like a pleasant
breeze.[7]

Half hidden in the mistiness the moon still glows

With love, which fills th' river and permeates the trees!

159

Songs of Weal and Woe

39. 登鹳雀楼

王之涣

白日依山尽，
黄河入海流。
欲穷千里目，
更上一层楼。

Ascending the Stork Tower[1]

Wang Zhihuan[2]

Lingering is th' dusky sun about the mount's height,

Surging is the Yellow River[3] eastwards to th' sea.

Aim higher and up th' tower take another flight

To hold a vision broader than one thousand *li*.

40. 春晓

孟浩然

春眠不觉晓，
处处闻啼鸟。
夜来风雨声，
花落知多少？

Spring Morn

Meng Haoran[1]

Awakening to a late morn of spring,

I hear the merry birds everywhere sing.

The winds and rains did splatter yesternight:

How many flowers have dropped in a plight?[2]

41. 宿桐庐江寄广陵旧游

孟浩然

山暝听猿愁，
沧江急夜流。
风鸣两岸叶，
月照一孤舟。
建德非吾土，
维扬忆旧游。
还将两行泪，
遥寄海西头。

To an Old Friend in Guangling —
Composed When Staying on the Tonglu River[1]

Meng Haoran

At dusk the river is hastily surging by,

When the gibbering of apes rouse a sense of plight.

The trees on both banks shiver while winds sough and sigh;

On the lonely boat the moon sheds a hazy light.

Stranded in a strange land which to me appears drear,

I can't help missing you in Weiyang, my old friend.

Therefore I dedicate two rolls of yearning tear,

Which to the Northern reach of th' River I will send.[2]

Songs of Weal and Woe

42. 黄鹤楼

崔颢

昔人已乘黄鹤去，
此地空余黄鹤楼。
黄鹤一去不复返，
白云千载空悠悠。
晴川历历汉阳树，
芳草萋萋鹦鹉洲。
日暮乡关何处是？
烟波江上使人愁！

咏情言志

The Yellow Crane Tower

Cui Hao[1]

Astride his Yellow Crane th' immortal has heaven-wards
flown[2],

Leaving behind him the Yellow Crane Tower all alone.

The crane has gone for ages, ne'er to hither come again;

But th' fleecy clouds have been expecting her e'er since in vain.

The Hanyang Plain[3] presents trees charming in the sun's warm
shine,

And th' Parrot Isle[4] competes by showing grass that's lush and
fine.

Where's hometown? In th' dusk of the evening there's no way
to know,

Only the misty river's seen in its saddening flow!

167

43. 出塞

王昌龄

秦时明月汉时关，
万里长征人未还。
但使龙城飞将在，
不教胡马度阴山。

咏情言志

168

Far Away on the Frontier

Wang Changling[1]

As in th' Qin and Han times lie th' same forts and shines th'
   same moon,

Yet we can't expect men to return from th' long march soon.[2]

Were th' Flying General[3] who'd struck th' Dragon Town[4] with
   fear

Still alive, th' Hun steeds[5] wouldn't trepass Yinshan[6]!

Songs of Weal and Woe

44. 山居秋暝

王维

空山新雨后，
天气晚来秋。
明月松间照，
清泉石上流。
竹喧归浣女，
莲动下渔舟。
随意春芳歇，
王孙自可留。

咏情言志

170

An Autumn Eve during My Stay in the Mounts[1]

Wang Wei[2]

The rain has lent a new charm to the heights,

And autumn's so real in the eve of day.

A serene moon through tall pines sifts her light;

A limpid spring on rough rocks winds its way.[3]

A bustle from the bamboos does announce

The girls' return from bleaching, and the leaves

Of lotus for a fishing boat make way,

Which seems to slide and bounce.

Though flowers may wither, and fall the leaves,

Princes would yearn to hither stay.

171

45. 相思

王维

红豆生南国，
春来发几枝。
愿君多采撷，
此物最相思。

The Love Pea[1]

Wang Wei

The love peas flourish in the southern clime;

In spring with tender twigs they reach their prime.

'Tis wished you gather plenty of their seed —

The token best of love sincere indeed!

46. 将进酒

李白

咏情言志

174

君不见，黄河之水天上来，
奔流到海不复回。
君不见，高堂明镜悲白发，
朝如青丝暮成雪。
人生得意须尽欢，
莫使金樽空对月。
天生我材必有用，
千金散尽还复来。
烹羊宰牛且为乐，
会须一饮三百杯。
岑夫子，丹丘生，
将进酒，杯莫停。
与君歌一曲，
请君为我倾耳听。
钟鼓馔玉不足贵，
但愿长醉不复醒。
古来圣贤皆寂寞，
惟有饮者留其名。
陈王昔时宴平乐，
斗酒十千恣欢谑。

A Toast[1]

Li Bai[2]

Haven't you seen the Yellow River pouring down from th' skies

And surging to the vast sea, never ever to return?[3]

Haven't you seen rich men in th' mirror, who with misty eyes

Grieve o'er their transient hair, which in a day did gray turn?[4]

Thus it follows that people should drink to their hearts' content

When possible, and ne'er leave their cups empty under th' moon.

'Tis natural gifts that prove of real worth; for th' money spent

One may be reimbursed with forthcoming wealth very soon.[5]

Cattle having been butchered, and ready being the meat,

To three hundred cupfuls of wine ourselves we ought to treat!

Mister Cen and you, Mister Yuan[6] — dear friends of mine,

Would you please have your cups filled and refilled with wine!

In th' meantime be all ears to me,

I'll sing you a song in high glee:

Of luxuries and delicacies one ought to make light,

'Tis devoutly to be wish'd to remain drunk day and night.[7]

From of old obscure have been distinguish'd saints and sages,

Whereas great drinkers' names have survived through all the ages.[8]

At th' Peace Palace Prince Chensi[9] had held many a high feast,

That wine's price shot up to ten thousand he cared not the least!

主人何为言少钱，
径须沽取对君酌。
五花马，千金裘，
呼儿将出换美酒，
与尔同销万古愁。

Why do you trouble 'bout the matter of money, my host?

Just exhaust the vendor's and continue to drink a toast.

Isn't there in the stable still the dapple steed?

And my fur coat is worth ten thousand coins indeed.

Ask your little ones to have them all sold

For good wine, with which we'll drown cares age-old![10]

47. 静夜思

李白

床前明月光，
疑是地上霜。
举头望明月，
低头思故乡。

咏情言志

In the Quiet of the Night[1]

Li Bai

The ground before my bed[2] presents a stretch of light,

Which appears to be a track of frost pure and bright.

I raise my head: a lonely moon is what I see;

I stoop, and homesickness is crying loud in me!

179

Songs of Weal and Woe

48. 早发白帝城

李白

朝辞白帝彩云间，
千里江陵一日还。
两岸猿声啼不住，
轻舟已过万重山。

Embarkation at Baidi Early in the Morning[1]

Li Bai

I left Baidi nestling in rosy clouds at break of day,

And in the eve I'll reach Jiangling a thousand *li* away[2]:

The jabbering of apes along the banks still seems to last,

Oho, ten thousand sweeps of mounts my swift skiff has flashed

past![3]

49. 望庐山瀑布
（其二）

李白

日照香炉生紫烟，
遥看瀑布挂前川。
飞流直下三千尺，
疑是银河落九天。

Watching the Waterfall in the Lushan Mountains (No. 2)[1]

Li Bai

Round th' sunlit Incense Burner[2] glows a purplish haze;

The waterfall o'er th' stream afar attracts my gaze:

Plunging down some three thousand *chi* it flies and flies[3]

As if it were th' Milky Way descending from th' skies[4]!

Songs of Weal and Woe

50. 塞下曲
（其一）

李白

五月天山雪，
无花只有寒。
笛中闻折柳，
春色未曾看。
晓战随金鼓，
宵眠抱玉鞍。
愿将腰下剑，
直为斩楼兰。

A Frontier Melody (No. 1)[1]

Li Bai

Th' snow in Tianshan[2] in th' fifth month[3] are not yet to melt;

No flowers are seen, but a bitter cold is felt.

The tune of Willow Twigs[4] is oft struck up on th' flute,

But not a sign of spring has anywhere been spelt.[5]

By day, spurred by the drum and gong we charge and fight;

Saddles in arms we sleep on the lookout at night.

We pledge, with th' sharpened swords we're wearing on the
waist,

To smash Loulan[6] and put th' foes in a fatal plight.

185

51. 题破山寺后禅院

常建

清晨入古寺，
初日照高林。
曲径通幽处，
禅房花木深。
山光悦鸟性，
潭影空人心。
万籁此俱寂，
但余钟磬音。

An Inscription on the Wall of the Back Compound of the Poshan Hill Temple

Chang Jian[1]

I visit th' temple at the break of day,

The sun lending the woods a lustre new.

The small path to seclusion winds its way;

Th' compound nestles 'midst trees of a vague hue.

The mountain scene suits th' birds' mentality[2];

The limpid pool could cleanse the human souls.[3]

Everything's in perfect tranquility,

Except at times resound th' bells' tuneful tolls.

Songs of Weal and Woe

52. 自京赴奉先县咏怀五百字（节选）

杜甫

多士盈朝廷，
仁者宜战栗。
况闻内金盘，
尽在卫霍室。
中堂舞神仙，
烟雾散玉质。
煖客貂鼠裘，
悲管逐清瑟。
劝客驼蹄羹，
霜橙压香橘。
朱门酒肉臭，
路有冻死骨。
荣枯咫尺异，
惆怅难再述。

Intonation of Five Hundred Characters —
Evoked on the Way from the Capital to
Fengxian County (an excerpt)[1]

Du Fu[2]

When evil's running rampant ere the throne,

Benevolence with daily fear does shake.[3]

'Tis said that gold utensils of th' crown's own

The Weis and Huos may at random take.[4]

The gauze light betrays the complexion fair

Of th' angels[5] dancing gracefully at th' hall;

The flutes and th' *se* resounding in the air,

Upon th' guests are lavished fur coats and all.

The stewed camel tendons please their taste,

And fruits of all seasons serve as dessert.

Behind red gates wine and meat go to waste;

On th' road those freezing to death lie in dirt.[6]

Oh, what a contrast 'tween Heaven and Hell!

Obsessed by grief more details I can't tell!

Songs of Weal and Woe

53. 春望

杜甫

国破山河在，
城春草木深。
感时花溅泪，
恨别鸟惊心。
烽火连三月，
家书抵万金。
白头搔更短，
浑欲不胜簪。

The Panorama in Spring[1]

Du Fu

The mounts and rivers still exist, the capital has fallen, tho!

Untended grass and trees—a dismal spring scene does the city
show.

Affected by the times I shed tears at the sight of flowers fair;

To this separation-stricken heart th' birds can only add
despair.[2]

The flames of war have raged for three months, causing
sufferings untold;

A letter coming far from home is worth ten thousand tael of
gold.

Repeated scratches out of trouble now have made my gray hair
thin —

'Tis so infirm and thin that it can hardly hold a pin.

54. 茅屋为秋风所破歌

杜甫

八月秋高风怒号，
卷我屋上三重茅。
茅飞渡江洒江郊，
高者挂罥长林梢，
下者飘转沉塘坳。

南村群童欺我老无力，
忍能对面为盗贼。
公然抱茅入竹去，
唇焦口燥呼不得。
归来倚杖自叹息。

俄顷风定云墨色，
秋天漠漠向昏黑。
布衾多年冷似铁，
娇儿恶卧踏里裂。
床头屋漏无干处，
雨脚如麻未断绝。
自经丧乱少睡眠，
长夜沾湿何由彻！

Sorrow over My Thatched Cottage Damaged by the Autumn Winds[1]

Du Fu

The furious autumn winds were howling past,

My thatched roof into pieces did they blast.

Flying was the thatch across the stream, oh my!

Caught on top of th' trees were some bits which flew high,

While in pits and depressions did others lie,

The kids took advantage of my age and th' chance for material
gain;

At ease across the stream the thatch they began to obtain.

With their booty they proudly stalked into the bamboo grove,

I shouted myself hoarse and tried to stop them but in vain.

On my return I heaved deep-drawn sighs, leaning on my cane.

When the winds subsided, the clouds darkened in hues.

Th' autumn day finally drew to a gloomy end.

My quilt now feels cold as iron due to long use,

To make it worse, cowering, my son did it rend.

With rainwater pouring down in threads and in streaks,

Not even a dry spot of the bed can I keep.

Drenched through, how am I to hold out until day breaks ?

Oh, e'er since the war[2] ne'er have I had enough sleep.

安得广厦千万间，
大庇天下寒士俱欢颜，
风雨不动安如山。
呜呼！
何时眼前突兀见此屋，
吾庐独破受冻死亦足！

How I wish millions of mansions may appear

To myriads of the suffering's great delight,

Relieving them from their constant worries and fear.

Oh, if only I could see such a happy sight,

How very cheerful and contented I would be —

E'en if my house should be ruined and I die in plight!

55.闻官军收河南河北

杜甫

剑外忽传收蓟北，
初闻涕泪满衣裳。
却看妻子愁何在，
漫卷诗书喜欲狂。
白日放歌须纵酒，
青春作伴好还乡。
即从巴峡穿巫峡，
便下襄阳向洛阳。

Poem Composed at the News of the Recapture of Henan and Hebei by the Royal Forces[1]

Du Fu

The news that North Ji[2] has been recaptured does spread

To this side of the Jianmen Pass[3], at which I shed

Delighted tears. My wife and son, wild with glee,

Are packing up books — no trace of care can I see.

In lovely daylight one deserves some songs and wine;

Spring's offer as company who shall decline?[4]

Through Gorge Wu to Xiangyang we'll sail from Gorge Ba here

And journey homeward to Luoyang[5], which I endear!

197

56. 绝句四首
（其三）

杜甫

两个黄鹂鸣翠柳，
一行白鹭上青天。
窗含西岭千秋雪，
门泊东吴万里船。

Four Short Poems
(No. 3)[1]

Du Fu

Two or three orioles tweeting midst th' willows green,

A flock of egrets are soaring up the skies blue.

The window en-frames[2] the age-old snow-clad West Ridge,

And th' door o'erlooks the anchored ships from th' distant Wu[3].

57. 弹琴

刘长卿

泠泠七弦上，
静听松风寒。
古调虽自爱，
今人多不弹。

Playing the *Qin*[1]

Liu Zhangqing[2]

Resounding from th' *qin*'s seven strings serene

Is the touching *Through th' Pines Rustle th' Winds Cold*[3].

For th' melody my love is as e'er keen,

Few moderns, though, enjoy such strains of old.

58. 枫桥夜泊

张继

月落乌啼霜满天，
江枫渔火对愁眠。
姑苏城外寒山寺，
夜半钟声到客船。

Mooring at the Maple Bridge for the Night

Zhang Ji[1]

The moon is set, the crows decrying dark and frosty skies;[2]
The maples vague[3], the fishing lamps are blinking ere mine
  eyes.
The ringing bells from Hanshan Temple[4] outside Gusu[5] float
Afar at mid-night to the sad and troubl'd napper's boat.

59. 滁州西涧

韦应物

独怜幽草涧边生，
上有黄鹂深树鸣。
春潮带雨晚来急，
野渡无人舟自横。

The West Brook in the Prefecture of Chuzhou

Wei Yingwu[1]

I keenly love the brook-side grass obscure and yet serene,

Rather than th' orioles warbling high up in th' woods deep
green.[2]

The spring tide, hastened by the rains, occurred last night so
swift

That th' ferry boat, unmanned, is left midst th' wilderness
adrift.

60. 塞下曲（其二）

卢纶

林暗草惊风，
将军夜引弓。
平明寻白羽，
没在石棱中。

A Frontier Melody (No. 2)[1]

Lu Lun[2]

The woods obscured, the grass in th' winds seeming to moan,

In th' dark his bow the general adeptly bent.

He found his arrow deep inserted in a stone

At dawn when he was tracking where the feathers[3] went.

61. 游子吟

孟郊

慈母手中线，
游子身上衣。
临行密密缝，
意恐迟迟归。
谁言寸草心，
报得三春晖。

Song of the Roamer[1]

Meng Jiao[2]

'Tis with threads in the loving mother's hand

That clothes are made as th' out-going son's wear.

For fear he may stay long in a strange land,

She's sewing stitch by stitch with love and care.[3]

Oh, th' gratitude of grass can ne'er repay

The spring sun's maternal warmth, I dare say![4]

62. 左迁至蓝关示侄孙湘

韩愈

一封朝奏九重天，
夕贬潮阳路八千。
欲为圣明除弊事，
敢将衰朽惜残年？
云横秦岭家何在？
雪拥蓝关马不前。
知汝远来应有意，
好收吾骨瘴江边。

To My Grandnephew Xiang—Composed on My Post-Demotion Journey via the Lantian Pass[1]

Han Yu[2]

My petition sent in to the throne at dawn, at th' close of day

Came th' edict of my removal to Chaoyang[3] far away.

Since 'tis my pledge to purge the reign of malpractice and sin,

How can I — though full of years — drift along to save my skin?[4]

Home's vanished beyond th' Qin Ridge covered with dark
　　clouds;

My horse balks at the Lantian Pass clad in snowy shrouds.[5]

'Tis th' fear that on th' rill of miasma[6] exposed my remains

Might lie, I guess, that's made you come from afar with great
　　pains.

63. 野老歌

张籍

老农家贫在山住，
耕种山田三四亩。
苗疏税多不得食，
输入官仓化为土。
岁暮锄犁倚空室，
呼儿登山收橡实。
西江贾客珠百斛，
船中养犬长食肉。

Song of the Poor Farmer

Zhang Ji[1]

An aged farmer, I live in poverty and in th' mounts[2],

The hillside fields I till below four *mu* by actual count.

The crops sparse, the taxes high, on nothing is left to be dined[3],

And yet my grain decays in state-owned barns as rent in kind.

In winter, when my shabby hut presents tools but no hope,

My poor sons have to gather acorns[4] on the mountain slope.

Oh, in striking contrast merchants on th' West River are worth

Millions of pearls, even their pets boast silver spoons from

    birth![5]

64. 春怨

金昌绪

打起黄莺儿，
莫教枝上啼。
啼时惊妾梦，
不得到辽西。

A Lady's Grievances in Spring

Jin Changxu[1]

I scare th' orioles off the trees, for fear

That they may in due time break my dream sweet:

I may not yet reach Liaoxi[2] the frontier

And meet my man if they warble and tweet.

65. 江雪

柳宗元

千山鸟飞绝，
万径人踪灭。
孤舟蓑笠翁，
独钓寒江雪。

The River Permeated with Snow[1]

Liu Zongyuan[2]

Thousands of mounts devoid of flying birds, no sign

Of men along a myriad of paths is found.[3]

On board a lone boat the man with his rod and line

Is braving th' snow, with which his hat and coat abound. [4]

66. 秋词（其一）

刘禹锡

自古逢秋悲寂寥，
我言秋日胜春朝。
晴空一鹤排云上，
便引诗情到碧霄。

咏情言志

218

Odes to Autumn (No. 1)[1]

Liu Yuxi[2]

Distress induced by autumn has long been a favoured theme,

But autumn time is lovelier than th' morns of spring, I'd say:[3]

Poetic inspiration in the azure seems to gleam

When up into the clouds soars a crane on a sunny day![4]

67. 乌衣巷

刘禹锡

朱雀桥边野草花，
乌衣巷口夕阳斜。
旧时王谢堂前燕，
飞入寻常百姓家。

咏情言志

220

The Black Coat Lane[1]

Liu Yuxi

Th' Rose-finch Bridge[2] looks desolate 'midst wild grass and

    plants;

Th' Black-coat Lane's obscure 'gainst the sun, which westward

    slants[3].

Th' swallows, which used to construct nests at th' splendid

    domes

Of th' Wangs' and Xies'[4], are darting into common homes.

221

68. 聚蚊谣

刘禹锡

沉沉夏夜兰堂开，
飞蚊伺暗声如雷。
嘈然欻起初骇听，
殷殷若自南山来。
喧腾鼓舞喜昏黑，
昧者不分聪者惑。
露华滴沥月上天，
利觜迎人着不得。
我躯七尺尔如芒，
我孤尔众能我伤。
天生有时不可遏，
为尔设幄潜匡床。
清商一来秋日晓，
羞尔微形饲丹鸟。

On Swarming Mosquitoes[1]

Liu Yuxi

The hall is open, night in summer drear;

Mosquitoes waiting in the dark now hum

At once, their sound so terrible to hear

As if from Mount Nan[2] fierce thunders had come.

Confusing fools, perplexing e'en the wise,

They clamour for the darkness they adore.

When dew descends and the moon does arise,

With sharp probosces men around they'll bore.

They are like awns, I'm seven *chi*[3] in height,

But they are in swarms and to th' bites I'm prone.

Now that they have their time in nature's light,

Confined to bed and net I'll hold my own.[4]

For autumn time is not far off indeed,

When fireflies on their tiny forms will feed![5]

223

69. 悯农二首

李绅

其一
春种一粒粟，
秋收万颗子。
四海无闲田，
农夫犹饿死。

其二
锄禾日当午，
汗滴禾下土。
谁知盘中餐，
粒粒皆辛苦？

咏情言志

224

Two Poems in Commiseration with the Farmers

Li Shen[1]

I

Every seed of millet they sow in spring

Will in autumn countless grains to them bring.

No field under the sun does idle lie, [2]

And yet of starvation the farmers die!

II

They're hoeing th' fields, the mid-day sun o'erhead;

Their sweat onto the soil is being shed.

Whoever knows that in the plate each grain

Of rice has come from much toil and much pain?[3]

225

70. 赋得古原草送别

白居易

离离原上草，
一岁一枯荣。
野火烧不尽，
春风吹又生。
远芳侵古道，
晴翠接荒城。
又送王孙去，
萋萋满别情。

The Grasses on the Ancient Plateau
Sending Me off

Bai Juyi[1]

Behold the grasses green and thick,

Which wither every year and thrive[2].

The prairie fires may burn and lick;

When breezes blow they'll yet revive.[3]

Their fragrance floats to th' ancient way,

Their luster tinctures th' ruins of town.

One more scion going away,

'Tis in the blues they themselves drown.[4]

71. 轻肥

白居易

意气骄满路，
鞍马光照尘。
借问何为者，
人称是内臣。
朱绂皆大夫，
紫绶悉将军。
夸赴军中宴，
走马去如云。
樽罍溢九酝，
水陆罗八珍。
果擘洞庭橘，
脍切天池鳞。
食饱心自若，
酒酣气益振。
是岁江南旱，
衢州人食人！

Steeds, Silks and Satins[1]

Bai Juyi

Overbearing are the riders all the way;

Th' steeds and saddles through the dust with splendour shine.[2]

People tell me 'tis the eunuchs that are they,

When I, much stunned, wonder what can be their line[3].

The scarlet robes mark officials ranking high,

While the purple ribbons the generals wear.[4]

Galloping like clouds under a windy sky,

They rush to an army banquet with foods rare.

Exquisite cups brim with nectar and nice wine,

Dainties from sea and land fill many a dish;

Upon tangerines from Mount Dongting[5] they dine,

Minced and braised is Heavenly Pool[6] fish.

Having eaten to their full, pleased they appear;

Tipsy, more supercilious now they grow.

Oh, th' south is stricken by a grave drought this year,

And hunger's killed and crazed thousands in Quzhou![7]

72. 卖炭翁

白居易

卖炭翁，
伐薪烧炭南山中。
满面尘灰烟火色，
两鬓苍苍十指黑。
卖炭得钱何所营？
身上衣裳口中食。
可怜身上衣正单，
心忧炭贱愿天寒。
夜来城外一尺雪，
晓驾炭车辗冰辙。
牛困人饥日已高，
市南门外泥中歇。
翩翩两骑来是谁？
黄衣使者白衫儿。
手把文书口称敕，
回车叱牛牵向北。
一车炭，千余斤，
宫使驱将惜不得。
半匹红绡一丈绫，
系向牛头充炭直。

The Charcoal Burner[1]

Bai Juyi

Behold the man, who in the mounts does hack

Wood and burn charcoal each and every day.

His wrinkled face is smeared, his fingers black,

And his hair on the temples brownish gray.[2]

In need of money his goods should be sold

To allay hunger and keep warm the skin,

He only wishes that it would grow cold,

Although the clothes he wears are worn and thin.[3]

He's filled with hope by last night's heavy snow,

For a good sale at dawn for town he makes.

At noon exhausted man and cattle grow,

And out of th' city gate a rest he takes.

Now come two riders with a haughty air,

One in yellow, th' other in a white gown[4].

Royal edict in hand, they do declare

The charcoal bought and make for th' north of town[5].

The cartload weighing o'er a thousand *jin*

Is own'd by th' court — claims as such none could duck[6]!

With a token payment of some gauze thin,

What else can he do but curse his bad luck?[7]

73. 鹦鹉

白居易

竟日语还默，
中宵栖复惊。
身囚缘彩翠，
心苦为分明。
暮起归巢思，
春多忆侣声。
谁能拆笼破，
从放快飞鸣。

The Parrot[1]

Bai Juyi

Taciturn by day she is oft lost in thought;

In the dead of night she wakes up with a start.

Beauty has been the bane of her being caught;[2]

Th' sense of justice results in an upset heart.

Homesickness at dark grows in intensity;[3]

Old friends' voice in spring oft becomes fresh in mind.

When smashed is this cage — a bar to liberty[4],

She'll freely sing and fly, leaving it behind!

74. 行宫

元稹

寥落古行宫，
宫花寂寞红。
白头宫女在，
闲坐说玄宗。

The Imperial Resort

Yuan Zhen[1]

The ancient palaces[2] present a rueful sight;

'Tis vainly that are blooming flowers red and bright.[3]

Those white-haired ladies[4], who've survived their mental pain,

Now sit at ease recalling Xuanzong and his reign.[5]

❧

75.题李凝幽居

贾岛

闲居少邻并，
草径入荒园。
鸟宿池边树，
僧敲月下门。
过桥分野色，
移石动云根。
暂去还来此，
幽期不负言。

Poem Inscribed on the Wall of Li Ning's
Secluded Cottage

Jia Dao[1]

The cottage has few neighbours, as one sees,

Thus th' garden looks deserted all the more.

Some birds are resting in the pond-side trees;

A monk is knocking at the moonlit door.[2]

'Tis wild that this side of th' bridge does appear,

Where th' clouds would waver if a rock you move.[3]

For the appointment I'll come again here,

And faithful to my word I'll surely prove.

76. 感讽（其一）

李贺

合浦无明珠，
龙洲无木奴。
足知造化力，
不给使君须。
越妇未织作，
吴蚕始蠕蠕。
县官骑马来，
狞色虬紫须。
怀中一方板，
板上数行书。
不因使君怒，
焉得诣尔庐。
越妇拜县官，
桑牙今尚小。
会待春日晏，
丝车方掷掉。
越妇通言语，
小姑具黄粱。
县官踏飧去，
簿吏复登堂。

Hard Times (No. 1)

Li He[1]

Hepu is now depriv'd of pearls for which it was once known;

Longzhou's depleted of its oranges so vastly grown.[2]

And thus the following conclusion is self-evident:

To satiate th' prefects, e'en Creator's incompetent![3]

Now that the wriggling silkworms are in such a tender stage,

In weaving the Yue housewife does not yet herself engage.[4]

Astride a horse a county official comes to her door,

Who with thick and curly beard looks ferocious all the more.

He draws a warrant from his bosom, on which several lines

Of words appear to leap. Who knows he comes for tax or fines?

"If the magistrate had not been so very much enraged,

"Why should I've bothered to come and be in this task engaged?"

"The housewife, after making a salute, to the official says:

"Lo, tender is the mulberry, and so the worms I raise!

"Could you, my lord, be kind enough to wait till th' end of spring,

"By which the task of weaving to a close we'll surely bring?"[5]

Her sister-in-law preparing a yellow millet meal,

She's trying every possible means to plead and appeal.

Oho, the sated man departs[6]. May nothing else befall!

But nay, just in his wake the bookkeeper has come to call![7]

77. 泊秦淮

杜牧

烟笼寒水月笼沙，
夜泊秦淮近酒家。
商女不知亡国恨，
隔江犹唱后庭花。

Mooring on the Qinhuai River

Du Mu[1]

The mist shrouding cold waters, th' moon dimly showing the
shore,[2]

I moor near wine-shops on the Qinhuai River after dark.

On the opposite bank a songstress, who knows not the sore

Over lost sovereignty[3], is singing "Flowers in th' Back Park."[4]

78. 山行

杜牧

远上寒山石径斜，
白云生处有人家。
停车坐爱枫林晚，
霜叶红于二月花。

A Mountain Scene[1]

Du Mu

A stony path's winding high up the chilly mount,

Where homes are set off by th' fleecy clouds' very fount[2].

Drawn by th' dusky maples th' cart to a halt I bring:

Th' frost-reddened leaves are brighter than th' flowers of

    spring[3].

79. 赤壁

杜牧

折戟沉沙铁未销，
自将磨洗认前朝。
东风不与周郎便，
铜雀春深锁二乔。

咏情言志

244

The Red Cliff [1]

Du Mu

The broken halberd has not yet been rusted out in th' sand;

In order to verify its times I wash it and scrub.[2]

That winter, if th' east wind had grudged th' gifted Zhou a free hand, [3]

By spring th' Bronze Fitch Stand would have seen the Qiao sisters locked up.[4]

80. 更漏子

温庭筠

玉炉香，红蜡泪，
偏照画堂秋思。
眉翠薄，鬓云残，
夜长衾枕寒。

梧桐树，三更雨，
不道离情正苦。
一叶叶，一声声，
空阶滴到明。

The Hydraulic Chronograph[1]

Wen Tingyun [2]

Th scent from th' burner and th' tearful red candle trace[3]
In th' well-adorned bower th' autumn sadness in the belle's face.
Her raven hair shaggy, her eyebrow pigment gone,
The bedding feels cold and the autumn night drags on and on.

Detached are th' Chinese parasols and mid-night rain,
Which sound unfeeling 'bout her departure-inflicted pain:
Th' trees send down leaf after leaf, th' rain falls drop by drop;
Ere dawn splattering on the door steps without any stop.[4]

247

81. 无题

李商隐

相见时难别亦难，
东风无力百花残。
春蚕到死丝方尽，
蜡炬成灰泪始干。
晓镜但愁云鬓改，
夜吟应觉月光寒。
蓬山此去无多路，
青鸟殷勤为探看。

An Untitled Poem[1]

Li Shangyin[2]

'Tis hard for us to meet, but separation's harder still.

When breezes languish, fall and wither all the flowers will.[3]

The silkworm ceases not to spin her thread before she's dead;

Unless burnt to ashes endless tears a candle'll shed.[4]

At dawn the mirror betrays my sole dread of aging hair;

Reciting poems at night you should feel th' moon's chill in the

    air.

As Mount Penglai is not very long a distance away,

Visits in my stead th' Blackbird must be kind enough to pay![5]

82. 官仓鼠

曹邺

官仓老鼠大如斗，
见人开仓亦不走。
健儿无粮百姓饥，
谁遣朝朝入君口？

The Rats at State-Owned Granaries[1]

Cao Ye[2]

The rats at the state granaries, as big as cats, are proud:

E'en when men enter from th' doors they don't deign to walk away.

"Hungry and needy are th' folk and soldiers ," I quiz aloud,

"Who's entitled you to eat your fill each and every day?"[3]

83. 蜂

罗隐

不论平地与山尖，
无限风光尽被占。
采得百花成蜜后，
为谁辛苦为谁甜？

咏情言志

252

To the Bees

Luo Yin[1]

On any pretty scene you can be found —
Be it a mountain peak or level ground.[2]
You are collecting pollen with such haste,
And yet the honey you make who will taste?[3]

84. 钱塘江潮

罗隐

怒声汹汹势悠悠，
罗刹江边地欲浮。
漫道往来存大信，
也知反覆向平流。
任抛巨浸疑无底，
猛过西陵只有头。
至竟朝昏谁主掌，
好骑赪鲤问阳侯。

咏情言志

254

The Qiantang Tide[1]

Luo Yin

As if Rakshas[2] were sending th' earth into the flow,

Roaring with a great momentum surges the tide.

Notwithstanding in good faith it does come and go,

And in due course it ebbs without traces of pride.

Bottomless the sea appears when its waves loom large,

And yet the west dyke marks the finish of its task.

Of the precept of the tide who is taking charge?

Riding on the Red Carp Yanghou I'll go to ask.[3]

85.新沙

陆龟蒙

渤澥声中涨小堤，
官家知后海鸥知。
蓬莱有路教人到，
亦应年年税紫芝。

A New Sandbar in the Bohai Sea

Lu Guimeng[1]

After th' roaring tides a nice and fat sandbar did appear,

Of which the throne had got wind ere th' seagulls were in the

know.[2]

E'en th' immortals would be taxed on magic herbs every year —

If to Penglai the collectors could find a way to go![3]

86.题菊花

黄巢

飒飒西风满院栽，
蕊寒香冷蝶难来。
他年我若为青帝，
报与桃花一处开。

To the Chrysanthemum

Huang Chao[1]

You flourish in the garden under the windy autumn skies;

With flowers cold and scent chilly you're snubbed by butterflies.

If someday I'd possess authority as God of Spring[2],

An equal chance to bloom at once with th' peach I'll to you

    bring![3]

87. 山中寡妇

杜荀鹤

夫因兵死守蓬茅，
麻苎衣衫鬓发焦。
桑柘废来犹纳税，
田园荒后尚征苗。
时挑野菜和根煮，
旋斫生柴带叶烧。
任是深山更深处，
也应无计避征徭。

The Widow Living Deep Deep in the Mountains

Du Xunhe[1]

Her thatched hut and gunny clothes shabby, and brown her hair, [2]

She has been widowed by the war and driven to despair.[3]

The mulberry trees untended, silk duties must still be paid;

Her fields uncultivated, under taxes is she laid.[4]

To alleviate hunger herbal plants with roots are stewed;

For lack of ready wood she burns leafed branches freshly hewed.[5]

Alas, the duties and taxes you'll find no way to dodge,

Even if in the deepest of remote mountains you lodge![6]

Songs of Weal and Woe

88. 虞美人

李煜

春花秋月何时了？
往事知多少。
小楼昨夜又东风，
故国不堪回首月明中。

雕栏玉砌应犹在，
只是朱颜改。
问君能有几多愁？
恰似一江春水向东流。

Yu the Beauty

Li Yu[1]

Th' autumn moon and spring flowers in their endless rounds,
Nostalgia seething in me seems to know no bounds![2]
When spring breeze revisited my building last night,
How sad I felt o'er th' lost kingdom under a moon so bright.[3]

Th' carved railing and jade steps must be there as before,
Yet the hue of youth, sicklied o'er, exists no more.[4]
How much distress do I have? If you'd care to know,
Just Behold the rill's spring waters in th' eastward flow.[5]

注释　Notes and Commentary

31. 人日思归　Homesickness on Man's Day

1　This poem, through enumeration of events in sequence of time and comparisons between different things (comparison between the poet's return and that of the wild geese, and comparison between homesickness and the trees in "budding"), subtly expresses the homesickness of the narrator, a northerner who has stayed in the south for two long years.

　　Since the Han Dynasty it has been customary for the Chinese to observe Man's Day on the seventh day of the first lunar month, a festival connoting the wish that Man may live in peace and contentment.

2　Xue Daoheng (540 AD–609 AD), who was from Jiankang — the present-day Nanjing, was an important poet of the Sui Dynasty.

3　In Chinese literature the wild goose, which begins its migration from the wintering area to the breeding ground in spring as a rule, is symbolic of the messenger or nostalgia.

32. 无向辽东浪死歌　Don't Go East to Liao and Die for Nothing in a Strange Land

1　In the present ballad, Wang Bo, leader of the uprising, calls upon the peasants to rise in revolt. It circulated in the area of the Mount Ever White. The description of the poet's heroic deeds and military spirit must have been encouraging, for tens of thousands of peasants had answered the call.

2　His lance ... /...of light.— These two lines, each involving a case of hyperbole, praise Wang for his valiance.

33. 咏鹅　The Goose

1　This rhyme, created by Luo Binwang in his childhood (at the age of seven, to be exact) is on the lips of billions of children. It vividly depicts how the goose gaggles while swimming in the limpidity.

2　Luo Binwang (c. 640 AD–c. 684 AD) was one of the Four Distinguished Poets of the Tang Dynasty. His poetry is known for its vigorous style.

3　The word "gaggle" (the mimicking of the goose's utterance) is a case of onomatopoeia, and the repetition of the word adds to the rhetorical effect of the line.

咏
情
言
志

264

34. 送杜少府之任蜀州　**Farewell to Du**

1　The complete title of the original, "Farewell to Du, Who's Faring forth for Shu to Fill the Position of Assistant County Magistrate," is shortened here for the sake of brevity. "Shu" is the short (or rather, the ancient name) for Sichuan, and "Du" is the surname of the poet's friend.

　　In terms of ideological content and subject matter, Wang had broadened the realm of poetry and had formed a style of his own. In this connection, "Farewell to Du" may serve as example. Totally free from the low-key tone and conventional pattern of send-off poetry, it is imbued with a positive feeling of optimism. That is why one couplet "So long as you have a friend devoted and dear, / E' if he's far away you'll e'er feel he's near" has become a celebrated dictum to cherish friendship.

2　Wang Bo (649 AD?–676 AD) was from Longmen of the now Shanxi Province. Exceptionally intelligent, he passed the highest civil examination at the age of fourteen. He had held several official positions. He got drowned at twenty-seven.

　　Wang is recognized as the most prominent of the "Four Distinguished Poets of the Early Tang Dynasty," who strove to break away from the formalist style typical of the poetry of the Qi and the Liang Dynasties and whose poetry displays the young intellectuals' initiative in the political reform as well as their resentment against repression.

3　th' capital — The capital of the Tang Dynasty, i.e. Chang'an.

4　the Three Qins — When Xiang Yu (232 BC–202 BC) toppled the Qin Dynasty, he divided the former territory of the Kingdom of Qin into three parts, usually termed the Three Qins.

5　... I gaze /... in the haze. — The Five Ferries, namely the Ferries of Baihua, Wanli, Jiangsu, Shetou and Jiangnan, are located in Shu (for which Du was leaving). Literally speaking, Shu, which was a long distance away from Chang'an, could not be visible, and yet in the mind's eye of the poet, the two places were closely linked up.

　　The opening couplet, which expresses the poet's deep concern for his friend's future, foreshadows the theme of the poem — a bosom friend afar brings a distance land near.

6　th' same career — the official career.

7　... shed womanly tears — ... shed tears as a woman does (a case of transferred epithet).

35. 滕王阁诗　The Tower of Prince Teng

1　In the year 675 AD, the poet took his way to Jiaozhi via Hongzhou (the now City of Nanchang), where he took part in a party held at the Tower of Prince Teng. At the party he wrote impromptu the well-known prose "Eulogy to the Tower of Prince Teng" and the present poem.

　　In this poem, he expresses his feelings, in a beautifully succinct style, about the change of times and events and about the situation in which talent is ignored.

2　th' pendant wearers — The pendant wearers refer to Prince Teng and his entourage.

3　Its painted ..., / ...West Hill. — Here the ridge-beams and curtains are personified.

4　At the tower ..., / ... now fast. —The prince is gone forever, and now who would set an eye by the mighty river?

266

36. 登幽州台歌　Ascent of the Youzhou Tower

1　Chen Zi'ang (661 AD−702 AD) was a poet and statesman from Xiehong of the now Sichuan Province. As the one, he had done significant pioneering work for the forthcoming flourish of Tang poetry: he was opposed to the formalist practice, advocating that verse should be vested with realistic political content; as the other, he was of wide vision and great resource: he had more than once remonstrated with the highest authority for the sake of the nation and people, without fearing to offend the powerful. He was framed up and died in gaol.

　　In the year 696 AD, he started as staff officer on an expedition against a rebel. He offered advice about saving a serious situation caused by the commander's mistakes, only to bring about his own demotion. Feeling upset and disappointed, the poet ascended the Youzhou Tower, on the site of which the wise King Zhao of Yan had, one thousand years before, constructed the Golden Platform to accord courteous receptions to talented people. The historic site inspired him to compose a poem which was to touch the hearts of millions.

　　The poem is a natural flow of feelings. In form and language, it shows the influence of the verse of Chu; in artistic conception and content, it bespeaks the originality of the poet.

2　the ancients —Here the poet is alluding to such wise rulers as King Zhao of Yan, who has shown great respect for and entrusted important tasks to such talented people as Yue Yi and Guo Wei.

3 moderns of the type — Contemporary rulers who are willing to follow the example of King Zhao.

The first couplet involves the device of antithesis (ancients versus moderns).

37. 回乡偶书　Random Lines on My Return to Hometown

1 He Zhizhang (659 AD–774 AD) had held the position of Adviser to the Crown Prince. He was unrestrained by the convention and often lent a helping hand to unrecognized young talents. When he was over eighty, he resigned office and returned to his hometown Yongxing of Yuezhou, the now Xiaoshan of Zhejiang Province.

The present poem, in which a quiet tone of pathos in undercut by the dramatic scene of the poet's meeting with the native children, expresses the mixed feelings of the poet about his hometown and the great change which time has effected in him.

2 Away at ... decayed — This line contains two cases of antithesis, namely "left" versus "return" and "at a tender age" versus "when decayed."

3 Although my accent's unchanged, — This implies that the poet's love of his hometown is as keen as before.

267

4 The children's smile only serves to set off the plaintive element of the poem, and the seemingly matter-of-course question must be quite a shock to the poet.

38. 春江花月夜　The Flower-Fringed River in a Moonlit Night

1 Poems under the title of "The Flower-Fringed River in a Moonlit Night" (the name of a Music-Institute song) are many, but this lyric of Zhang's excels in that the five scenic elements involved (spring, river, flower, moon and night) are skillfully integrated with the feelings of the narrator so true to life. As a subtle manifestation of a melancholic lady's amorous yearnings for her man on a charming moonlit night, it imparts a perception of feminine beauty. The first stanza (the first twelve lines) depicts the beautiful scene, the second stanza (the succeeding twelve lines) describes the young lady's feelings evoked by that scene, and the last stanza is devoted to sublimation of the lady's feelings, bringing forward the thematic idea that the lady's youth-hood, like the flower, may be transient, but her true love for her man will remain as boundless

Songs of Weal and Woe

as the moonlight.

The metric pattern of this poem allows a sonorous reading. Without being turgid, the language is elegant; without being showy, the style is elevated. Activated by the pertinent use of rhetorical devices the picturesque scene harmoniously changes with the mood of the character, presenting an irresistible aesthetic and artistic appeal to the readers.

2　Zhang Ruoxu (c.666 AD−c.720 AD) was from Yangzhou. He is known as one of the Four Talents of Wu (the other three being He Zhizhang, Zhang Xu and Bao Rong).

3　The elfish moon ..., /... absentee. — Why does the lovely moon become elfish in the lady's mind's eye? Because it shows up the dressing table of the lady's beloved, who is absent, and thus making her sad.

4　Th' swans ...; / ... just ripples appear. — These couplet shows how disappointed the lady is when no letter from her man is received and when she awakens to the reality that she cannot fly with light to meet her man.

In Chinese literature, the images of the fish and the swan are metaphoric of messengers.

5　The fallen flowers are suggestive of the elapse of time.

6　Jieshi and Xiaoxiang — Jieshi, a place in North China, is far away from Xiaoxiang in the south. Here the two place names do not necessarily refer to the specific places in which the lovers respectively stay, but are used to denote "the north and the south" (a case of metonymy).

7　May there be ... breeze. — Here the narrator wishes that there be men who have come home to enjoy a happy reunion with their wives. By endowing the lady with a sympathetic heart, the poem itself attains a lofty realm of thought.

39. 登鹳雀楼　Ascending the Stork Tower

1　This poem, written in a simple, natural and vigorous style, represents the splendor of Nature and reflects the enterprising spirit which prevailed in the Early Tang Dynasty. It was composed when the poet was ascending the Stork Tower, which commands a good view of the Zhongtiao Mountains and the Yellow River. Its well-constructed conceptual realm imparts to us that, only when we attain a lofty realm of thought, can we see further ahead. The last couplet has become a celebrated dictum for inspiring people to make unremitting efforts in their pursuit of truth, knowledge and success.

2   Wang Zhihuan (668 AD−742 AD) was born to an established family in the Prefecture of Jinyang, the now Taiyuan of Shanxi. He had held some minor official positions and spent much of his life time travelling. He is best known for his four-line metrical poems, most of which deal with frontier landscapes.

40. 春晓   Spring Morn

1   Meng Haoran (689 AD−740 AD) was from Xiangyang of the now Hubei Province. As a pastoral poet, advantageous points lie in short poems which depict natural scenery.

    The connotations of poetry proliferate in the course of circulation. On the surface, the poem merely reflects the ease of reclusive life; in the deep level, however, it implies the sympathetic feeling for the fallen flowers — beauty brutalized by the evil forces embodied in the shattering winds and rains.

2   The winds ...; /... in a plight? — Awakening from slumber, the poet at first hears the birds sing and, on recalling the winds and rains of the night, cannot help thinking — with a touch of pathos — of the flowers which may have been broken into shatters.

    As time progresses, the last couplet has acquired a figurative meaning and may be cited to expressing sorrow for the beautiful and / or virtuous trampled upon by the evil forces.

41. 宿桐庐江寄广陵旧游   To an Old Friend in Guangling — Composed When Staying on the Tonglu River

1   The poet expresses how keenly he is missing his old friend through a vivid description of surrounding scenery, which serves as a foil to the poet's feelings. Traditionally, whether one is sincere and devoted to his friends constitutes an important factor for the judgement of his moral integrity.

    Tonglu is a county located in Zhejiang, and the present-day Yangzhou was referred to as Guangling or Weiyang in ancient times.

2   In this couplet tear is a metaphor for message, and the north reach of the Yangtze River refers to where the poet's friend stays.

42. 黄鹤楼   The Yellow Crane Tower

1   Cui Hao (704 AD?−754 AD) was from the prefecture of Bian — the now

Kaifeng of Henan Province. He became an official candidate in the Reign of Kaiyuan, and was appointed a court official in the Reign of Tianbao.

Many of his early compositions were tumid. As luck would have it, he had immediate contact with frontier life in his later years, which effected a significant change in his style.

In the present piece, the poet's imagination soars between legend and reality, up to the sky and down to the earth, and from the past to the present, creating a fascinating aesthetic entity which is formed by images of the Yellow Crane, the immortal, the fleecy clouds, the dominant tower, the wooded plain, the grassy isle, the misty river and the nostalgic poet himself.

This poem has enjoyed great popularity. The great poet Li Bai thought highly of it. It is said that he was struck with admiration when he first read the poem, which was inscribed on the wall of the tower in question. The famous critic Yan Yu of the Southern Song Dynasty points out that it is "beyond doubt the best of long seven-character metrical poems of the Tang Dynasty."

2 Astride ... flown — This is an allusion to the Chinese legend, which goes that Zi'an, an immortal who flies astride his Yellow Crane, often alights to take a rest on the Yellow Crane Rock of the Snake Hill, where the Yellow Crane Tower is located.

3 The Hanyang Plain is on the north bank of the Yangtze River opposite to the City of Wuchang, where the Snake Hill lies.

4 th' Parrot Isle is situated on the Yangtze River north to Wuchang.

43. 出塞　Far Away on the Frontier

1 Wang Changling (698 AD?−757 AD?) was from the capital Chang'an (the now Xi'an). Since he passed the highest civil examination in 727 AD, he had held some minor positions. He wrote excellent short metrical poems with five-character lines about frontier life, departure and feminine grievances, which are his favourite subjects.

In the present piece, which derives its title from a Music-Institute song, the poet, in a succinct and implicit style, expresses his deep concern about national defense and satirizes the Tang rulers who failed to choose competent warriors for guarding the borders.

2 As in ...; /... soon. — These two lines, by alluding to history, deplore the age-long problem of suffering from invasions by the nomads from the

north.

3   th' Flying General — This refers to Li Guang of the Han Dynasty, who had been acclaimed as the Flying General for his bravery and resource.

4   th' Dragon Town had been the religious and political centre of the Huns.

5   The "Hun steeds" is the metonymy for " the Hun cavalry."

6   Yinshan — a chain of mountains in the north of ancient China, which had provided a natural strategic position for defence.

44. 山居秋暝 An Autumn Eve during My Stay in the Mounts

1   The present poem, a word picture of a country scene in autumn, expresses the poet's love of nature and enjoyment of the reclusive life that he lived in his later years. It flows with natural ease. The English version follows the rhyme scheme of *Ode to a Nightingale* by John Keats.

2   Wang Wei (701 AD–761 AD), a great poet, painter, calligrapher and musician, was from Qi of Taiyuan, the now Qi County of Shanxi Province. His political career was an involved one: he passed the highest civil examination in 721 AD, had held in succession the positions of Counselor and Official Supervisor before he was demoted for lack of moral courage when An Lushan's forces captured the capital, and he was promoted to the position of deputy premier in charge of one of the two divisions of the cabinet. Wang is the most distinguished representative of the Landscape School (of course that doesn't mean he is confined to landscape portrayal). On the whole his verse features an elegant style, a fresh conceptual world and beautiful sentiments.

3   A scene moon .../... winds its way. — In Chinese prosody, this is called an antithetical or parallel couplet, one in which the words and phrases in the corresponding positions of the two lines should be neatly matched in their tones, senses and parts of speech. An eight-line metrical poem involves two such couplets (the second and the third couplets), as is the case with the original of the present poem.

45. 相思 The Love Pea

1   This poem was written to the famous musician Li Guinian, who was leaving for the south. By taking advantage of the symbolic meaning of the love pea, the poet expresses a profound love for his friend and wishes that their friendship be forever cherished.

    The poem is marked by the successful use of symbolism (with the love pea representing friendship).

The love pea is a tree which grows in the south of China. According to a Chinese legend, the seed of the tree is the incarnation of the lady who, overcome by grief over her husband's death on the frontier, cried bitterly and at last died under the tree. Hence the love pea has come to symbolize love and / or friendship.

46. 将进酒　A Toast

1　The present poem, which derives its title from a Music-Institute song, belongs in "Classical Verse", i.e. verse without strict rules governing the tonal pattern, rhyme scheme and number of syllables in a line. It was composed around 752 AD, eight years after the poet was squeezed out of the political and cultural centre Chang'an.

This poem express the poet's indignation at the stern reality, in which vile characters hold sway while the noble-minded and talented are reduced to obscurity. On the one hand, it manifests the poet's sunny outlook on life, which grows out of self-confidence, aspirations and love for the people and nature; on the other hand, it reveals the poet's pessimism, which stems out from setbacks, suppression and, of course, from the limitation of his times. The issue as to how far the poet is carried away by pessimism has remained controversial. Some allege that the poet has reached the point of decadence; Others argue that heroic spirit and optimism are the mainstream, that such proposals to toast as "people should drink to their hearts' content / When poss'ble and ne'er leave their cups empty under the moon" should not be regarded as a demonstration of the poet's ideas, and that some lines are based on the same thought as "How can I bend my proud head and stoop to serving the powerful vile / At the sacrifice of a dignified smile?" (quoted from another poem by the poet), which only shows the poet's contempt for the powerful flew, etc.

This poem is marked by its ingenious use of rhetorical devices (metaphor, hyperbole, allusion, etc.), natural flow of ideas and unconstrained style. As one of Li's masterpieces, its artistic value is generally recognized.

2　Li Bai (701 AD−762 AD) was born in Suiye of Anxi Prefecture, which was in the now Kazakhstan (his ancestral home was in Chengji of Longxi). At the age of five he went with his father to Mianzhou — the now Mianyang of Sichuan, where he received his education. At twenty-five he left the place to make extensive travels. Early in the Reign of Tianbao he went to Chang'an and was bestowed upon the title of Hanlin (an honour for renowned scholars) on the recommendation of Wu Jun, a Daoist. What with his unrestrained personality and what with his opposition to corrupt politics, he incurred repeated attacks from powerful bureaucrats and was euphemistically "allowed to return with gold in reward", i.e. compelled to leave the capital. When the rebellion under An Lushan and Shi Siming broke out, he served as aide-de-camp to Li Lin, the Prince of Yong, only to be involved in the conflict among the royalty and sentenced to a banishment to Yelang. The banishment was remitted when he was on the way to Yelang, the poet, however, had been physically and psychologically wrecked. He began to lead a wandering life. He visited Li Yangbin (magistrate of Dantu County) at his residence, where he put up till he died at the age of sixty-two.

Li Bai, generally revered as "a banished celestial being" and "the Immortal Muse", is one of the greatest poets. He had made an unrivalled contribution to bringing romanticism to its zenith of prosperity. His poetry, more than one thousand pieces in all, is marked by masculine grandeur, natural grace, unconstrained boldness, fantastic vision and singular conception. Du Fu sings the praises of Li in some ten poems. The well known essayist Han Yu and the renowned critic Yan Yu highly appraise Li's attainments. People world-wide cherish the memory of Li Bai not only for his wonderful contribution to the sum of cultural heritage, but also for his lofty personality, as was incarnated in his ardent love for his people and nation, in his tireless pursuit of freedom and justice, and in his daring spirit to revolt against the vicious and powerful.

273

3   Haven't you seen ... /... never ever to return? — This is a rhetorical question, which helps to emphasize the idea. To say that the Yellow River is "pouring down from th' skies" is a case of hyperbole, and the river is a metaphor for time which, once lost, can not be regained.

4   Haven't you seen .../... turn? —This question suggests that life is transient and that time wait for no one — not even the mansion dwellers.

To say that hair turned white in a day is another case of hyperbole.

5   'Tis natural gifts ..., /... very soon. —This couplet demonstrates the poet's values and attitudes: he treasures gifts, believing that some day his talent will be brought into play, and he makes light of money, for it can come

and go.

It would be interesting to make a comparison between the outlook of the poet and that of quite a few people in modern society, who are haunted by the craze of money worship.

6 Cen and Yuan respectively refer to Cen Xun and Yuan Danqiu.

7 'Tis devoutly ... night. — The world is so unbearably confounded and unjust that the poet can only wish that he could remain unconscious of it! Note the sarcastic tone of the poet.

8 From of old ..., /... all the ages. — The world has been turned upside down: the saints and sages are denied the opportunity to render talent to society and reduced to obscurity, while drinkers can make a name for themselves.

9 Prince Chensi — Namely Cao Zhi, who was given to the bottle because his talent only roused the jealousy of the monarchs.

10 ..., with which we'll drown cares age-old! — To drown cares in drink is passive practice. On the other hand, we can see what trouble the poet's mind are not merely personal cares. A man with a sense of historic mission, the poet has the ill-fated nation at heart.

47. 静夜思　In the Quiet of the Night

1 Hu Yinglin, critic of the Ming Dynasty, says that Li Bai's four-line verse is "spontaneously superb." The present piece may serve as an example. More often than not travellers found themselves stranded in a strange place in ancient China, which had a vast territory but poor transport facilities, and thus homesickness provided a subject for versification. This poem, for one, describes the poet's seething nostalgia in the quiet of a moonlit night.

With its simplicity, natural grace and ingenious artistic conception this poem has acquired an unbroken popularity.

2 ... before my bed — This attributive phrase, seemingly trivial, carries a subtle implication. It may set the careful reader wondering whether the poet is suffering from insomnia. The word "bed" suggests an late hour of the night, as the title does.

48. 早发白帝城　Embarkation at Baidi Early in the Morning

1 It is believed that this poem was written in 759 AD, when the poet was returning under amnesty from Baidi to Jiangling along the Yangtze River.

Written in a breezy and picturesque style, this poem effectively expresses the lofty sentiments of the light-hearted poet who, absolved from banishment, is parting with his woeful past and advancing towards a less gloomy future in spite of all the snags and whirls. An optimistic boldness overflows between the lines, and the image of the poet is suggestive of a flying angel. It possesses "a momentum which could check the fury of the elements and work up the mental fervour of the gods", says Yang Shen, critic of the Ming Dynasty, in praise of the poem.

It is an old story that honesty and virtue invite attack and persecution, and a little optimism is indispensable for the survival of people with integrity. Perhaps we could learn something from this poem: if we had a gloomy today, just think that there might be a bright tomorrow yet.

2   To be more accurate, the distance between Baidi (in Sichuan) and Jiangling (in Hubei) measures 1,200 *li*.

3   The jabbering of apes ..., /... has flashed past! — In Chinese literature, the jabbering of apes (which was typical of the Wu Gorge in ancient times) imparts a feeling of sorrow and the boat sometimes symbolizes "cause" or "resolution."

49. 望庐山瀑布（其二） Watching the Waterfall in the Lushan Mountains（No. 2）

1   This poem, which features a novel hyperbole and a vigorous imagination, is one of Li Bai's masterpieces. By picturing a beautiful and romantic scene of the Lushan Mountains, the poet shows a deep love for Mother Nature.

2   Incense Burner, named from its shape, is one of the many peaks. In this poem it forms the beautiful background of the scene.

3   Plunging down some three thousand *chi* — This is a case of hyperbole: the height is exaggerated. *Chi* is the Chinese unit of length approximately equalling 33.3 centimetres.

4   As if ... descending from th' skies — This line contains a simile: the waterfall is likened to the descending Milky Way. From the diction we can see what unbounded imagination the poet possesses.

50. 塞下曲（其一） A Frontier Melody（No. 1）

1   The poet has written six pieces under the title "A Frontier Melody", of

which the present poem is the first.

This poem reflects the rigour of frontier life, eulogizes the heroic spirit of frontier guards and expresses the ardent patriotism of the poet, who is concerned about the fate of his nation.

Li Bai, while opposing himself to the Tang rulers' abuse of force, hated the rebellions under regional aristocrats. For this matter the readers may refer to his "Song of the White-Horse Rider(《白马篇》)", "Song of the Eastward Advance under Prince Young(《永王东巡歌》)", etc.

2 Tianshan — The Tianshan Mountains, which is the metaphor for "frontier."

3 th' fifth month — the fifth month in the lunar calendar

4 Willow Twigs — the name of an ancient melody

5 But not a ... spelt. — But not a sign has anywhere been spelt（= meant）for spring.

6 To smash Loulan ... — This is an allusion to history: The king of Loulan had more than once ordered his men to intercept and kill envoys of the Han Empire, who were dispatched to the Western Regions to establish friendly relations. Fu Jiezi, at the order of Marshal Huo Guang, tactfully subdued the kingdom and thus ensured a safe passage to the regions.

51. 题破山寺后禅院　An Inscription on the Wall of the Back Compound of the Poshan Hill Temple

1 Chang Jian (?−?) was from Chang'an. He became an official candidate in 727 AD. He abandoned his chequered official career and lived a seclusive life. His poetry is marked by its concise language and fresh conception.

The present poem is Chang's representative work. By giving a vivid description of a mountain scene, the poet shows his quiet mentality and ardent love of nature.

2 ... suits th' birds' mentality — Here the birds are personified.

3 The limpid pool ... souls. — From this we can see that the poet has a deep understanding of human weaknesses and that he himself is indifferent of fame and gain.

52. 自京赴奉先县咏怀五百字（节选）　Intonation of Five Hundred Characters — Evoked on the Way from the Capital to Fengxian County (an excerpt)

1 The present excerpt is taken from a poem written in 755 AD, when the

rebellion under An Lushan was in brew. Despite the forthcoming crisis Emperor Xuanzong indulged in pleasures together with his concubine Yang Yuhuan at the Huaqing Resort in Mount Lishan. When the poet went past that mountain on his way to Fengxian County to visit his family, he could not help feeling both worried about the fate of his nation and indignant at the dissipation of the rulers. Upon arriving home, he learned that his little son had been starved to death. All sorts of feeling welling up his heart, the poet, at this stage well prepared in artistry, ideology and life experience, took up his writing brush to elaborate a long poem, which vividly reflects the grim reality and sharp class contradiction of the High Tang Dynasty. Rich in content, profound in thought, compact in framework and succinct in language, it has remained a masterpiece of realistic poetry.

2   Du Fu (712 AD−770 AD) was born to an official's family, which had moved from Xiangyang (in the now Hubei Province) to Gongxian County of Henan. He had shown a keen inclination for literature and calligraphy since his childhood. He stayed in Luoyang for some time in the Reign of Tianbao, when he made the acquaintance of and formed a lasting friendship with Li Bai. At the age of thirty-five he went to Chang'an in the hope of getting a position, but his ten years' stay there proved fruitless for that matter. During the An-Shi Turmoil he was appointed attendant remonstrant, but because of his divergence with the emperor he was demoted to a minor position in Huazhou Prefecture, which he relinquished not long afterwards. He moved first to Qinguan and then to Tonggu, and finally settled down in Chengdu, where he built a thatched house with the support of friends and relatives. On the recommendation of Yan Wu (military governor of Jiannan), under whom he had served as a staff officer, Du was appointed an official in the Ministry of Works in 764 AD, but he abdicated the post soon afterwards. His later years saw him haunted by poverty and wandering about with his family. He died of illness on the voyage along the Xiang River.

Du Fu was a great humanist. Without mercy he condemns the evils of the corrupt, fatuous and predatory few; with great sympathy he airs the sufferings of the poverty-stricken, famine-haunted and war-worn millions. "When evil's running rampant ere the throne, / Benevolence with daily fear does shake", he laments. "Behind red gates wine and meat go to waste; / On th' road those freezing to death lie in dirt", he thus pictures the striking contrast between the rich and the poor. His immense works — more than 1,400 verses and over 20 essays — offer a most complete realistic picture of the High Tang Dynasty and of its decline, and they are lauded as "history recorded in verse".

Armed with a wide range of erudition, Du has epitomized the best of all preceding versification. His poetry takes on various forms and covers a wide scope of subjects. On the whole his style features solemnity, simplicity, vigour and boldness, though there is no lack of examples of breezy and elegant works. As to the language and metre, they are brilliant and perfect. Du Fu, a golden combination of humanism, genius and industry, certainly merits the name of "sage-poet" — for he has added valuable contributions to the treasure house of human civilization.

Just as Li Bai tops the peak of romanticism, so Du Fu treads the summit of realism. Du Fu will forever be remembered as a great friend of the people.

3　When evil's ..., /... does shake. — Here "evil" and "benevolence" are cases of synecdoche, which respectively denote "vicious court officials" and "noble-minded or kind-hearted people."

4　The Weis and Huos ... — This is an allusion to the history of the Han Dynasty. Wei Qing and Huo Qubing, being relatives of Emperor Wudi, had enjoyed both authority and privilege. The poet is actually exposing by innuendo the misdeed of Yang Yuhuan's kinsmen.

5　th' angels — This refer to Yang Yuhuan and her cousin, who found favour with the emperor.

6　Behind red gates ..., / ... lie in dirt. — This couplet, by way of typical images condensation, reflects the striking contrast between the rich and the poor.

53. 春望　The Panorama in Spring

1　This metrical poem was written in 757 AD, when the poet had been taken prisoner and incarcerated in Chang'an by the rebelling troops under An Lushan. It represents the desolation of the capital after looting and expresses the poet's feelings — his yearning towards his family, his sorrow over the fall of the capital and his love for the motherland.

Three unities are achieved: the unity of the ideological content and aesthetic form, the unity of profound thought and succinct language, and that of the description of scenes and the expression of feelings.

2　Affected by the times ...; /...add despair. — Here the poet employs what seems to be abnormal to express what is natural. As a rule birds and flowers can cheer people up, but there are times when people's saddened hearts refused to be appeased. Only when we take the poet's sentiments and circumstances into consideration, can we realize that it stands to reason for him to feel all the more distressed at the sight of flowers and upon hearing the singing of birds. Examined logically, thematically or psychologically, the interpretation of the birds and flowers as the subjects (i.e. the doers of the acts of shedding tears and feeling distressed), doesn't seem to hold water.

54. 茅屋为秋风所破歌　Sorrow over My Thatched Cottage Damaged by the Autumn Winds

1　This poem was composed in 761 AD. It consists of three stanzas: the first narrating how the poet's thatched house was shattered by the autumn winds; the second relating the wretched conditions of the family after the house was destroyed and since the An-Shi Turmoil broke out; and the last stanza manifesting the breadth of mind and lofty ideal of the poet, who associates his own misfortune with the adversities of the common people whom he loves, wishing that the ill-fated millions be well sheltered.

　　The varied rhyme scheme and the irregular length of lines adequately ensure a smooth and natural flow of feelings, and the poet's deep concern and hearty consideration for the populace attain an ideological height. All those factors bespeak why the poem has a far-reaching impact on people of later generations.

2　the war — the An-Shi Turmoil

55. 闻官军收河南河北　Poem Composed at the News of the Recapture of Henan and Hebei by the Royal Forces

1　This metrical poem was written in 763 AD, when the recapture of Henan and Hebei from the rebelling forces knelled the complete failure of the Rebellion under An Lushan and Shi Siming, which had lasted for over seven years. In a bold and flowing style the poet describes the jubilation of his family at the exciting news, showing his yearning for and love of peace. As it expresses the feeling of the average refugee from war and turmoil, this poem has touched the heart of millions.

2　North Ji — the northern part of Hebei

3　this side of the Jianmen Pass — This refer to central Shu, which lay

Songs of Weal and Woe

south to the Pass.

The poet was at the time taking refuge in Zizhou.

4　Spring's offer ... decline? — This is a rhetorical question, which means "Nobody shall decline the offer of spring to accompany him on the journey." Here spring is personified.

5　And journey homeward to Luoyang — And travel to Luoyang, where my home is located.

56. 绝句四首（其三） Four Short Poems (No. 3)

1　In 764 AD, Du Fu moved back to his thatched house in Chengdu when he learned that his old acquaintance Yan Wu had resumed the position as military governor of that city. The An-Shi Turmoil having ended in a complete failure for the rebels, the poet felt relieved and was in a cheerful frame of mind. Fascinated by the spring scene, which signalled hope and peace, he wrote four quatrains to express his feelings, the present piece being the third.

This poem is composed of two antithetical couplets: the first imparting an aesthetic perception of spring, which is full of life; the second depicting the thrilling sights attained through the window and the door. Words implicitly or explicitly denoting the sounds (e.g. tweeting), the motions (e.g. soaring) and the colours (e.g. white, yellow, green, silvery, blue) are used to vividly describe the vitality of spring, and the picturing of the snow-clad ridge and the ships from afar creates a sense of grandeur and impetus.

2　Here the word "en-frame" is an example of the the poet's masterly use of verbs, which is one of the distinctive features of this poem. A window en-framing the snow-clad West Ridge may naturally be associated with a beautiful picture hanging on the wall.

3　Wu, also called the Eastern Wu, refers to the region around the lower reaches of the Yangtze River.

57. 弹琴 Playing the *Qin*

1　The *qin* is a pluck musical instrument with seven strings. The poem "Playing the Qin" manifests the poet's undaunted spirit to persevere in his own values in spite of the general current of thought, and touches the issue whether valuable traditions should be maintained. In times of drastic social changes, not all the people will cherish what they have already owned, and some will even dump the "baby" out with "bath." In this regard the poem is of omnipresent significance.

2　The poet Liu Zhangqing (709 AD?-780 AD?) was from Hejian in what is now Hebei Province. He had held such positions as Official Supervisor and Prefect of Suizhou, and had more than once been demoted for giving offence to his superiors or rather, for his honesty. His poetry, mainly dealing with his political setbacks and social upheavals, is of a succinct and implicit style.

3　"Through th' Pines Rustle th' Winds Cold" is the name of the music.

58. 枫桥夜泊　Mooring at the Maple Bridge for the Night

1　Zhang Ji was from Xiangzhou, the now Xiangyang of Hubei. He obtained his candidature in 753 AD. His poetry is mostly devoted to travels and landscape portrayal.

　　The present metrical quatrain is Zhang's representative work. The scenic elements, well chosen and vividly pictured, effectively serve the theme of the poem — the loneliness of a passenger who is stranded in a strange place. The style is elegant and yet unaffected.

2　... the crows decrying ... — The crying of crows usually sounds plaintive, and when the personified crows are made to decry the dark and frosty skies, a striking effect is produced.

3　The maples vague — In Chinese poetry, green maples have acquired the connotation of sadness.

4　The Hanshan Temple, located a short distance away from the Maple Bridge, is a scenic spot of the Suzhou City.

5　Gusu — another name for Suzhou

59. 滁州西涧　The West Brook in the Prefecture of Chuzhou

1　Wei Yingwu (737 AD-791 AD?) was from Chang'an. He had been the prefect of Chuzhou, Jiangzhou and Suzhou in sequence of time. As an official, he enjoyed an unsullied reputation; as a poet, he won recognition for his excellent idylls. The great poet Bai Juyi comments that Wei's poetry "demonstrates an exceptional artistic talent" and that it "tends to be analogical and satirical in style."

　　The present metrical quatrain is among the most popular of Chinese poems. By picturing a country scene after spring rains, the poet not only shows his love of Nature, but also expresses his contempt for the time-servers and his indifference to fame or gain.

2   I keenly love ..., /... deep green. — The interpretation of this couplet has remained controversial. Some people think that the poet is likening crafty time-servers to orioles and that the brook-side grass is a metaphor for the noble-minded people, who are reduced to obscurity, whereas others hold that this couplet is a mere description of the scene.

Obviously the poet adores the grass in preference to the orioles, which may be understood as a manifestation of aloofness from worldliness.

60. 塞下曲（其二） A Frontier Melody (No. 2)

1   The present poem eulogizes the archery and velour of a frontier soldier, whose poetic image is given a romantic colouring by means of hyperbole. The poet draws inspiration from a legend about the famous general Li Guang, which goes that Li Guang once shot at something midst the grass, which he mistook for a tiger, only to find his arrow submerged in a stone.

2   Lu Lun (748 AD?−798 AD?) was from Puzhou of Hezhong, the now Yongji County of Shanxi. He was the most prominent of the "Ten Talents in the Reign of Dali." His frontier poetry, which reflects the hardships of frontier life and the militant spirit of the soldiers, has a robust flavour and is of a vigorous style.

3   the feathers — Feathers form the tail of an arrow. The technique which involves the substitution of the part for the whole (as is the case with the present example), or the whole for the part, is rhetorically known as synecdoche.

61. 游子吟 Song of the Roamer

1   Unlike some of his poems, which are marked by deep words, the present piece — a classical poem — features freshness and simplicity. It eulogizes profound maternal love through a commonplace and yet typical incident and expresses sincere filial gratitude by means of metaphor. Filial piety constitutes the basis of traditional ethics.

2   Meng Jiao (751 AD−814 AD) was from Wukang of Huzhou Prefecture, i.e. the now Deqing County of Zhejiang. He didn't obtain his official candidature until he was forty-six. As a man of moral integrity, he was opposed to worldliness and led a very hard life.

Meng's strength lies in five-character metrical poems. His works reflect the social contradiction, air the grievances of the common people, and lay bare the dissipation of the rulers and the separatist military governors. His style is unique. In popularity and artistry he ranks along with the great poet-essayist Han Yu.

3 For fear ..., /... with love and care. — This couplet not only describes what and how the mother does (act) for her outgoing son, but it also reveals her inner being (thought), which enhances the artistic effect of the poem.

4 Oh, ... / ... I dare say! — Grass is a metaphor for the son, and the spring sun stands for the mother.

62. 左迁至蓝关示侄孙湘　To My Grandnephew Xiang — Composed on My Post-Demotion Journey via the Lantian Pass

1 As the poet says in the title of the original, this poem was written on his way through the Lantian Pass after demotion.

In 819 AD, Han admonished Emperor Xianzong against his decision to preserve a relic of Buddha in the Imperial Palace, saying in his petition that what the emperor desired to do would "corrupt public morals and become a subject of ridicule. " As a result he was relegated to the position of Prefect of Chaozhou. On his way to Chaozhou the miserable poet met first with a snow storm and then with his respectful grandnephew Han Xiang, who came out of his way to accompany him on the journey. Inspired by the incidents, he wrote the present poem to express his distress and political ideal.

In spite of the sorrowful tone, this poem has attained a lofty realm of thought.

2 Han Yu (768 AD−824 AD) was from Heyang of Henan. Since he obtained his official candidature in 792 AD, he had held the positions of Official Supervisor in the Supervisory Bureau, Professor at the Imperial Academy, Deputy Minister of Justice, Deputy Minister of Official Personnel, etc.

As an official, Han displayed an involved character. On the one hand he was opposed to the superstition about Buddhism, to military separatism and to the stale style of writing; on the other hand, siding with the eunuch Ju Wenzhen and his like he was against the political reformers headed by Wang Shuwen. He was, anyhow, true to himself.

In terms of literature, Han was gifted in many ways. In prose writing, he was a trail-blazing pioneer in the reformation later known as the

Classical Prose Movement and, among the Eight Greatest Essayists of the Tang and the Song Dynasties, he was second to none. In versification, he was the most prominent representative of the Han-Meng (i.e. Meng Jiao) School and has made a far-reaching impact by breaking fresh ground. His poetry flies its own colours: the creative diction, an original prose flavour, a fantastic conceptual world, and a breach of outmoded traditional rules governing pattern, structure and scheme, ... all of which combine happily to give a sense of wonderfully wild beauty. Some of his poems, however, show the weakness of being recondite.

3   Chaoyang — the now Chaozhou City in the east of Guangdong.

4   How can I ... save my skin? — How can I — though coming of age — drift with the tide for the sake of my life?

5   My horse balks ... shrouds. — This line, by creating the image of the balking horse, reveals the poet's miserable state of mind and his reluctance to go forward.

6   th' rill of miasma — This refers to the river later known as the Han River, which has been named after the poet.

63. 野老歌 Song of the Poor Farmer

1   Zhang Ji (768 AD?–830 AD) was from the Prefecture of Wu, the now Suzhou City. He obtained his official candidature in 799 AD. He has occupied such positions as Eulogist in the Bureau of Sacrificial Rites, Functionary of the Department of Navigation and Irrigation, and Professor-Cum-Vice-Chancellor of the Imperial Academy.

Zhang was a great supporter of the New-Music-Institute Movement initiated by Yuan Zhen and Bai Juyi. He successfully employs the colloquialism of his day in this poetry, which reflects in a simple and succinct style the avarice of the ruling class and the misery of the common people.

The present poem is Zhang's representative work. By making a poignant contrast between the extreme poverty of the farmers and the luxury of the wealthy merchants, it reveals the cruel exploitation of farmers and the sharp class contradiction of the day.

2   ... live in poverty ... th' mounts — Here the verb "live" collocates with to two phrases, with one figuratively (i.e. in poverty) and with the other literally (i.e. in th' mounts). Such a figure of speech is rhetorically known as zeugma or syllepsis. The same is the case with "... my shabby

hut presents tools but no hope".

3 Nothing is left to be dined on.

4 acorns—the nuts of the oak tree, which provide a substitute for grain in times of famine.

5 even their pets boast silver spoons from birth! — This clause, which is suggestive of the idiomatic expression "a silver spoon in one's mouth", means that even their pets are leading a comfortable life.

64. 春怨 A Lady's Grievances in Spring

1 Jin Changxu was from Yuhang, which was in the now Zhejiang Province. Little is known about his life.

The present poem is a classic. By narrating how a young lady yearns to see her husband at the front, it reflects people's adversities inflicted upon by war and by the feudal system of military service.

This poem is marked by its unusual artistic conception and folk-song colouring. The first couplet sets the reader wondering why the lady (narrator) should scare the tuneful orioles off the trees around her house. The second couplet sheds light on the reason: since it is impossible for her to meet her man in reality, the narrator can only hope to do so in a dream, and thus she won't let the twittering birds disturb her dream.

2 Liaoxi — the region west to the Liao River. Here Liaoxi is the antonomasia for the frontier.

65. 江雪 The River Permeated with Snow

1 In this poem, by picturing a lone man angling in the snow, the poet successfully creates the image of a dauntless pursuer of truth.

2 Liu Zongyuan (773 AD−819 AD) was from Hedong, the now Yongji of Shanxi Province. After he obtained his official candidature in 793 AD, he became a senior official in the Ministry of Codes and Protocol. He was an ardent participant in the political reforms under the leadership of Wang Shuwen. As a result, he was demoted to the position of a subordinate to the Prefect of Yongzhou when the reforms were crushed. Latter he was advanced to a prefecture.

Liu was one of the "Eight Greatest Essayists of the Tang and the Song Dynasties". He is ranked with Han Yu as co-leader of the Classical Prose Movement. His works, prose and verse alike, lay bare the social contradiction and criticize the corrupt officialdom.

As far as his poetry is concerned, Liu has a style of his own: fresh, simple and succinct. His word paintings are often his inner world incarnate. In the present poem, the severe weather symbolizes the deplorable political situation the poet is in, and in the image of the angler who braves the snow we find the person of a reformer: dauntless, aloof and imbued with moral strength.

3   Thousands of mounts ..., /... is found. — This couplet describes the bleakness of the world. "Thousands of mounts" and "a myriad of paths" are cases of hyperbole used to heighten the artistic effect.

4   On board a lone boat ... / ... abound. — On board a boat a lone man is engaged in angling regardless of the driving snow, with which his bamboo hat and coir coat abound. In the past, protective clothing was usually made of coir.

66. 秋词（其一） Odes to Autumn (No. 1)

1   What autumn could bring to the world was but bleakness in the mind's eye of many an ancient poet, who had been inclined to chant their songs of sorrow at the sight of frost or withered plants. Liu Yuxi, however, was able to appreciate the unique beauty if autumn, to which he wrote two odes, the present piece being the first.

If we compare this poem with Liu Zongyuan's "The River Permeated with Snow", we'll see that the broad-mindedness, dauntlessness and optimism were the fine qualities the reformers had in common: though their reforms had been crushed and they themselves relegated, they remained high-spirited.

This poem express the poet's lofty sentiments in a fresh, sonorous and magnificent style.

2   Liu Yuxi (772 AD−842 AD) was from Pengcheng, the now Xuzhou of Jiangsu Province. He was appointed Official Supervisor after the obtained his candidature in 793 AD, but was to be demoted for his advise participation in the political reforms under the leadership of Wang Shuwen. Later he rose in succession to be Adviser of the Prefecture, Tutor to the Crown Prince and Minister of Codes and Protocol. He was a progressive thinker.

Liu has a fresh, familiar and succinct style. His poetry, which lays bare the dark reality, has opened up new ground for the development of Tang Poetry.

3 Distress ..., /... I'd say: — This couplet brings forth the poet's anti-conventional attitude by means of implicit comparison.

4 Poetic inspiration ... /... on a sunny day! — In this couplet, the poet's peculiar vision and lofty aspirations are shown by way of simile ("... seems to gleam") and the creation of the image of the crane, which soars high up into the clouds.

67. 乌衣巷　The Black Coat Lane

1 "The Black Coat Lane" is one of the "Five Topics on the City of Jinling", a group of poems which, by picturing the five places of historic interest, express the poet's feelings about the rise and fall of dynasties and reflections upon historical events.

　　In this poem, which had won the admiration of Bai Juyi, Liu subtly employs the images of swallows, which are supposed to have witnessed the prosperity and decline of the reputable families, as links of connection between the past and the present. The poet's feelings are implied in the description of the scene.

2 Th' Rose-finch Bridge, a bridge in Nanjing (Jinling) across the Qinhuai River, is historically connected with the Black Coat Lane, which was inhabited by illustrious families in the Eastern Jin Dynasty. The construction of the tower with two bronze rose-finches on the bridge was sponsored by Xie An.

3 The setting sun here symbolizes decline.

4 The Wangs' and the Xies' were the most distinguished families of the Black Coat Lane. Wang Dao was the founder and prime minister of the Eastern Jin Dynasty, and Xie An was the prime minister who had had command of the eastern Jin army in the well-known Feishui Campaign, which ended in the defeat of the Preceding Qin forces from the north.

68. 聚蚊谣　On Swarming Mosquitoes

1 The poet often makes oblique and yet rapier thrusts. In the present poem, he attacks the sinister officials who are opposed to the political reforms by likening them to the mosquitoes, whose abominable characteristics are vividly described. This poem, symbolic and metaphoric, also shows the poet's broad-mindedness and optimistic outlook.

2 Mount Nan — short for Mount Zhongnan.

3 The *chi* is a unit of length equaling 33.33 centimetres.

4   ... I'll hold my own. — I'll keep my position even if attacked.

5   The ancients believed that fireflies fed on mosquitoes.

69. 悯农二首   Two Poems in Commiseration with the Farmers

1   Li Shen (772 AD–846 AD) was from Wuxi. He had occupied the positions of scholar at the Imperial Academy, prime minister, and military governor of Huainan.

Li, a literary talent, was one of the ardent advocates of the New-Music-Institute Movement. His poetry had earned the praises of Yuan Zhen and Bai Juyi.

The present poems in "Commiseration with the Farmers" have been on the lips of billions. In a classic style it lays bare the cruel exploitation of the farmers and expresses the poet's great sympathy for and high praise of those who have created the wealth of society by the sweat of their brows.

2   No field ... does idle lie, — No field remains uncultivated.

3   Whoever knows ... /... much pain? — This couplet, which contains a mild satire upon the idle classes, is often cited to exhort people to thrift.

70. 赋得古原草送别   The Grasses on the Ancient Plateau Sending Me off

1   Bai Juyi (772 AD–846 AD) was from Xiagui, the now Weinan County of Shaanxi Province. He became Scholar at the Imperial Academy and Attendant Remonstrant after obtaining his official candidature in 800 AD, but was later demoted to the position of a functionary to the Prefect of Jiangzhou. In time he was to rise to such positions as Prefect of Hangzhou, Prefect of Suzhou, Professor to the Crown Prince, and Deputy Minister of Justice.

Bai, with a sum of more than 3,000 poems, was the most prolific of the Tang poets. He launched, together with Yuan Zhen, the New-Music-Institute Movement, which had made a notable impact on literature and art, advocating that "Essays should reflect the times and poems should centre upon current affairs" — a principle which he himself had put into practice.

Bai's poetry covers a wide range of subjects and contains substantial content. His ten-piece "Recitations in Qin" and fifty-piece "New-Music-Institute Songs", mostly masterpieces if realist poetry, extensively reflect the life of all social strata, while "Eternal Grief" and "Song of a Pipa Player", Bai's best-known narrative poems, respectively relate the romances of Emperor Xuanzong and his favourite Concubine, Lady Yang, and of the poet's chance meeting with an ill-fated *pipa* player. In many of his poems Bai fearlessly slashes on the dark society and expresses his great sympathy for the common people. In his later years, however, the social critic in him ebbed. With all his limitations Bai remains to be a great poet of the people.

The present poem, which takes departure as a theme but in essence extols the great vitality of the grasses, is a lyric composed when the poet first came to Chang'an. It is said that, when Bai and the old poet Gu Kuang first met, the latter had punned upon the former's name, saying, "Everything being so expensive, it'd not be easy for you to make a living in Chang'an." After reading this poem, however, the old poet observed, "Such poetic talent will warrant one in making a living anywhere in the world."

2 Which wither every year and thrive — Which wither and thrive annually.

3 The prairie fires ...;/... they'll yet revive. — What matters if the devastating fires should burn and lick? When spring comes they'll surely resurrect.

This couplet has become a celebrated dictum often used to describe the great vitality of progressive forces or new-born things.

4 'Tis in the ... drown — They are given to the sadness caused by the departure of one more scion.

In this line three techniques are involved:

a) that of punning — the word "blue" has a double meaning denoting sadness and the color blue;

b) that of personification — the grasses are, so to speak, made to think and feel; and

c) that of transferred epithet — the phrase "in the blues", which should rightly modify the poet, is used to describe the grasses to which it does not really apply.

71. 轻肥　Steeds, Silks and Satins

1 This poem is one of the "Recitations in Qin", a group of ten poems composed in the Reigns of Zhenyuan and Yuanhe, during which the poet lived in Chang'an. The title, borrowing from *The Analects*, is a metonymy for "luxurious life".

This poem exposes the arrogance and extravagance of the eunuchs and expresses the poet's sympathy for the suffering. The language is simple but vivid, and such devices as simile, exaggeration, periphrasis and contrast are employed.

2   Th' steeds ... shine. — Through the dust kicked up, the horses and saddles shine with splendour.

    This line, which contains a case of exaggeration, shows what luxury the riders live in.

3   ... what can be their line — ... what their occupation is; ... what they are

4   The scarlet robes mark ..., /... the generals wear. — Those in scarlet robes are high-ranking officials, and those who wear purple ribbons are generals.

    Early in the Reign of Emperor Xuanzong, the power of eunuchs began to expand. Later on the eunuchs assumed not only political power, but also power of the sword.

5   Mount Dongting, situated in the Taihu Lake area, was known for its tangerines, which were of a rare and precious species.

6   Heavenly Pool — This is a periphrasis denoting the oceans.

7   Oh, th' south ..., / ... in Quzhou! — This couplet turns to a completely different situation, which forms a sharp contrast with the heartless spree of the eunuchs. Hidden in between the lines lies the poet's indignation at the dark reality.

72. 卖炭翁　The Charcoal Burner

1   "The Charcoal Burner" is taken from "The New-Music-Institute Songs", a collection of fifty poems composed on the Reign of Yuanhe, during which the poet held the position of Attendant Remonstrant. By narrating the mishap of an old man, who is forced into accepting some cheap and thin textile in barter with his cartload of charcoal, it exposes the evil nature of Court Purchasing.

    The so-called "Court Purchasing" was in essence plunder conducted by the emperors' errand-runners, who "purchased" things for the royal family either with a payment unworthy of the goods or without any payment at all.

    The poet vividly creates the image of the old charcoal burner by describing his looks, acts and psychology, which serves the theme of the poem. The language is simple, and the style vigorous.

2   His wrinkled face ... /... brownish gray. — These two lines, which picture

the charcoal burner's looks, are suggestive of the hardship the man has experienced.

3　In need of ..., /... worn and thin. — These four lines reveal the psychology if the old man — For a good sale of his charcoal he wished it might get cold, though he is not properly protected in terms of clothing.

4　One in yellow, th' other in a white gown — Emperor Dezong entrusted his eunuchs with "purchases." Eunuchs of higher ranks wore yellow robes, and those without a rank, white ones.

5　... make for th' north of town — ...make for the palaces.

　　The palaces were located in the north of Chang'an, while the two major market-places — the East Market and the West Market — were in the southern part of the city.

6　The clause "claims as such none could duck" expresses the feeling of helplessness in face of tyranny. To duck means to dodge.

7　The old man had expected to get some cash for his charcoal to "allay hunger and keep warm the skin", who knows he should get a token payment? Like others he can find no way to avoid the looting, hence he can only curse his own luck.

73. 鹦鹉　The Parrot

1　This poem expresses the sentiments of an honest talent — his great detestation of officialdom, ardent love of nature and strong longing for freedom. It is marked by the unique artistic conception and skillful employment of symbolization.

　　The parrot symbolizes the poet, and the cage is the feudal institution incarnate.

2　Beauty ... being caught; — He is bound up in fetters (metaphor for officialdom) just because she is beautiful.

3　Homesickness ... in intensity; — Homesickness grows more and more intense when night falls.

4　... this cage — a bar to liberty — ... this cage, which is an obstruction to liberty.

74. 行宫　The Imperial Resort

1　Yuan Zhen (779 AD−831 AD) was from Henan (the now Luoyang of Henan). He obtained his official candidature in 793 AD. He had been appointed to such positions as Official Supervisor, Deputy Minister of

Songs of Weal and Woe

Works, Imperial Envoy to Zhedong, Military Governor of Wuchang and Co-Premier.

Yuan and his bosom friend to Bai Juyi co-chaired the New-Music-Institute Movement. He set store by the political function of poetry, advocating that poetry should reflect popular plight and current affairs of the times. He applied that notion to his artistic creation with great zeal and with a simple style.

The present poem, by depicting the sorrowful sight of the imperial resort and the inhabitants within, carries a sharp criticism of the pleasure-seeking Emperor Xuanzong, with a touch of melancholy over the bygone golden age of the Tang Dynasty. Hong Mai, critic of the Song Dynasty, points out that, "brief in word and yet rich in substance", it "leaves a wonderfully long-standing aftertaste."

2   the ancient palaces — These refer to one of Emperor Xuanzong's resorts, i.e. the Shanyang Palaces in Luoyang.

3   'Tis vainly that...bright. — The flowers, though beautiful, are only blooming in vain, as people who used to enjoy them are long gone.

Here the poet employs the technique of setting off the melancholic by depicting what is pleasant (the flowers).

4   those white-haired ladies — Those used to be young beautiful girls when chosen as court ladies, whose duty was to wait on the emperor once he came to stay at the palaces. They had been, so to speak, jailed in the inhuman palaces, lonely and loveless — at least most of them all their lives or all of them most of their lives. The poet is sympathetic with them.

5   ... recalling Xuanzong and his reign. — This line may evoke a series of connections: the emperor's romances and versatility; the social stability and prosperity in the early and middle stages of his reign; the An-Shi Turmoil, which might partly be attributed to the emperor's fatuousness and self-indulgence, etc.

75. 题李凝幽居   Poem Inscribed on the Wall of Li Ning's Secluded Cottage

1   Jia Dao (779 AD−843 AD) was from Fanyang Prefecture of Hebei. As a poet of the Elaborate School, which set store by the choice of words, he enjoys equal popularity with Meng Jiao. His works are of a singularly fresh style.

The presents poem, which features a tranquil conceptual world, narrates the experience of an unsuccessful visit to the poet's friend.

2   Some birds ...; /... moonlit door. — This celebrated couplet creates a sense of tranquility.

The monk refers to the poet himself.

An anecdote goes that Jia Dao couldn't make up his mind as to which word he should choose — "knock" or "push", until he consulted the famous scholar Han Yu, who pointed out that the word "knock" might be preferable in that it was capable of producing a sound effect.

3   Where th' clouds ... you move. — This side of the bridge is so tranquil that the air seems frozen and the clouds seem connected to the rocks, thus if you move a rock, the clouds would be disturbed.

76. 感讽（其一） Hard Times (No. 1)

1   Li He (790 AD−816 AD), a remote descendant of the Prince of Zheng, was from Changgu of Fuchang, the now Yiyang County of the Henan. He cherished lofty aspirations and progressive ideals, which were to be thwarted. He died young.

Li's poetry, which feature fantastic imagination, peculiar conception and rich colouring, expresses the feelings of an upright man about the social reality of the Tang Dynasty, which was then on the turn for the worse. The impact of Li's romantic style has been great.

The present poem, by narrating a typical incident and creating typical images, lay bare the insatiable greed of the ruling class and expresses the poet's sympathy for the common people, who live under cruel exploitation and oppression.

2   Hepu (a place in the now Guangxi) and Longzhou (the now Hanshou County of Hunan) are respectively looted, so to speak, of the pearls and oranges. In this poem exploitation in different places are mentioned to show the universality of the malpractice.

3   To satiate ... incompetent! — Even the Creator would not be able to satisfy the needs of the greedy prefects!

4   ... the Yue housewife ... engage. — The woman living in Yue (the region around the now Zhejiang) has not yet begun weaving.

5   By which ... we'll surely bring? — By that time we'll have finished weaving, and thus will be able to pay you the tax, could you be kind enough to postpone the urge?

6   The sated man departs. — The man, having eaten to his full, goes away.

7   But nay, ... come to call! — But against the wish that no more mishaps may befall, the bookkeeper has come for extortion in the wake of the official!

77. 泊秦淮   **Mooring on the Qinhuai River**

1   Du Mu (803 AD–852 AD) was from Wannian (万年) of the Capital City (i.e. the now Xi'an City). He obtained his official candidature in 828 AD and he had in succession held the position of Supervisor in the Supervisory Bureau, Prefect of several places, Secretary of Merits in the Ministry of Official Personnel, and Adviser to the Cabinet.

One of the most important poets of the late Tang Dynasty, he is honoured as Du the Junior (vs. the great Poet Du Fu as Du the Senior). He holds that, in prose and verse alike, "Ideas and thoughts should be put in command, while feelings should play the role of auxiliaries. As to the words, sentences (lines), paragraphs (stanzas) and the colouring, they are supposed to be the entourage." His poetry has a vigorous and refined style and contains trenchant criticism of the governance.

The present poem is a masterpiece. By narrating that the poet, when mooring on the Qinhuai River, hears a songstress caroling a smutty song against the gloomy setting of a misty night and a dim moon, it satirizes the pleasure-seeking select society and expresses the poet's deep concern over the fate of the Tang Empire. Its language is simple, its style vigorous, and the thought it expresses profound.

2   The mist ... the shore, — This line vividly present the poetic images of the mist-shrouded river and the dim moon, which are suggestive of a hopeless gloomy situation.

"The mist shrouding cold waters" , meaning "The mist enveloping cold waters like shrouds" , involves a case of metaphor.

3   ... who knows not the sore/Over lost sovereignty, ... — who does not know the agony which people of a conquered country feel.

The songstress merely catered to the audience which, more often than not, was made up of the rich and powerful, and it was the audience that chose the song which would best please its taste. That the songstress "knows not the sore / Over lost sovereignty" is a periphrasis implying that the upper-class society shows not the least concern about the destiny of the nation.

4　"Flowers in th' Back Park" — short for "Jade Trees and Flowers in the Back Park", the title of a smutty song composed by the last sovereign of the Southern Dynasties, who had indulged in pleasures and finally lost his sovereignty.

78. 山行　A Mountain Scene

1　This poem presents a word picture of a splendid autumn scene: against the background of a mountain, in which some homes are nestling admit the fleecy clouds, the maples, whose leaves have been reddened by frost, display such a fantastic beauty as would outshine that of spring flowers; and in order to feast his eyes on the charming woods the poet suspends his tour by bringing the carriage to a halt.

　　Full of life and free from the stereotyped sentimentalism about autumn, it demonstrates the poet's ardent love of nature and optimistic attitude towards life.

2　fount — source; the place where something begins or comes from
3　Th' frost-reddened ... of spring — Here the poet eulogizes the maples for their beauty by making a fanciful comparison between them and the bloom of spring.

79. 赤壁　The Red Cliff

1　This poem conveys a brief comment on a historical event, i.e. the war between the Kingdom of Wei and the Kindom of Wu. It bears a natural and sonorous style.

　　In the year 208 AD, Cao Cao, with a powerful army under his command, intended to cross the Yangtze River and subjugate the Kindom of Wu, and the Red Cliff Campaign broke out. Cao's strategy was thwarted, though, by the resourceful Zhou Yu, Commander in Chief of the Wu forces, who took advantage of an east wind that was very unusual during that time of the year and burnt up Cao's warships. Thus the campaign ended in the victory of Wu.

　　The poem begins by making a connection between an unearthed relic (a broken halberd) and the famous campaign, and subtly expresses the poet's belief that lucky chance can sometimes be a decisive factor of success.

2　... I wash it and scrub. — ... I wash and scrub it.
3　... if th' east wind had ... a free hand — ... if the east wind hadn't offered

General Zhou a helping hand.

Here the east wind is personified.

4   By spring ... locked up. — The next spring the Qiao sisters would have been captured and locked up at the Bronze Finch Stand.

The Bronze Finch Stand, constructed in honour of Cao Cao, was situated in the City of Ye. On the stand was a tower with a huge bronze finch atop.

Of the two Qiao sisters (said to be very beautiful ladies), one was Sun Ce's widow (Sun Ce was the late king of Wu), and the other was Zhou Yu's wife. Their supposed capture would have signify the fall of Wu.

80. 更漏子 The Hydraulic Chronograph

1   This is the tune of music to which the present *ci*-poem (a masterpiece) is set. The poem lays bare the inner world of a lady, who is suffering from loneliness in a sleepless autumn night.

2   Wen Tingyun (812 AD?–870 AD?) was from Qi of Taiyuan, i.e. the now Qi County of Shanxi. Though highly gifted, he had been denied any important position because of his irreverent attitude towards the powerful and of his unconstrained life style. Being the first poet devoted to the creation of *ci*-poetry, he is honoured as Father of the Floral School, who had contributed much to the maturity of that genre as a serious literary form. His favourite themes are departures and such delicate feelings as feminine grievances, etc., and his style is flowery. As the critic Hu Zi of the Song Dynasty points out, Wen, who possesses an elegant style, is a master in diction.

3   Here the scent from the burner and the candle are personified. The candle, with tear-like wax-drops, may be suggestive of inner suffering, selfless devotion, tenacious pursuit of truth, etc., according to the specific context.

4   This line implies that the lady, sensitive to the sounds, stays awake the whole night through.

81. 无题 An Untitled Poem

1   The present poem, which expresses the narrator's deep affection for and unwavering faithfulness to her lover, is perhaps the most popular of Li's works. Its worth lies not only in the realm of thought attained, but also in the artistry displayed — the soaring imagination, the subtle use of

rhetorical devices, the fanciful comparison and the phonological charm, etc., all of which combine to make this classic of love lyrics capable of touching the human heart and cleansing the human soul.

There are, however, other interpretations as to the purport of the poem. Some people regard it as an expression of the poet's faith to his political beliefs and his longing for the demoted prime minister Li Deyu; others take it as an elegy dedicated to the poet's deceased wife. In any case, the artistry of the poem has remained unchallengeable.

Judging from the awareness of the aging hair and the presumption of night recitation in the third couplet and the allusion to the mythology in the fourth, the narrator should be of the tender sex, hence the poem is rendered accordingly.

2   Li Shangyin (813 AD–858 AD?) was from Henei of Huaizhou (the now Qinyang of Henan). He obtained his official candidature in 837 AD. He had worked as Assistant County Magistrate, Secretary at the Imperial Library and Senior Secretary at the Ministry of Works. He cherished lofty aspirations, and had encountered repeated setbacks in his political career.

An important poet of the late Tang Dynasty, Li was honoured as Li the Junior (in connection with Li Bai as the Senior Li). His poetry covers an extensive range of subjects. He opposes himself to the tyranny of the eunuchs and the dissipation of the rulers, expresses his sorrows over his own mishaps, and sings the praises of fine qualities. As a master in making allusions, he has a refined romantic style and an original conception. Somewhere, though, he's somewhat obscure and sentimental.

3   When breezes ... the flower will. — In the Chinese mind's eye, the spring breeze is the champion incarnate for the just and beautiful, while the flower symbolizes what is ideal, e.g. love or truth.

4   The silkworm ...; /... a candle'll shed. — Here the silk thread, believed to be from the bosom of the silkworm, is a metaphor for unbounded sincere love, and the personified candle, giving off its altruistic light, is compared to a devoted lover, with its wax-drops suggestive of suffering or agony.

This couplet, a celebrated dictum, has been quoted and re-quoted to express sincere love, utter devotion, steadfast faith to a cause, or the spirit of self-sacrifice.

5   As Mount Penglai ..., /... pay! — Here Mount Penglai (a fairyland said to be located in the distant ocean in light of the Chinese myth)

is an antonomasia for the place where the narrator's lover lives, the employment of which constitutes an implicit comparison of the man to an immortal. "Penglai is not a long distance away" is an understatement showing the bright side of the narrator's outlook.

The Blackbird is a mythological bird, which is said to have been sent by the Heavenly Queen as her envoy to pay a complimentary visit to Emperor Wu of the Han Dynasty. The "Blackbird" is at the same time an allusion and an antonomasia for "messenger."

82. 官仓鼠　The Rats at State-Owned Granaries

1　The present poem is a poignant satire directed at the corrupt officials, who abuse their authority and batten on the blood of the working men and are ingeniously likened to the insatiable and audacious rats in state-owned granaries. It involves a case of exaggeration to say that the rats are "as big as cats." The language is vivid and colloquial, and the style metaphoric and allegoric.

2　Cao Ye (816 AD?−875 AD?) was from Guizhou, i.e. the now Guilin of Guangxi. Since he obtained his official candidature in 850 AD, he had been appointed in succession Doctor in the Bureau of Sacrificial Rites, Director of the Department of Religious Affairs under the above-mentioned Bureau, and Prefect of Yangzhou.

Quite a number of Cao's poems reflect the seamy side of the society, and the present poem is a case in point.

3　This is a rhetorical question, which challenges the "rats" to justify their malpractice.

83. 蜂　To the Bees

1　Luo Yin (833 AD−909 AD) was from Yuhang, i.e. the now Hangzhou of Zhejiang. He had been a Courtier, whose duty was to dispose of documents before they were presented to the crown.

Luo, an important writer of the late Tang, is better known for his essays, almost all of which, as Lu Xun has pointed out, "are strong protects and indignant condemnations." His poetry also contains sharp criticisms of the society. The present piece, for one, lays bare the irrational reality in which working men are deprived of their fruit of labour.

The allegory of the working people to the bees is excellent. Likewise the English poet Shelley (1792 AD−1822 AD) calls his people "Bees of

England" in his *Song to the Men of England*.

2 Be it ... ground. — No matter it is a mountain peak or flat ground.

3 And yet ... who will taste? — This is a rhetorical question, meaning "It is others that will enjoy the fruit of your labour."

84. 钱塘江潮　The Qiantang Tide

1 This poem, which engages the techniques of metaphor, allusion, personification, etc., vividly presents a word picture of the sensational Qiantang Tide. As one of the best poems about the tide, it might develop the whims into phantasmagorias in the reader's mind.

2 Rakshas is a ferocious Man-eating demon in Hindu mythology.

3 According to Chinese mythology the Red Carp is a draught animal capable of flying across lakes and rivers, and the immortals can ride on its back and move about freely and easily, and Yanghou is the legendary God of Wave.

85. 新沙　A New Sandbar in the Bohai Sea

1 Lu Guimeng (?−881 AD?) was an important writer from Gusu, i.e. the now Suzhou. He became known for his literary talents when young, but he failed to obtain official candidature. His essays and poems are mostly criticisms of the Establishment.

    The present piece tells that the officials, alert to anything exploitable, had learned of the new sandbar even before the sharp-eyed seagulls discovered it. Needless to say, they were reckoning on the tax to be imposed upon it once it was cultivated, and the immortals would have inevitably been taxed if the tax collector had been able to approach the fairyland. Beneath the surface of amusement lies a satire as sharp as a razor — a satire directed at the bloodsucking officialdom.

2 This line involves a case of exaggeration.

3 ... th' immortals ... /... to go! — If the officials could have found a way to go to Penglai, a fairyland, they would also levy a tax on the glossy ganoderma (said to be a magic herb) that the immortals have collected. If even the all-mighty immortals failed to dodge the snatch, the snatcher should be very crafty.

86. 题菊花　To the Chrysanthemum

1 Huang Chao (?−884 AD) was from Yuanju of Caozhou, i.e. the now

Heze of Shangdong. In the late Tang Dynasty, people lived in an abyss of misery. In 875 AD Huang rose in rebellion against the Tang Empire and was crowned in 880 AD. The next year the rebels under his command captured the capital Chang'an. In 884 AD, the uprising was suppressed, and Huang took his own life in Mount Tai.

Written in a vigorous and symbolic style, the present poem overflows with romantic enthusiasm. It expresses the poet's sympathy with the suffering and aspiration to change the status quo. It also embodies the peasants' naïve concept of equality and people's longing to take their fate in their own hands. The chrysanthemum, traditionally a symbol of aloof dignity typical of men of letters, takes on an original image in this poem to represent the common folk struggling to survive in the cold wind of tyranny. The poet pledges that once he is able to, he will allow the flower an equal right to enjoy the warmth of spring.

2 God of Spring — a god in Chinese myth taking charge of everything related to spring.

3 An equal chance ... bring! — I'll enable you to bloom at the same time as the peach tree does.

87. 山中寡妇   The Widow Living Deep Deep in the Mountains

1 Du Xunhe (846 AD−907 AD) was from Chizhou of Shidai, the now Shitai of Anhui. He didn't obtain official candidature until 891 AD. His poetry reflects the tyranny of the rulers and the sufferings of the people in the midst of social upheavals of the late Tang Dynasty. He possesses a lucid and lively style.

The present poem, through the image of an ill-fated window, condemns the evil of war and exposes the cruelty of the rulers in reducing the common people to dire poverty. The language is vivid, and the style vigorous. The artistic effect is greatly heightened by such emphatic expressions as "leafed branches freshly hewed" and "the deepest of remote mountain", etc.

2 Her thatched hut ... hair, — This line describes the woman's features and living conditions, which point to her poverty and anxieties.

3 She ... driven to despair. — This line lays bare the cause of the widow's misery, i.e. war in addition to exploitation and oppression.

4 The mulberry trees ...; / ... under taxes is she laid. — This couplet exposes the inequity and inhumanity of taxation.

5   To alleviate ...; /... branches freshly hewed. — This couplet vividly pictures the widow's wretched life: she allays her hunger with wild herbs and, as she doesn't have fuel in store, she burns newly-hewed branches with leaves still attached to them.

6   Alas, the duties and taxes you'll find ..., /... you lodge! — In this couplet lies the conclusion that one can never find a place free from the cruel grip of the Establishment.

88. 虞美人　Yu the Beauty

1   Li Yu (937 AD−978 AD) was the last sovereign of the Southern Tang Dynasty (923 AD−936 AD), which was completely conquered by the Song Empire in 975 AD. Just as his person underwent an abrupt turn from emperor to captive, so his poetry effected a drastic change in subject matter and style: the pleasure of royal life was replaced by the sorrows over lost sovereignty, a flavour of the Floral School was superseded by a refined and vivid style. In terms of artistic effect, Li had attained a height so far unprecedented. He had played an important role in the development of the *ci*-poems.

The present *ci*-poem expresses Li's unbounded grief over his lost kingdom by means of contrast, comparison and images. Some critics deem it "king of *ci*-poems" on account of its artistic appeal and attainment. The last two lines, which create a magnificent artistic realm of tragic beauty, have become a celebrated dictum.

2   Th' autumn moon ..., /... no bounds! — These opening lines imply that, just as the panorama of seasons is unending, the poet's nostalgia is boundless.

3   When spring breeze..., /... a moon so bright. — The arrival of spring and the brightness of the moon only add to the poet's distress, for they remind him of the past, which forms a sharp contrast with the present.

4   Th' carved railing ... /... no more. — The palace of the lost kingdom, with its carved railing and jade-like steps, may remain the same as before; the hue of my youth, however, has been sicklied over and has faded away.

These two lines present a contrast between the long-standing world and transient human life, with a touch of self-pity. The expression "sicklied over" is a borrowing from Shakespeare's Hamlet, Prince of Denmark (... And thus the native hue of resolution / Is sicklied o'er with the pale cast of thought, ...).

5 How much distress ... /... eastward flow. — Here the poet ingeniously compares his distress to the spring waters of the river. As these two lines touch the problem of distress — a universal issue man is confronted with, the appeal they make has been great.

302

Chapter Five　Poetry of the Song Dynasty

Introductory Remarks

The founding of the Song Dynasty (960 AD−1279 AD) ended the drastic situation of the Five Dynasties (907 AD−960 AD), restored social stability and revitalized the nation's economy. Such philosophers Zhang Zai (1020 AD−1077 AD) Zhu Xi (1130 AD−1200 AD), and Cheng Hao (1032 AD−1085 AD) sprang up to acclaim Neo-Confucianism. The philosophy consisted majorly of two schools, the Rationalist School represented by Zhu Xi, which dealt with the origin and the law of the universe, and The Psychological School headed by Lu Jiuyuan (1139 AD−1193 AD), which investigated the realization of conscience and the relationship between knowledge and practice.

The social changes allowed but did not assure the prosperity of verse. For nearly forty years since the establishment of the empire the world of poetry had been reigned over by the frivolous Xikun School, which was given to the ornate representation of the leisurely and luxurious life of courtiers.

The above-mentioned school met its fate only after Ouyang Xiu and Mei Yaochen launched the Literary Reform Movement which, unlike the two aborted political reforms respectively initiated by Fan Zhongyan, Ouyang Xiu and by Wang Anshi, had turned out to be a great success. Ouyang, leader of the literary world, and Mei, pioneer of Song poetry, advocated the theory that verse should mirror the reality and at the same time serve as a social corrective, and in terms of artistry they pursued the aesthetics of simplicity, profundity and natural ease. The movement grew in strength with the participation of Wang Anshi and Su Shunqin, and reached its climax when the literary genius

Su Shi entered the poetical world.

The *ci*-poetry is a verse form that had come into being in the Sui Dynasty and taken shape in the Tang Dynasty. The *ci*-poems are also termed as "song words" or "long-and-short lines." As those names suggest, the *ci*-poems, mostly of uneven line-length, are originally set to music to be sung. The music had various tune names, and the poem set to a particular tune follows a tonal pattern and rhyme scheme of its own. The *ci*-poetry had formerly been exclusively given to romance subjects. Poets of the Sentimentalist School followed that tradition but assumed a more serious attitude towards love than those of the Flower-Shade School of the Five Dynasties. Fan Zhongyan and Ouyang Xiu made successful attempts to open up new realm of thought, and Liu Yong variegated its form by creating "long tunes." On the foundation laid by the forerunners, Su Shi enlarged the conception governing the function of the *ci*-poetry, sublimating it into a powerful instrument capable of expressing all kinds of sentiments and describing all kinds of social life. Su's Unconstrained School, which ushered in the golden age of *ci*-poetry, has produced a far-reaching impact on Chinese poetry and, in a broad sense, on Chinese literature.

The Literary Reform Movement split up after Su Shi's death. Huang Tingjian (1045 AD−1105 AD) and Chen Shidao (1053 AD−1101 AD) founded the Jiangxi School; Qin Guan and He Zhu (1063 AD−1120 AD) flew their own colours; and Zhou Bangyan (1057 AD−1121 AD) pioneered the Metrical School.

In the early years of the Southern Song Dynasty (1127 AD−1279 AD), patriotism became the accepted theme of progressive literature. The poets of the Xin School, such as Lu You, Xin Qiji,

Chen Liang (1143 AD–1194 AD), Liu Guo (1154 AD–1206 AD) and Liu Kezhuang (1187 AD–1269 AD), represented the mainstream of the Powerful and Unconstrained School. Their works are not only imbued with white-hot patriotism, but they also present an irresistible aesthetic and artistic charm. Other important patriotic poets of the time were Yue Fei, Zhang Yuangan, Zhang Xiaoxiang, Fan Chengda and Yang Wanli (1127 AD–1206 AD). The great poetess Li Qingzhao (1084 AD–1151 AD) and the famous poet Chen Yiyi (1090 AD–1138 AD), respectively belonging to the Sentimentalist and the Jiangxi Schools, had also taken part in the concerto of patriotism and struck touching notes.

The history of Song Poetry was brought to a solemn and stirring close by Wen Tianxiang, whose immortal "Song of Righteousness", "Crossing the Lonely Bay" and "Libation to the Moon over the Rill", like the excellent works of others, have an important bearing on the character of the Chinese nation. Owing to the unique charm in its artistic form, *ci*-poetry still boasts an irresistible appeal to contemporary poets and readers.

89. 渔家傲

范仲淹

塞下秋来风景异，
衡阳雁去无留意。
四面边声连角起，
千嶂里，
长烟落日孤城闭。

浊酒一杯家万里，
燕然未勒归无计。
羌管悠悠霜满地，
人不寐，
将军白发征夫泪。

Pride of the Fisherman[1]

Fan Zhongyan[2]

Th' frontier unfolding an autumn scenery of its own,

Without hesitation the wild geese to Hengyang have flown.

The bugle calling, th' steeds neighing, th' winds now scream

and now groan.

The sun drooping down perilous peaks, columns

Of smoke rising to th' sky, th' town, with all its gates shut,

stands lone.

A cup of wine drowns not my yearning, for home's far away;

But ere my name's carved on Mount Yanran, nothing will me

sway![3]

Frost's everywhere; melancholic strains the *Qiang* flutes[4] do

play.

What have th' countless sleepless nights been witnessing?

The frontier guards shedding tears, th' general's hair turning

gray.

90. 雨霖铃

柳永

咏情言志

寒蝉凄切。对长亭晚，骤雨初歇。

都门帐饮无绪，留恋处、兰舟催发。

执手相看泪眼，竟无语凝噎。

念去去、千里烟波，暮霭沉沉楚天阔。

多情自古伤离别。更那堪、冷落清秋节。

今宵酒醒何处，杨柳岸、晓风残月。

此去经年，应是良辰好景虚设。

便纵有、千种风情，更与何人说。

Bells in the Rain[1]

Liu Yong[2]

Cicadas decrying the chill which befalls

In th' wake of the rain, the pavilion[3] ahead

Bedims in the dusk as if it had a sorrowful heart.

The boat now relaying its urge in the calls,

At th' send-off out of the city in a shed,

Neither of us are in th' mood for wine, as I'll soon part.

We are full of tears but short of word;

Sobbing, we just grasp each other's hand:

Destination lies beyond the waves which are blurred

By the mist hanging low over the southern land.[4]

Love's haunted by separation from of old,

Moreo'er, I'm leaving on an autumn day so cold.

What shall I see when wine's effect weakens after the night?

Bank and willows under a pale setting moon — a strange sight.[5]

I'll stay away for long long years, during which lovely days

And thrilling scenes would mean nothing to such a lonely

    heart.

Affections in me henceforward may seethe and burn and blaze[6],

And yet to whom could I my tender sentiments impart?

91. 陶者

梅尧臣

陶尽门前土，
屋上无片瓦；
十指不染泥，
鳞鳞居大夏。

The Potters[1]

Mei Yaochen [2]

People who've exhausted their doorway clay[3]
For kilning under tile-less roofs do stay[4];
While the drones, who've ne'er to earthwork applied
Their fingers, in spacious mansions reside.

92. 菩萨蛮

张先

哀筝一弄《湘江曲》，
声声写尽湘波绿。
纤指十三弦，
细将幽恨传。

当筵秋水慢，
玉柱斜飞雁。
弹到断肠时，
春山眉黛低。

Buddhist Dance[1]

Zhang Xian[2]

On th' plaintive *zheng*[3], *Song of th' Xiang River* she plays.

At first th' limpidity each note lively portrays,

Then in detail th' pent-up grief she does impart.

Her nimble fingers on th' thirteen strings dart,

Till the waters in front slow down for th' plight,

And wild geese from Jade Hill droop in their flight.

At last she strikes up the most plaintive strain,

When th' mountains seem to knit their brows for pain.

93. 戏答元珍

欧阳修

春风疑不到天涯，
二月山城未见花。
残雪压枝犹有橘，
冻雷惊笋欲抽芽。
夜闻归雁生乡思，
病入新年感物华。
曾是洛阳花下客，
野芳虽晚不须嗟。

Jocular Response to Yuanzhen's Verse[1]

Ouyang Xiu[2]

The second moon as it is, no flowers have yet been seen;

Will spring to this remote mountain town[3] never come about?

Snows weighing on their branches, th' orange trees stand lively
green;

The thunders, crashing th' frozen air, spur bamboo shoots to
sprout.

Th' cawing of south-bound wild geese touch my homesick
heart at night;

The splendour of the New Year, though, enlivens my weak
frame.

As one who's seen th' Luoyang peonies — a marvelous sight,

For th' flowers late blooming in th' wilderness he bears no
blame![4]

Songs of Weal and Woe

94. 生查子

欧阳修

去年元夜时，
花市灯如昼，
月上柳梢头，
人约黄昏后。

今年元夜时，
月与灯依旧。
不见去年人，
泪湿衣衫袖。

Hawthorns in the Wilderness[1]

Ouyang Xiu

On th' eve of th' Lantern Festival last year,
The flower fair was lit up bright as noon.
We rendezvoused when dark night drew near
And to th' top of th' willows arose the moon.
Of this year's Lantern Festival on th' eve,
The moon and the lanterns remain as bright.[2]
But tears have wetted either of my sleeve,
For th' soul of my heart[3] is far out of sight.

319

95.蚕妇

张俞

昨日入城市，
归来泪满巾。
遍身罗绮者，
不是养蚕人。

The Woman Silk-Worm Raiser[1]

Zhang Yu[2]

To the city yesterday she did go,

On her return her scarf was wet with tears.

For of those who are wrapped from top to toe

In silk and satins, none are worm raisers!

96. 阮郎归

司马光

渔舟容易入春山，
仙家日月闲。
绮窗纱幌映朱颜，
相逢醉梦间。

松露冷，海霞殷。
匆匆整棹还。
落花寂寂水潺潺，
重寻此路难。

322

The Return of Ruan the Youngster[1]

Sima Guang[2]

My fishing boat somehow haps to reach Dale Ever-Green,

O'er which to move at leisure th' sun and th' moon seem.

Charming is she, set off by th' carved window and gauze screen!

And our rendezvous is quite a perfect dream.

The morn dew on th' pines cold, and th' clouds thick in the eve.

My oar ready, I prepare in haste to leave.

Now fallen flowers stay soundless and gurgles th' stream,

And 'tis hard to follow the same route, I deem.

97. 泊船瓜洲

王安石

京口瓜洲一水间，
钟山只隔数重山。
春风又绿江南岸，
明月何时照我还？

Anchoring at Guazhou

Wang Anshi[1]

Beyond the River lies Jingkou[2], from which Zhongshan[3]

Is but a span of several mountains away.

Now that the spring breezes have re-greened the south bank,[4]

When will the bright moon see me on my home-bound way?

325

98.元日

王安石

爆竹声中一岁除，
春风送暖入屠苏。
千门万户曈曈日，
总把新桃换旧符。

326

New Year's Day[1]

Wang Anshi

In th' midst of firecrackers[2] goes the past year,

And spring breeze lends warmth to the Tusu wine[3].

At countless doors new peach-wood charms[4] appear

In stead of th' old ones, th' world bath'd in th' sun's shine.

99. 桂枝香

王安石

登临送目，正故国晚秋，天气初肃。
千里澄江似练，翠峰如簇。
征帆去棹残阳里，背西风，酒旗斜矗。
彩舟云淡，星河鹭起，画图难足。

念往昔、豪华竟逐。
叹门外楼头，悲恨相续。
千古凭高对此，谩嗟荣辱。
六朝旧事随流水，但寒烟衰草凝绿。
至今商女，时时犹唱，后庭遗曲。

Fragrant Is the Cassia Twig[1]

Wang Anshi

Late autumn's chill felt in th' ancient capital, I gaze afar on
high.

Th' lengthy rill's like a ribbon; th' clusters of green peaks rise
to th' sky.

Ships sailing in th' setting sun, wine-shop sign-flags in th' west
wind, painted yachts,

Fleecy clouds, and egrets flushing from th' isles — all these do
paintings defy[2].

The bygone days had witnessed men vie for power and wealth
and fame.

Besieged, th' monarchs still embraced their belles, and as a
result disgrace came.

I sigh over th' rises and falls, of which history, as it were,
makes game.

Only withered grass and mist are seen, gone are th' Six
Dynasties for aye,

And yet the songstresses are still singing the captured throne's
song[3] today.

100.饮湖上初晴后雨（其一）

苏轼

水光潋滟晴方好，
山色空濛雨亦奇。
欲把西湖比西子，
淡妆浓抹总相宜。

Drinking on the West Lake in a Changing Weather (No. 1)[1]

Su Shi[2]

Oh, you are pretty, shimmering when 'tis fine,

And charming against the murky hills in rain.[3]

I would liken you to Xishi[4], who did shine

No matter her make-up was heavy or plain.

101. 水调歌头

苏轼

明月几时有，
把酒问青天。
不知天上宫阙，
今夕是何年？
我欲乘风归去，
又恐琼楼玉宇，
高处不胜寒。
起舞弄清影，
何似在人间！

转朱阁，
低绮户，
照无眠。
不应有恨，
何事长向别时圆？
人有悲欢离合，
月有阴晴圆缺，
此事古难全。
但愿人长久，
千里共婵娟。

Prelude to Melody of Flowing Waters[1]

Su Shi

When did the brilliant moon come into being?

Raising my cup I ask the azure sky.

And what year's tonight in, I wonder, in light of

The calendar of the palace on high[2]?

The dread that it'd be too cold in the firmament

Gives me pause[3] — otherwise riding on the zephyr

To the crystalline palace[4] I would fly.

And further, whom might I dance with up there but my shadow?

With this regard[5] the fancy for celestial life seems wry.

Creeping from th' other side of th' mansion,

Through the carved window on the sleepless

The moon mischievously casts its light.

Why should she ironically grow full when people part,

As if upon men she were venting a spite?

Ay, but who can e'er change the course of nature?

As the moon may wax or wane and grow dim or bright,

So men thrive or decline, and part or reunite.[6]

'Tis devoutly to be wished that we may live long

And share — though far apart— the Beauty's gentle light[7].

102. 念奴娇·赤壁怀古

苏轼

大江东去，
浪淘尽、
千古风流人物。
故垒西边，
人道是三国周郎赤壁。
乱石穿空，
惊涛拍岸，
卷起千堆雪。
江山如画，
一时多少豪杰。

遥想公瑾当年，
小乔初嫁了，
雄姿英发。
羽扇纶巾，
谈笑间，
樯橹灰飞烟灭。
故国神游，
多情应笑我，

Fair Is Niannu — Reflections on Historical Events at the Red Cliff[1]

Su Shi

The great River to the east surges high,

Washing th' fame of th' heroes of yore away.[2]

West to th' ancient fortress th' Red Cliff does lie,

Where Zhou Yu[3] of th' Three Kingdoms, people say,

During the great campaign had made a name.

Lo, the jugged rocks are rising to th' skies,

And terrifying waves slashing on th' shore,

Rolling up a thousand piles of foam th' same

As snow. In a land fair as paradise,

How many of th' era are held in awe?

Tracing back to th' time of General Zhou,

Who, having just linked a conjugal tie

To Xiao Qiao[4], with life and wit did o'erflow.

Feather fan in hand and in spirits high,

He had th' foe's ships burnt to ashes in th' stream.

One might jest that, so carried away

By th' reflections, I'd have my hair grayed soon.

Songs of Weal and Woe

早生华发。
人生如梦，
一尊还酹江月。

Oh, be soft now! As life's like a brief dream,

In libation, a cup of wine I may

As well offer to th' river-lighting moon.

103. 江城子 · 密州出猎

苏轼

老夫聊发少年狂，
左牵黄，右擎苍。
锦帽貂裘，
千骑卷平冈。
欲报倾城随太守，
亲射虎，看孙郎。
酒酣胸胆尚开张，
鬓微霜，又何妨！
持节云中，
何日遣冯唐？
会挽雕弓如满月，
西北望，射天狼。

Riverside Town — Hunting in Mizhou Prefecture[1]

Su Shi

For th' moment to display the craze of th' young I'm bound:

Holding a falcon and the leash to a hound.

A thousand horsemen in hunting suits in th' wake

Come, sweeping across mountains and level ground.

I'll play th' part of Sun Quan[2], tiger shooter renown'd,

For the whole town pour out for the event's sake.

What matters if there are a few gray hairs on th' crest?

Reinforced by wine I feel at my best.

Oh, th' Feng Tang[3] of today when will the throne send

As an envoy to reinstate the depressed?

In time aiming my arrow at th' Wolf[4] in th' northwest,

My bow into a full moon I shall bend!

104. 江城子 · 乙卯正月十二日夜记梦

苏轼

十年生死两茫茫，
不思量，自难忘。
千里孤坟，
无处话凄凉。
纵使相逢应不识，
尘满面，鬓如霜。

夜来幽梦忽还乡。
小轩窗，正梳妆。
相顾无言，
惟有泪千行。
料得年年肠断处：
明月夜，短松冈。

Riverside Town — A Record of My Dream[1]

Su Shi

Alas! It's been ten years since you did depart,

Over which grief has been gnawing at my heart.

You lie in the grave a thousand *li* away,

Without any means your loneliness to impart;

And I am so reduced as to give you a start —

Should we meet — my face dusty, and my hair's frost-gray.

I dreamed I suddenly went home yesternight

And saw you making up at the table right

Behind th' window, that our tears rolled down like threads

Of beads, and that we were both dumb-founded for th' plight.

Oh, I can tell how sad you are each year this night

On th' hill-lock, where on th' pines a wretched light[2] th' moon

sheds.

Songs of Weal and Woe

105. 蝶恋花

苏轼

花褪残红青杏小。
燕子飞时，绿水人家绕。
枝上柳绵吹又少，
天涯何处无芳草！
墙里秋千墙外道。
墙外行人，墙里佳人笑。
笑渐不闻声渐悄，
多情却被无情恼。

The Butterfly Fluttering around the Flowers[1]

Su Shi

Swallows darting, th' limpid stream does past th' house flow;

Flowers fading, hanging are unripe apricots green.

Fewer are willow catkins, for winds oft blow,

Yet everywhere fragrant grass and plants are seen!

On this side of th' fence th' passer-by is on his way,

And a maid giggles on the swing on the other side.

When no giggle is heard and footsteps fade away,

His fondness for th' silent th' loving can hardly hide![2]

343

Songs of Weal and Woe

106. 望江南·超然台作

苏轼

春未老，
风细柳斜斜。
试上超然台上看，
半壕春水一城花。
烟雨暗千家。

寒食后，
酒醒却咨嗟。
休对故人思故国，
且将新火试新茶。
诗酒趁年华。

Yearning for the South — Composed at the Detachment Tower[1]

Su Shi

Spring still in its prime,

waving in the breeze are the willows trim[2].

To take a look the Detached Platform I climb:

Th' town's full of spring and th' trench is about to brim,

Though countless households th' mist and th' rain bedim.

After Cold Food Day[3],

I sigh and lament when sober from wine.

About old home to old friends you just nothing say,

To start a new fire and make new tea 'tis fine,

For wine and verse just to youth-hood incline.[4]

107. 临江仙

苏轼

夜饮东坡醒复醉，
归来仿佛三更。
家童鼻息已雷鸣。
敲门都不应，
倚杖听江声。

长恨此身非我有，
何时忘却营营？
夜阑风静縠纹平。
小舟从此逝，
江海寄余生。

咏情言志

346

Immortals over the River[1]

Su Shi

Th' East Slope saw me drunk and sober now and again,

When I came back it was around th' third watch[2] or four.

Th' servant's thundering snores formed an unbroken chain:

My knocks at the door he appeared to ignore.

On my cane I went to listen to th' tide's roar.

That I can't be true to self 'tis a life-long shame.

When can I rid myself of worldly affairs?

Now that the night's deep, the weather calm and th' rill tame,

How I wish there were a little boat that bears

Me to the seas — and to a life free from cares!

347

108. 鹧鸪天

苏轼

林断山明竹隐墙，
乱蝉衰草小池塘。
翻空白鸟时时见，
照水红蕖细细香。

村舍外，古城旁，
杖藜徐步转斜阳。
殷勤昨夜三更雨，
又得浮生一日凉。

Partridges in the Sky[1]

Su Shi

Mounts clear on th' woods' verge, 'midst bamboos th' hut does lie;

Th' grass around th' pool languish, and cicadas yell.

The white birds hover From time to time in th' sky;

Th' scent of lotus flowers comes spell after spell.

From the huts to the ancient town, on my cane

I take a long walk at sunset at leisure.

Thanks to the mid-night rain I can once again

Enjoy, in my drifting life[2], a day's pleasure.

109. 定风波

苏轼

三月七日沙湖道中遇雨。雨具先去，同行皆狼狈，余独不觉。已而遂晴，故作此词。

莫听穿林打叶声，
何妨吟啸且徐行。
竹杖芒鞋轻胜马，谁怕？
一蓑烟雨任平生。

料峭春风吹酒醒，微冷，
山头斜照却相迎。
回首向来萧瑟处，归去，
也无风雨也无晴。

Taming the Waves and Winds[1]

Su Shi

On 7th of the third moon, I was caught in rain on my way
to the Sandy Lake. As the rain gear had been sent to the
destination in advance, all the company felt awkward except
me. I composed this *ci*-poem when the rain stopped .

What matters if on the woods and leaves splatters th' rain?
I may well recite poems while pacing on the cane
And in sandals, which better than horseback have me eased.
Howe'er could one with dread be seized,
When his sanguine coir coat has braved life's wind and rain? [2]

I feel the chill when th' breezes sober me from wine,
But then a soothing sun atop the hill does shine.
I glance back at the place that I am to return,
There's th' seclusion for which I yearn:
'Tis secure and quiet, be th' weather rough or fine !

Songs of Weal and Woe

110. 清平乐

黄庭坚

春归何处？
寂寞无行路。
若有人知春去处，
唤取归来同住。

春无踪迹谁知？
除非问取黄鹂。
百啭无人能解，
因风飞过蔷薇。

Celebrating Peace and Order[1]

Huang Tingjian[2]

Oh! Where is Spring?

I know not where to go in lonely dismay.

Would anyone who knows Spring's whereabouts kindly bring

Her word, requesting that with me she should stay?[3]

Alas! Who knows, as no trace is to be found?

To seek th' oriole's advice I may well try.

Yet unfathomable is th' bird's tweeting sound;

With a gust of wind o'er th' rose bush th' fowl does fly![4]

111.鹊桥仙

秦观

纤云弄巧，
飞星传恨，
银汉迢迢暗度。
金风玉露一相逢，
便胜却、
人间无数。

柔情似水，
佳期如梦，
忍顾鹊桥归路。
两情若是久长时，
又岂在、
朝朝暮暮。

Celestial Beings on the Magpie Bridge[1]

Qin Guan[2]

Her yearning in th' clouds th' Girl Weaver subtly weaves,

While the shooting stars display how th' Cowherd grieves.[3]

Across the Milky Way they meet

But once out of a year's so many eves!

Howe'er, no secular love can e'er compare

With th' holy sentiments they for a time share.[4]

Their tender feeling is like a long long stream;

Their rendezvous is like a transient dream.

Their hearts may bleed now that they part

At th' Magpie Bridge[5] — men are inclined to deem.

But nay, so long as steadfast love will stay,

Whereat should they be bound up each night and day?[6]

355

112. 踏莎行·郴州旅舍

秦观

雾失楼台，
月迷津渡，
桃源梦断无寻处。
可堪孤馆闭春寒，
杜鹃声里斜阳暮。

驿寄梅花，
鱼传尺素，
砌成此恨无重数。
郴江幸自绕郴山，
为谁流下潇湘去？

Walking on Grassland[1] — Composed at the Inn in Chenzhou

Qin Guan

Towers lost in the mist of plight,

The ferry vague in a moon that looks pale,

The Dale of Peach Blossom[2] is out of sight.

In th' lonely inn spring cold does me assail;

At dusk to th' setting sun th' cuckoo does wail.

The silk scrolls stuck in th' fish bellies

And all the flowers sent by post[3], oh lo!

Pile up tall as my countless grievances.

Round th' Chenshan Hill the Chen Rill ought to go:

Whereat does it to th' Xiao and th' Xiang Rills flow?[4]

113. 鹧鸪天

贺铸

重过阊门万事非，
同来何事不同归？
梧桐半死清霜后，
头白鸳鸯失伴飞。

原上草，露初晞，
旧栖新垄两依依。
空床卧听南窗雨，
谁复挑灯夜补衣？

358

Partridges in the Sky[1]

He Zhu[2]

Reentering th' Changmen Gate[3], everything changed I find;

Since we'd shared life, why not share it through? Why leave me

    behind

Like a Chinese parasol half dead after hoary frost,

Or a lone white-haired mandarin duck flapping with th' mate

    lost?[4]

The grasses on the plain must still be wet with dew at dawn?

'Tis for you in th' new grave that I in th' old nest[5] always mourn.

I groan, listening to th' pelting rain on th' half-vacant bed[6]:

Whoever could mend my coat in the lamplight in your stead?[7]

114. 行路难

贺铸

缚虎手，悬河口，
车如鸡栖马如狗。
白纶巾，扑黄尘，
不知我辈可是蓬蒿人？
衰兰送客咸阳道，
天若有情天亦老。
作雷颠，不论钱，
谁问旗亭美酒斗十千？
酌大斗，更为寿，
青鬓常青古无有。
笑嫣然，舞翩然，
当垆素女十五语如弦。
遗音能记秋风曲，
事去千年犹恨促。
揽流光，系扶桑，
争奈愁来一日却为长！

Life's Journey Is Perilous[1]

He Zhu

I have tiger-taming hands and a silver tongue, though,

In a coop-like carriage drawn by dog-like horses I'll go

To th' capital. I'll prove that I'm no mediocrity,

Though my headband now suggests of no post and dignity .

The magnolias taken off their bloom, with th' folks I part

For Xianyang, o'er which Heaven would age if it had a heart.

Like Lei the Crazy[2] wealth I'll make light. About price who'd
care?

Even ten thousand taels for a *dou* of wine I won't spare!

For th' sake of life to a large wine-cup I will henceforth hold:

Whose temple hair has remained black for ever from of old?

By the way, in watching performances there is no harm:

The girls' smiles and dances and silver tongues exude with charm.

Song to th' Autumn Winds fresh in our minds, a thousand years
have passed

Since it was composed. Isn't life transient? And isn't time too
fast?

With this regard I'd tie the sun to Fusang Tree[3] with beams of light.

Howe'er, I'd find a day too long to endure in a wretched plight.[4]

115. 苏幕遮

周邦彦

燎沈香，消溽暑。
鸟雀呼晴，
侵晓窥檐语。
叶上初阳干宿雨。
水面清圆，
一一风荷举。

故乡遥，
何日去？
家住吴门，
久作长安旅。
五月渔郎相忆否？
小楫轻舟，梦入芙蓉浦。

Temple Music[1]

Zhou Bangyan[2]

Eagle-wood is burned to dispel

Heat; The peeping birds from the eaves

Twitter of a fine day to tell.

In th' morning sun th' raindrops on th' lotus leaves

Shrink. Green in colour and round in shape they appear

To be held high above the waters clean and clear.

My hometown is far far away,

Oh, whenever can I return?

Why should a Wumen native stay

Long in Chang'an? Ah, do th' fishermen yearn

For me still? I row to Lotus Pool down the stream

In a skiff to meet them, which turns out a dream!

363

116. 好事近

朱敦儒

摇首出红尘，
醒醉更无时节。
活计绿蓑青笠，
惯披霜冲雪。
晚来风定钓丝闲，
上下是新月。
千里水天一色，
看孤鸿明灭。

A Blessing at Hand[1]

Zhu Dunru[2]

After a shake I've cast off th' shackles of worldliness,

And now at my own sweet will I get drunk, or sober grow.

I love my bamboo hat, my coir coat and my business,

And more oft than not I tread the frost and brave the snow.

Th' wind calm at dusk, my fishing line resumes its serenity;

Either in th' sky or waters is seen a new moon bright.

Boundless waters and skies merging into an entity,

A care-free wild goose[3] is now in sight, now out of sight.

117. 病牛

李纲

耕犁千亩实千箱，
力尽筋疲谁复伤？
但得众生皆得饱，
不辞羸病卧残阳。

The Sick Farm Cattle[1]

Li Gang[2]

I've plowed lots of land and filled the barns with grain;

When tired out no comfort I expect to gain.

I lie at ease, though feeble when the sun's set:

If I've helped suffice th' folk, why should I regret![3]

118. 六幺令·次韵和贺方回金陵怀古，鄱阳席上作

李纲

长江千里，
烟淡水云阔。
歌沈玉树，
古寺空有疏钟发。
六代兴亡如梦，
苒苒惊时月。
兵戈凌灭，
豪华销尽，
几见银蟾自圆缺。

潮落潮生波渺，
江树森如发。
谁念迁客归来，
老大伤名节。
纵使岁寒途远，
此志应难夺。

Liuyao Melody — Reflections on History Improvised at the Banquet on the Boyang Lake in Reply to He Fanghui with the Same Rhyme Sequence[1]

Li Gang

Th' thousand-*li* Yangtze River lies long

 And vast in the haze, and its waves roll.

Gone has been "Trees of Jade"[2], the lusty song;

Just the bells from th' temples in time toll.

How time flies! The rises and falls, it seems,

Of Six Dynasties were but transient dreams.

The flames of war were gone for aye,

And sumptuousness didn't long stay,

But th' moon still waxes and wanes in its own way.

Th' waters boundless, th' tide ebbs and flows, and behold,

The riverside trees are as dense as hair.

Who could have thought that I should have returned old

And dismissed, having fallen into th' snare?

E'en if the way is long and the times are hard,

My pursuit of th' goal nothing can retard.

高楼谁设，
倚阑凝望，
独立渔翁满江雪。

On the top of the tall tower I lean

Against the railing, as to gaze afar I'm keen,

When braving th' snow o'er th' rill a fearless angler's seen.[3]

119. 减字木兰花

李清照

卖花担上，
买得一枝春欲放。
泪染轻匀，
犹带彤霞晓露痕。

怕郎猜道，
奴面不如花面好。
云鬓斜簪，
徒要教郎比并看。

咏情言志

372

The Lily Magnolia (A Simplified Version)[1]

Li Qingzhao[2]

From the peddler I choose and buy

A spray of flowers alive with spring hue.

It beams, like a lass sweet and shy,

With th' tinctures of rosy clouds and morning dew.[3]

For fear my boyfriend might not grant

That my features are as th' flowers as fair,

I wear it on th' temple on th' slant

To make it easier for him to compare!

120. 一剪梅

李清照

红藕香残玉簟秋。
轻解罗裳,
独上兰舟。
云中谁寄锦书来?
雁字回时,
月满西楼。

花自飘零水自流。
一种相思,
两处闲愁。
此情无计可消除,
才下眉头,
却上心头。

A Spray of Plum Flowers[1]

Li Qingzhao

Th' mat's chill, and autumn's taken off th' lotus' bloom;

Intending to chase away my gloom,

I go alone on deck th' orchid yacht.

When back, I ascend th' moon-lit tower, to spot

The wild geese[2] flying over the skies

Without bringing me a great surprise!

The petals drift and th' stream flows in their own way.

Though in different places we stay,

The same ardent affections we share.

Away from such feelings you just can not tear:

For whenever from the brows they part,

They all at once come into the heart.[3]

Songs of Weal and Woe

121. 声声慢

李清照

寻寻觅觅，
冷冷清清，
凄凄惨惨戚戚。
乍暖还寒时候，
最难将息。
三杯两盏淡酒，
怎敌他、晚来风急。
雁过也，正伤心，
却是旧时相识。

满地黄花堆积，
憔悴损、如今有谁堪摘。
守着窗儿，
独自怎生得黑？
梧桐更兼细雨，
到黄昏、点点滴滴。
这次第，
怎一个愁字了得。

Beats Slowing Down[1]

Li Qingzhao

Fumbling and searching, at a loss I feel,

At a loss in such lonely melancholy

And plaintive solitude as seem unreal.

Th' turn of cold and warmth is, incredibly,

The most miserable time to endure.

Of th' chill of evening winds how can I cure

Myself with a few cups of wine impure?

'Tis heart-rending to see th' wild geese in th' sky,

My acquaintances of old, elsewhere fly!

Chrysanthemums now flourish here and there,

But who would care to pluck them, feeling blue?

Sitting alone at th' window in despair,

Ere night falls I know not how to pull through.

Now dripping and dropping incessantly

On the Chinese parasols is the rain.[2]

Alas, much much more than anxiety,

At such a time, is what one must sustain.

122. 醉花阴

李清照

薄雾浓云愁永昼，
瑞脑消金兽。
佳节又重阳，
玉枕纱厨，
半夜凉初透。

东篱把酒黄昏后，
有暗香盈袖。
莫道不消魂，
帘卷西风，
人比黄花瘦。

Tipsy in the Shade of Flowers[1]

Li Qingzhao

Mist followed by dark clouds, I have been sad all day,

Watching the incense in th' censer burning away.

The Double Ninth Festival has now come again,

Yet in th' gauze screens and on th' jade pillow I up stay,

Feeling at mid-night th' chilly loneliness and pain.

'Midst chrysanthemums I took a drop[2] in the eve,

Which have left a wisp of light fragrance in each sleeve.

That love-sickness is not consuming who can say?[3]

When it rolls up the curtain, the west wind would grieve

At a soul thinner than th' yellow flower of th' day.[4]

123. 武陵春

李清照

风住尘香花已尽，
日晚倦梳头。
物是人非事事休，
欲语泪先流。

闻说双溪春尚好，
也拟泛轻舟。
只恐双溪舴艋舟，
载不动、许多愁。

Spring in Wuling[1]

Li Qingzhao

Th' wind subsides, dust smelling of fallen flowers here and
   there;
Th' sun's high up, but I can find no mood to comb my hair.
Gone is everything with my man, though his things still
   remain.
Before I can utter a word down roll tears of pain!

'Tis said that the Twin Brook still maintains a pretty spring
   scene,
And I somehow think of canoeing on which I'm keen.
However, I doubt whether there is a vessel big enough there
That can bear the weight of so much sorrow and despair![2]

Songs of Weal and Woe

124. 夏日绝句

李清照

生当作人杰，
死亦为鬼雄。
至今思项羽，
不肯过江东。

Four-Line Poem Composed in Summer[1]

Li Qingzhao

Be a man of men with mettle while alive,

And a soul of souls even if doomed to die![2]

Xiang Yu, who would rather perish than survive

By crossing th' River,[3] is held in esteem high!

125. 渔家傲·题玄真子图

张元干

钓笠披云青嶂绕，
绿蓑细雨春江渺。
白鸟飞来风满棹。
收纶了。
渔童拍手樵青笑。

明月太虚同一照。
浮家泛宅忘昏晓。
醉眼冷看城市闹。
烟波老。
谁能惹得闲烦恼。

Pride of the Fisherman — An Inscription on the Portrait of Genuine Meta-Physician[1]

Zhang Yuangan[2]

Clouds fleeting o'erhead, in a coir-coat you sail in the rill

In spring, which is walled on both sides with many a green hill.

When the white birds hover around, your cabin the winds fill.

Lo, the fishing line is pulled up!

Yutong th' boy claps his hands and Qiaoqing[3] th' maid with
   laughs does thrill .

The bright moon in the great void on all men alike has shone.

In your floating life you ignore whether it's dusk or dawn.

You love wine, but clamorous city life you hold in scorn.

While th' haze and waves are at their best,

From th' racketing world who could afford to invite a thorn[4]?

385

Songs of Weal and Woe

126. 满江红

岳飞

怒发冲冠，
凭栏处，
潇潇雨歇。
抬望眼，
仰天长啸，
壮怀激烈。
三十功名尘与土，
八千里路云和月。
莫等闲，
白了少年头，
空悲切！

靖康耻，
犹未雪；
臣子恨，
何时灭。
驾长车，
踏破贺兰山缺。
壮志饥餐胡虏肉，
笑谈渴饮匈奴血。

咏情言志

386

The River All Red

Yue Fei[1]

I lean on the railings,

Bristling in righteous wrath,

Th' spattering rain beginning to withdraw.

With pent-up aspirations seething in me,

I gaze afar

And skyward roar.

I make light of the ranks and merits won in thirty years,

Together with countless encounters in the flames of war![2]

Waste not my youth,

For if my raven hair for nothing turned gray,

Grief and regret would my heart gnaw.[3]

We've not yet avenged th' Humiliation

Of Jingkang[4] upon the enemies;

Howe'er can we officials to the crown

Our burning indignation appease?[5]

Riding on chariots over Mount Helan,

Enemy forts we'll crush and seize.

We are pledged to sweep away the savage Hun invaders,

And relentlessly smash their provisions into pieces,

待从头，
收拾旧山河，
朝天阙！

Until we have recovered

Our sacred territories,

When we can be present at Court at ease.

127. 游山西村

陆游

莫笑农家腊酒浑，
丰年留客足鸡豚。
山重水复疑无路，
柳暗花明又一村。
箫鼓追随春社近，
衣冠简朴古风存。
从今若许闲乘月，
拄杖无时夜叩门。

咏情言志

390

Visiting the Shanxi Village[1]

Lu You[2]

Disdain not their home-brew for its impurity,

The farmers will make up th' treat in a bumper year.

Facing the chains of mounts and rills one may feel lost;

Midst trees and flowers a new vista will appear.[3]

The simple clothing signifies old-time values;

Th' drums and flutes announce Spring Offering's drawing
   near.[4]

Had I th' freedom to saunter every moonlit eve,

Supported by a cane I'd frequent th' doors so dear!

128. 鹧鸪天

陆游

家住苍烟落照间，
丝毫尘事不相关。
斟残玉瀣行穿竹，
卷罢黄庭卧看山。

贪啸傲，任衰残，
不妨随处一开颜。
元知造物心肠别，
老却英雄似等闲！

Partridges in the Sky[1]

Lu You

In th' greenish mist and soft sunset rests my home,

Which from the dust of worldly affairs is free.

Th' nectar sipped, ' midst the bamboo groves I roam;

Th' Daoist Scripture closed, I watch the mounts with glee.

Firm and proud, about ups and downs I don't care,

Amuse myself here and there as well I may.[2]

Creator has a varied heart, I'm aware,

To whom it's nothing to let heroes decay.[3]

393

Songs of Weal and Woe

129. 鹧鸪天

陆游

懒向青门学种瓜，
只将渔钓送年华。
双双新燕飞春岸，
片片轻鸥落晚沙。

歌缥渺，舻呕哑，
酒如清露鲊如花。
逢人问道归何处，
笑指船儿是我家。

Partridges in the Sky[1]

Lu You

The melon grower of the Green Gate who cares
To copy? [2] In fishing I shall find delight.
The swallows dart about the spring banks in pairs,
And hosts of gulls on the evening sand alight.

The oars creaking, songs are resounding in th' air,
Th' dishes seem to bloom, and as dew th' wine's as clear.
Smiling and pointing to the boat, when asked where
I live, I proudly reply: " My home's right here!"

395

Songs of Weal and Woe

130. 钗头凤

陆游

红酥手，
黄縢酒，
满城春色宫墙柳。
东风恶，
欢情薄，
一怀愁绪，
几年离索。
错，错，错！

春如旧，
人空瘦，
泪痕红浥鲛绡透。
桃花落，
闲池阁。
山盟虽在，
锦书难托。
莫，莫，莫！

Phoenix Hairpin[1]

Lu You

Reaching out her beautiful pinkish hand,

She poured wine which is of a famous brand;

We enjoyed a parkful of spring where willows green did stand.

But alas, th' spiteful east wind[2] played th' mischief;

Harmonious conjugal life was cut brief.

A few years of cruel separation

Has made our hearts aching without relief.

What grief, grief, grief![3]

Spring, as usual, now has come again,

However, both have grown haggard in vain,

The satin handkerchief being wet with tears of great pain.

Th' ponds and pavilions desolate for long,

Peach flowers now fall down throng after throng.

Although to oaths we'll for aye remain true,

'Tis hard e'en for letters to cross th' bars[4] strong.

All's wrong, wrong, wrong!

Songs of Weal and Woe

131. 诉衷情

陆游

当年万里觅封侯，
匹马戍梁州。
关河梦断何处，
尘暗旧貂裘。

胡未灭，鬓先秋，
泪空流。
此身谁料，
心在天山，身老沧洲。

Relating Heartfelt Sentiments[1]

Lu You

For merits worthy of enfeoffments, alone on horseback I did go
Ten thousand *li* away to serve in the army in Liangzhou.
Passes and fortresses appear just in dreams, but when awake
I find my army coat tarnished by dust, which worn out does
  grow.

My hair has turned gray, and yet the foe
Is still ferocious. My tears in vain flow!
Who could have expected that one who aspires to fighting
In Tianshan should get older and older still in Cangzhou![2]

132. 鹊桥仙

陆游

茅檐人静，篷窗灯暗，
春晚连江风雨。
林莺巢燕总无声，
但月夜，常啼杜宇。

催成清泪，惊残孤梦，
又拣深枝飞去。
故山独自不堪听，
况半世，飘然羁旅。

Immortals on the Magpie Bridge[1]

Lu You

’Round th’ thatched eaves and th’ window — all’s still;

The lamp is dim and the night is deep.

In late spring the winds and rains befall the rill.

The orioles and swallows always silent keep,

But on moon-lit nights cuckoos[2] will disturb my sleep.

Ere they into deep woods disappear,

Their plaintive voices will break up dreams

And arouse th’ lonely wanderer’s sorrowful tear.

Hardly can men — e’en ’midst their native mounts and
    streams —

Bear th’ cries, let alone one who with misery teems!

133.鹊桥仙

陆游

一竿风月，
一蓑烟雨，
家在钓台西住。
卖鱼生怕近城门，
况肯到红尘深处？

潮生理棹，
潮平系缆，
潮落浩歌归去。
时人错把比严光，
我自是无名渔父。

Immortals on the Magpie Bridge[1]

Lu You

My fishing rod has witnessed sweats and pains;
Th' coir-coat has experienced winds and rains.[2]
West to th' Fishing Terrace[3] my home does lie.
When going for fish-sales of th' city gate I'm shy,
Wherefore to worldly affairs should I myself tie?

When th' tide comes in, to hoist sail I prepare ;
When th' tide's appeased, of mooring I take care;
And I return singing when th' tide is tame.
People tend to regard me and Yan Guang[4] as th' same,
When[5] I'm a fisherman who makes light of a name.

403

Songs of Weal and Woe

134. 鹊桥仙

陆游

华灯纵博，
雕鞍驰射，
谁记当年豪举？
酒徒一半取封侯，
独去作江边渔父。

轻舟八尺，
低蓬三扇，
占断萍洲烟雨。
镜湖元自属闲人，
又何必官家赐与！

Immortals on the Magpie Bridge[1]

Lu You

I'd played round camp fire to my heart's content,

And on horseback strong bows I had oft bent.

Those heroic deeds who remembers still?

Even stupid drunkards o'er their enfeoffments thrill,

While I should have become a fisherman on th' rill.

My little boat measures eight *chi* in length,

Its three thatched awnings lacking in strength.

Yet it has the scenery to its own:

As favour to the commons that nature has shown,

The Mirror Lake has nothing to do with the throne[2]!

135. 卜算子·咏梅

陆游

驿外断桥边,
寂寞开无主。
已是黄昏独自愁,
更著风和雨。

无意苦争春,
一任群芳妒。
零落成泥碾作尘,
只有香如故。

咏情言志

406

The Diviner — Ode to the Plum Flower[1]

Lu You

By the broken bridge beyond the post[2] you bloom
In solitude, expecting none to flatter.[3]
At dusk the rains spatter, when you suffer lonely cares,
And the blasting winds do boom and you shatter.

As you have ne'er vied with the favoured[4] in spring,
What matters if they should envy you and blame?
You may wither, fall and be ground to dust, your fragrance[5],
However, will remain as before the same!

407

Songs of Weal and Woe

136. 示儿

陆游

死去元知万事空，
但悲不见九州同。
王师北定中原日，
家祭无忘告乃翁。

咏情言志

408

Will to My Sons[1]

Lu You

Everything is over when life's sands run out[2], I'm aware,

Except the invading hoofs will leave a posthumous pain.[3]

Forget not, while offering sacrifice[4], to let me share

Th' news if th' loyal troops have recovered th' Central Plain[5].

137. 四时田园杂兴（其三十一）

范成大

昼出耘田夜绩麻，
村庄儿女各当家。
童孙未解供耕织，
也傍桑阴学种瓜。

Idyllic Life of the Four Seasons
(No. 31)

Fan Chengda[1]

Twisting hempen threads at night or weeding the fields by day,

Each son and daughter of th' farmer has got a role to play[2].

E'en the grandson, who is too young to actual work know[3],

Is learning in the shade of mulberry to pumpkins grow[4].

411

Songs of Weal and Woe

138. 念奴娇·和
徐尉游口湖

范成大

湖山如画，
系孤篷柳岸，
莫惊鱼鸟。
料峭春寒花未遍，
先共疏梅索笑。
一梦三年，
松风依旧，
萝月何曾老。
邻家相问，
这回真个归到。

绿鬓新点吴霜，
尊前强健，
不怕衰翁号。
赖有风流车马客，
来觅香云花岛。
似我粗豪，
不通姓字，

Fair Is Niannu — Composed at the Kouhu Lake in the Same Rhyme Sequence with Xu Wei's Poem[1]

Fan Chengda

The lake and th' hills rival paintings in charm;

I moor my boat by the willow-fringed bank with care,

Thus the birds and fish I may not alarm.

Early spring chill, th' chance of blooming not all th' plants share,

With th' plums I may as well myself entertain.

A dream of three years[2] since I went away,

During which of aging th' moon shows no sign

And th' same as before th' pines and winds remain!

My former neighbours salute me and say:

"At last you're really home, for which we pine!"

New frost is added to what was raven hair;

So long as I can propose and reply toasts,

E'en if I'm nicknamed "senile chap" I won't care.

Moreo'er, refined and tasteful riders come in hosts

To enjoy the isles and plants and rosy haze.

Unconstrained and ignorant of the ways

Of th' world, which I not the least treasure,

只要银瓶倒。
奔名逐利，
乱帆谁在天表。

I take the bottle as my only pleasure:

Among those who hanker after wealth and fame,

Whoever could leave behind a good name?[3]

139. 鹧鸪天

范成大

嫩绿重重看得成，
曲阑幽槛小红英。
酴醿架上蜂儿闹，
杨柳行间燕子轻。

春婉娩，客飘零。
残花残酒片时清。
一杯且买明朝事，
送了斜阳月又生。

Partridges in the Sky[1]

Fan Chengda

The green and tender leaves are growing deeper in hue;

The railed corridor gladly greeting th' buds red and new.

Atop the raspberry trellises th' bees buzz and hum[2];

Between rows of willows th' swallows deftly go and come.

I deplore my wandering life when spring wears away,

And resort to left-o'er wine and flowers to sane stay.

Oh! Isn't one more cup be nice for tomorrow's sake?

But lo! The moon arises in the setting sun's wake! 417

Songs of Weal and Woe

140. 眼儿媚

朱淑真

迟迟春日弄轻柔,
花径暗香流。
清明过了,
不堪回首,
云锁朱楼。

午窗睡起莺声巧,
何处唤春愁。
绿杨影里,
海棠亭畔,
红杏梢头。

Charming Eyes[1]

Zhu Shuzhen[2]

A faint fragrance drifts along the flower-fringed path in th' air;

The sun shining, th' breeze caresses th' willows with care.

After Pure Brightness I can't bear,

However, to recall the days of th' past,

When with dark clouds the tower's overcast.

The melodious voices of warblers, which to my ear

Sound like cries of grief after my noon nap, appear

To be coming from far and near:

From th' willows green, from th' apricots in red,

And from th' begonias beside the shed.[3]

141. 浣溪沙

张孝祥

霜日明宵水蘸空，
鸣鞘声里绣旗红。
淡烟衰草有无中。

万里中原烽火北，
一樽浊酒戍楼东。
酒阑挥泪向悲风。

咏情言志

420

Rinsing Yarn in the Brook[1]

Zhang Xiaoxiang[2]

Th' waters of th' lake melting with the clear frosty sky,

Th' whips whiz and whir, and th' embroidered banners are red.

Thin mist and withered grass now and then catch my eye.

North to th' beacon on th' sacred land th' invaders tread.

At th' defence works out of th' east gate, I drink a cup

Of turbid wine, and 'gainst th' north winds sad[3] tears I shed!

Songs of Weal and Woe

142. 生查子·独游雨岩

辛弃疾

溪边照影行，
天在清溪底。
天上有行云，
人在行云里。
高歌谁和余？
空谷清音起。
非鬼亦非仙，
一曲桃花水。

Hawthorns in the Wilderness — Touring Yuyan the Dripping Cliff Alone[1]

Xin Qiji[2]

In the limpid brook is my figure cast,

And on th' bottom is reflected the sky,

Where fleecy clouds are seen floating me past,

And I appear to be walking on high.

Who is singing in reply to my song?

A sweet melody comes from th' hollow vale.

Is it th' ghost, or th' fairy? [3] But both are wrong:

Th' peach trees in bloom a stream's gurgling to hail.

143. 青玉案·元夕

辛弃疾

东风夜放花千树，
更吹落，星如雨。
宝马雕鞍香满路。
凤箫声动，
玉壶光转，
一夜鱼龙舞。

蛾儿雪柳黄金缕，
笑语盈盈暗香去。
众里寻他千百度，
蓦然回首，
那人却在，
灯火阑珊处。

咏情言志

424

The Desk of Green Jade — The Lantern Festival[1]

Xin Qiji

As if the east wind had brought a thousand trees in bloom,

Which soon fall like hosts of shooting stars in their full glare,

Fireworks of all sorts crack and boom.

Scent and music floating in the air,

Painted lanterns arousing delight,

"Fish" and "dragons"[2] dance all through the night.

The steeds and gold-trimmed carriages flash ahead with grace;

Th' well-adorned belles, shedding smiles and perfume, giggle by.

'Tis for her I've searched many a place,

And yet when I chance to glance back, why[3],

Right in the place where lanterns are few,

Th' soul of my heart does come into view!

144. 西江月·夜行黄沙道中

辛弃疾

明月别枝惊鹊，
清风半夜鸣蝉。
稻花香里说丰年，
听取蛙声一片。

七八个星天外，
两三点雨山前。
旧时茅店社林边，
路转溪桥忽见。

The Moon over the West River — A Night Trip through the Yellow Sand Hills[1]

Xin Qiji

The magpies flush out of th' branches in the minor light[2];
The breeze conveys th' chirping of cicadas at night.
The air filled with th' scent of rice flowers, I gladly hear
The frogs chorusing to herald a propitious year.[3]

Some seven or eight stars the cloudy skies still reveal,
And on this side of th' hill two or three raindrops down steal[4].
I make a turn and hurry o'er th' bridge; to my delight,
A familiar inn beside th' village temple comes in sight![5]

427

145. 清平乐·村居

辛弃疾

茅檐低小，
溪上青青草。
醉里吴音相媚好，
白发谁家翁媪？
大儿锄豆溪东，
中儿正织鸡笼。
最喜小儿无赖，
溪头卧剥莲蓬。

Celebrating Peace and Order — Country Life[1]

Xin Qiji

Th' thatched hut low

And small verges on[2] the brook-side with grass green.

Th' grey-haired couple are talking o'er the cups, which does show

A strong Wu accent and an affection keen.

East of th' stream the eldest son is hoeing weed

For th' beans; Th' second's braiding a coop of bamboo;

Th' youngest, lying upstream, is naughty indeed:

He's picking from a lotus-pod for a chew.[3]

429

146. 菩萨蛮·书 江西造口壁

辛弃疾

郁孤台下清江水，
中间多少行人泪？
西北望长安，
可怜无数山。

青山遮不住，
毕竟东流去。
江晚正愁余，
山深闻鹧鸪。

The Buddhist Dancers — An Inscription on the Cliff of Zaokou in Jiangxi[1]

Xin Qiji

Below the Yugu Terrace th' Clear River[2] gushes ahead,

Containing boundless bitter tears which refugees have shed!

I gaze into the northwest, where Chang'an[3] lies,

But alas, ranges of mountains block my eyes.

The river, leaping and rolling, surges east,

By the mountains its current will ne'er be ceas'd.[4]

My heart with sorrow the dusky river fills,

When partridges are heard deep deep in the hills.[5]

431

Songs of Weal and Woe

147. 永遇乐·京口北固亭怀古

辛弃疾

千古江山，英雄无觅孙仲谋处。
舞榭歌台，风流总被雨打风吹去。
斜阳草树，寻常巷陌，人道寄奴曾住。
想当年，金戈铁马，气吞万里如虎。

元嘉草草，封狼居胥，赢得仓皇北顾。
四十三年，望中犹记，烽火扬州路。
可堪回首，佛狸祠下，一片神鸦社鼓。
凭谁问：廉颇老矣，尚能饭否？

The Joy of Lasting Acquaintanceship — Reflecting on Historical Events at Beigu Pavilion in Jingkou[1]

Xin Qiji

Across this ancient land such great heroes
As Sun Quan[2] are not to be found again;
The splendour of the great halls and stages
Has long been eroded by th' wind and rain.
Behold the trees and grass in th' dusk: 'tis said
That Jinu had lived in th' commonplace lane.
In command of an armoured cavalry,
He had swept across the land in his reign.[3]

The hasty expedition in Yuanjia
Turned out the panicked king's remorseful sore.[4]
Fresh in my mind's Yangzhou being devoured
Forty-three years ago by th' flames of war.[5]
Whoe'er can bear to see Foli Temple
Bustling with pomposity any more?[6]
Alas, but who would deign to ask Lian Po:
"Is your appetite as good as before?"[7]

Songs of Weal and Woe

148. 摸鱼儿

辛弃疾

更能消几番风雨，匆匆春又归去。
惜春长怕花开早，何况落红无数。
春且住！见说道、天涯芳草无归路。
怨春不语，算只有殷勤，
画檐蛛网，尽日惹飞絮。

长门事，准拟佳期又误，蛾眉曾有人妒。
千金纵买相如赋，脉脉此情谁诉？
君莫舞！君不见、玉环飞燕皆尘土。
闲愁最苦，休去倚危栏，
斜阳正在，烟柳断肠处。

434

Fumbling for Fish[1]

Xin Qiji

How much wind and rain is left of spring,

Which will in a hurry disappear?

Th' fallen pedals come to me as a sting;

For love of th' season th' early blooming I oft fear.

"Oh, Spring[2]! Please stay a while. It is said

That even the remotest end of th' world is spread

With flowers, thus you will just find no path to tread."

Spring leaves, giving me no reply, and within sight

Are spiders' webs catching catkins from morn till night.

Like th' empress's appointment in th' Changmen Event[3],

Th' rendezvous is cancelled, for th' belles are jealous at heart.

Even if a thousand taels of gold could be spent

For Xiangru's *fu*, to whom can I my grievances impart?

Oh, don't be so complacent as to dance yet. Haven't you learned

Of th' much favoured Yuhuan and Feiyan, who have both to

dust turned? [4]

Oh, lingering grief is th' most consuming of all,

And so keep off the railing of a tower tall:

On th' weeping willows th' setting sun's casting its light,

Which now constitutes the utmost heart-rending sight.

Songs of Weal and Woe

149. 破阵子·为陈同甫赋壮词以寄之

辛弃疾

醉里挑灯看剑，
梦回吹角连营。
八百里分麾下炙，
五十弦翻塞外声。
沙场秋点兵。

马作的卢飞快，
弓如霹雳弦惊。
了却君王天下事，
赢得生前身后名。
可怜白发生！

咏情言志

Undermining the Battle Array — To Chen Tongfu as an Encouragement[1]

Xin Qiji

Tipsy, to watch my saber I raise the wick of the lamp;

In my dream, th' bugle horns are resounding from camp to camp.

Grill is portioned out to subordinates without delay;

Frontier martial airs the band do majestically play.

Autumn sees the warriors ready in battle array.

Our steeds are galloping as fast as the Dilu breed[2] rare,

The arrows like stunning lightning are whizzing in the air,

I've been keenly longing to accomplish the wish of th' throne

To win back our sovereignty and become forever known.

Ah, it turns out to be a dream, and my hair has grey grown!

150. 水调歌头·送 章德茂大卿使虏

陈亮

不见南师久，
谩说北群空。
当场只手，
毕竟还我万夫雄。
自笑堂堂汉使，
得似洋洋河水，
依旧只流东？
且复穹庐拜，
会向藁街逢。

尧之都，舜之壤，禹
　之封。
於中应有，
一个半个耻臣戎。
万里腥膻如许，
千古英灵安在，
磅礴几时通？
胡运何须问，
赫日自当中！

Prelude to Melody of Flowing Waters 一 To Zhang Demao, Out-Going Deputy Minister of Justice in the Capacity of Envoy to the Enemy State [1]

Chen Liang[2]

Don't presume that in Northern Ji there is no steed,[3]

Though the absence of Southern forces has been long.

The out-going official of mettle, for one, is indeed

More than a match for ten thousand men strong.

'Tis funny to fancy th' envoys of th' Han Dynasty

Should ever conduct themselves beneath their dignity,

As if they were waters which follow the preset trend!

On your departure for a call at th' yurt[4] I gladly send

You off, for Gao Street[5] will see the foe itself spend.

439

In Yao's land, Shun's domains and Yu's territories,

There must be quite a few men of spine, who won't sink

Into submission and cater to th' enemies.

On a myriad *li* of land sheep's smells now stink.

Once th' heroes' dauntless spirit is brought into play again,

Our sovereignty we shall undoubtedly regain.

Sooner or later the sun of justice will shine bright,

And the looters will be put in a wretched plight!

Songs of Weal and Woe

151. 念奴娇

陈亮

危楼远望，
叹此意、
今古几人曾会？
鬼设神施，
浑认作、
天限南疆北界。
一水横陈，
连岗三面，
做出争雄势。
六朝何事，
只成门户私计。

因笑王谢诸人，
登高怀远，
也学英雄涕。
凭却长江管不到，
河洛腥膻无际。
正好长驱，
不须反顾，
寻取中流誓。
小儿破贼，
势成宁问强对。

Fair Is Niannu[1]

Chen Liang

I gaze on high into the vast land,

Sighing over my strategy sound[2],

Which from of old few could understand.

'Tis strange that th' strategic vantage ground

Should have been deemed as bounds between!

What a place for striking out for peace:

The River of a thousand *li* it does face,

And it is backed up by the mountains green.

Oh, it's incredible that th' petty household ease

Th' Six Dynasties should have taken with a good grace!

Thus th' Wang's and th' Xie's in scorn I hold,

Who atop the tower undue tears shed.

Th' stream's no excuse for inaction when woes untold

The folks suffered under the smelly nomads tread.

Just gallop ahead, when 'tis the right time to make

A long drive, without hesitation the least! Oh,

Be gallant like Zu Ti[3] who, to recover th' land,

Crossed the stream, and our warriors will surely take

The initiative and defeat the foe!

For integrity we must get the upper hand!

152. 扬州慢

姜夔

淳熙丙申至日，予过维扬。夜雪初霁，荠麦弥望。入其城，则四顾萧条，寒水自碧，暮色渐起，戍角悲吟。予怀怆然，感慨今昔，因自度此曲。千岩老人以为有"黍离"之悲也。

淮左名都，
竹西佳处，
解鞍少驻初程。
过春风十里，
尽荠麦青青。
自胡马窥江去后，
废池乔木，
犹厌言兵。

Song of Yangzhou with a Slow Rhythm[1]

Jiang Kui[2]

On the Winter Solstice in the year of Bingshen (1176 AD) during the Reign of Chunxi, I passed by Weiyang, when the sky had just cleared up after the night snow. In sight was the sorry country overgrown with rampant weeds such as buckwheat, and a desolated city with the cold stream running ruefully on its own. When dusk fell, the panicking bugle horns began to whine. The present and the past constitute a wretched contrast. Sorrow-stricken I composed the present poem, which is regarded by Qianyan the Revered as "sounding of the grief expressed in *The Millet.*"

In th' great city south of th' Qinhuai,
Where th' Zhuxi Pavilion does lie,
I alight from the horseback for a brief stay.
What used to be a ten-*li* broad way
Is now overgrown with all kinds of weeds.
Since to th' river came the covetous steeds[3],
E'en th' trees and desolate ponds may dread
Th' mention of th' flames of war, which had o'er-spread

渐黄昏、清角吹寒，
都在空城。

杜郎俊赏，
算而今、重到须惊。
纵豆蔻词工，
青楼梦好，
难赋深情。
二十四桥仍在，
波心荡冷月无声。
念桥边红药，
年年知为谁生？

Th' land. In th' looted city, when dusk draws near,
Signal horns sound plaintive and drear.

Du Mu [4], who extols the place in his verse,
Would be stunned if he were alive, I deem;
And I'd defy his gifts to vent his grief o'er th' curse,
Though nice are his poems on reality and dream.
Oh, the Twenty-Four-Arch Bridge still lies there;
The waters shimmer in the silent glare
Of th' cold moon, and by th' bridge the peonies rare
Grow. Alas, I wonder for whom
The flowers from year to year bloom?

Songs of Weal and Woe

153. 清平乐

刘克庄

风高浪快，
万里骑蟾背。
曾识姮娥真体态，
素面元无粉黛。
身游银阙珠宫，
俯看积气濛濛。
醉里偶摇桂树，
人间唤作凉风。

Celebrating Peace and Order[1]

Liu Kezhuang[2]

Fast as waves and as winds swift,

I fly myriads of *li* and to th' Toad's back[3] I myself lift,

Where I made th' acquaintance of the Goddess Chang'e [4]

before —

Without powder and pigment, she's a beauty all adore.

The palaces of silver and pearls I tour in high glee;

Gazing down, the earth surrounded by mist and cloud I find.

Tipsy, I give a casual shake to the Laurel Tree,

Which sends down what is termed as breeze by the humankind.

154. 题临安邸

林升

山外青山楼外楼，
西湖歌舞几时休？
暖风熏得游人醉，
直把杭州作汴州！

An Inscription at a Lin'an Hotel

Lin Sheng[1]

Mountains undulate, and buildings stand in proud array[2];

Whether song and dance on West Lake will cease who should

    know?[3]

Sightseers are so charm'd by th' drowsy breezes[4] that they

Simply take Hangzhou for th' fallen capital — Bianzhou![5]

155. 游园不值

叶绍翁

应怜屐齿印苍苔，
小扣柴扉久不开。
春色满园关不住，
一枝红杏出墙来。

Shut without the Garden

Ye Shaoweng[1]

My clog-prints on greenish moss must have incurred the spite:

I knock at th' wooden gate, but there's no answer after all.[2]

A gardenful of spring can't be shut up, though, within sight

A twig of apricot flowers is flaming out o'er th' wall![3]

156. 过零丁洋

文天祥

辛苦遭逢起一经，
干戈寥落四周星。
山河破碎风飘絮，
身世浮沉雨打萍。
惶恐滩头说惶恐，
零丁洋里叹零丁。
人生自古谁无死？
留取丹心照汗青。

Crossing the Lonely Bay[1]

Wen Tianxiang[2]

Since my rise for th' knowledge of classics I've met with
  endless plights;

Battles having been sporadic for four years, resistance[3] blights.

Like the catkin in the wind land's being lost, which gives me
  pain;

While my life suggests the duckweed being spattered by the
  rain.[4]

On the Panic Shoal, remarks on being panic I forth sent;

Crossing the Lonely Bay, over loneliness I now lament.[5]

Death befalls all; I would, e'en if longevity could come true,

Prefer a loyal life that will shine in th' tablets of bamboo![6]

453

Songs of Weal and Woe

157. 酹江月·和友驿中言别

文天祥

乾坤能大，
算蛟龙、
元不是池中物。
风雨牢愁无著处，
那更寒虫四壁。
横槊题诗，
登楼作赋，
万事空中雪。
江流如此，
方来还有英杰。

堪笑一叶漂零，
重来淮水，
正凉风新发。
镜里朱颜都变尽，
只有丹心难灭。
去去龙沙，

Libation to the Moon over the Rill — In Reply to Deng Guangjian in the Same Rhyme Sequence

Wen Tianxiang

Of all in the universe vast and wide,

The dragon[1], which is not to be confined

To the little pond, is th' genuine pride.[2]

In addition to deep grief on my mind,

Crickets chirp in th' cell, rains pour and winds blow.

Oh, th' ambitious Cao, who wrote a poem, spear in hand,

Turned into th' distressed Wang who, atop th' tower tall,

Composed *fu*, when all the efforts melted down like snow![3]

Howe'er, like waters in th' rill, in this land

More heroes are yet to come, after all.

As if a drifting leave I come to th' side

Of th' Qinhuai River again, at a time

When the north wind is puffed up with pride.

In the mirror no more signs of my prime

Are left, yet royal the heart does remain.

On my way north to Longsha, I back turn

To see the lost territories that lie

江山回首，
一线青如发。
故人应念，
杜鹃枝上残月。

Like a ribbon blue, which does lend me pain.

On th' tree at dim nights, friends who show concern

'Bout me might see th' Unyielding Cuckoo cry.[4]

注释 Notes and Commentary

89. 渔家傲 Pride of the Fisherman

1 "Pride of the Fisherman" is the name of the tune, which is irrelevant to the theme of frontier life. The present piece was composed during the poet's term of office as Deputy Plenipotentiary to Shaanxi. It pictures the peculiar scene of the north, describes the hard life of frontier guards and expresses the poet's firm resolution to defeat the harassing forces of the Western Xia regime — a constant threat to the security of the border regions. It is deemed a pioneering work of the Unconstrained School of *ci*-poetry.

2 Fan Zhongyan (989 AD-1052 AD), courtesy name Fan Xiwen, was from Wu County, i.e. the now Suzhou. He was at the same time a statesman, philosopher, writer, educator, philanthropist and military strategist. He had been appointed Deputy Plenipotentiary to Shannxi (陕西), Vice-Premier and Imperial Envoy to Hedong and Shannxi, etc.

    Fan was honest and upright. He advocated political reforms and was concerned about people's livelihood. His famous saying "Take the lead in tackling people's concerns and pains, and bring up the rear in sharing the world's joys and gains," which bears the Daoist faith in charity, has been taken by billions as a maxim.

    Fan's poetry, magnificently conceived, has a bold and vigorous style. It had produced a notable impact on such poets of the Unconstrained School as Su Shi.

3 But ere my name's carved ... nothing will me sway! — But before my name is engraved in Mount Yanran for my meritorious service, nothing will sway my resolution to safeguard the borders!

    This line alludes to the heroic event that General Du Xian who, having defeated the invading Huns, ascended Mount Yanran and had an account of the victory engraved on a rock.

4 The *Qiang* flute is a wind musical instrument of the western regions.

90. 雨霖铃 Bells in the Rain

1 This is the tune name of the present piece — Liu's representative work which expresses the poet's deep and manifold feelings: his reluctance to part from his love, his sorrow at the parting, his frustrations in life and

his bewilderment about the future. The description of the bleak autumn scene is in perfect harmony with the narration of feeling and incidents.

2   Liu Yong (987 AD?–1053 AD?) was from an illustrious family in Chong'an, the now Chong'an County of Fujian. He was the first *ci*-poetry composer by profession, who wrote words for musicians and songstresses to set to music and sing. Deemed to be lacking moral principle, he didn't obtain his official candidature until 1034 AD, when he changed his name. He had held some minor positions.

Liu, representative of the Sentimentalist School, has established an important place in the history of *ci*-poems with his great artistic attainments and pioneering work in the creation of long *ci*-poems. His works mostly deal with the departure of lovers, personal grievances and the dissipated life of the upper class.

3   the pavilion — the travellers' pavilion, i.e. one constructed on the roadside for the travellers' rest and protection.

In the ancient times, a travellers' pavilion was built every ten *li* along the main roads.

4   Destination ..., /... the southern land. — These two lines symbolically imply that the future is dim.

5   What shall I see...?/... a strange sight. — When I become sober at daybreak tomorrow, I'll find myself a stranger in an exotic scene consisting of a pale setting moon and a willow-fringed bank.

In Chinese literature, the willow is symbolic of departure.

6   seethe and burn and blaze — These synonyms, which differ in intensity, are used for emphasis (a case of climax).

91. 陶者   The Potters

1   The present poem, through contrast, lays bare the stern reality in which the working people are deprived of the fruit of their labour. Its style is succinct and vernacular.

2   Mei Yaochen (1002 AD–1060 AD) was from Xuancheng of the present-day Anhui. He was granted an official candidature after an imperial interview and was appointed at first Lecturer at the Imperial Academy and then Deputy Director of a department in the Ministry of Justice.

Mei, honoured as "trail-blazing pioneer" of a new era of Song poetry, was the champion for the poetic reformation. His poetry reflects the popular plight and social contradictions of the time. Profound in thoughts, he is simple and implicit in style.

3　This line involves a case of hyperbole.

4　A tile-less roof is one without a tile, e.g. a thatched roof.

92. 菩萨蛮　Buddhist Dance

1　The present *ci*-poem, in the tune name of "Buddhist Dance", describes the artistic realm the woman musician has attained. Her plaintive strains are so fascinating that even the birds, hills and rills, which are personified, are deeply touched.

2　Zhang Xian (990 AD−1078 AD), courtesy name Zhang Ziye, was a poet renowned for his exquisite style.

3　The *zheng* is a pluck musical instrument. The word plaintive, which is actually used to modify the song, is a transferred epithet.

93. 戏答元珍　Jocular Response to Yuanzhen's Verse

1　The present poem was written in response to Ding Yuanzhen, when the poet had been relegated to the position of Magistrate of Yiling in the now Hubei. While expressing his grievance about the frustration, the poet shows his moral courage, which is embodied in the snow-clad orange trees, the crashing spring thunder and the bamboo shoots ready to sprout against the cold. The style of this poem, as is true of the poet, is simple and natural.

2　Ouyang Xiu (1007 AD−1072 AD), courtesy name Ouyang Yongshu and style name Old Drunkard, was from Luling, the now Ji'an of Jiangxi. Since he obtained his official candidature at the age of twenty-four, he had held several positions, the highest being that of Vice-Premier. He showed concern for people's livelihood and supported Fan Zhongyan and other reformers, which resulted in his relegation. In his later years, however, he was critical of the political reform initiated by Wang Anshi.

　　Ouyang, who was at the same time an established historian, a famous poet, a learned literary critic and one of the "Eight Greatest Essayists of the Tang and the Song Dynasties", had led the world of letters in the Northern Song period and had played an important role in the development of literature. His poems feature freshness and clarity.

3　Here "mountain town" refers to Xiazhou.

4　As one ..., /... he bears no blame! ── As a person who has seen much of the world and enjoyed the marvelous peonies of Luoyang, I'll not blame the flowers in the wilderness for their late blooming.

These lines lay bare the poet's broad-mindedness and the sunny side of his outlook on life: while readily adapting himself to the adverse circumstances, he cherishes the belief that spring will come in the course of time.

94. 生查子　Hawthorns in the Wilderness

1　This poem airs the narrator's keen yearning for the soul of his heart. By picturing similar scenes and events on similar occasions, it brings the happiness of the past and the separation-induced sorrow of the present into a sharp contrast.

2　The chain repetition of the moon, the festival and the lanterns highlights the mood of the poet.

3　"Th' soul of one's heart" is a case of metaphor denoting one's beloved.

95. 蚕妇　The Woman Silk-Worm Raiser

1　The present poem, by narrating why the woman is sad and how she comes to realize the grim reality that those who enjoy the fruit of labour are non-labourers. Simple as it is, the poem lays bare the sharp class contradiction of the time and expresses the poet's sympathy for the labouring people.

2　Zhang Yu (? − ?) was from Yizhou, i.e. the now Pi County of Sichuan. He gave up an official position and lived a secluded life in the Qingcheng Mountains. Rich in realistic social content, his poetry features a colloquial style.

96. 阮郎归　The Return of Ruan the Youngster

1　This tune name is derived from a legend, which goes as follows: In order to gather medical herbs, Liu Chen and Ruan Zhao made for Mount Tiantai but went astray. On a brook they met two belles, who invited them to put up where they lived. When they returned to their native place half a year later, they found that everything had changed and that they knew nobody, for actually a period of seven generations had past since they left.

Is the present piece a poetic version of the legend or a reminiscence of the poet's romance? So far there's no definite answer for the question.

2　Sima Guang (1019 AD−1086 AD), courtesy name Sima Junshi, was a famous writer and historian. As prime minister he had authored the monumental work *History as a Mirror for Governance*.

97. 泊船瓜洲　Anchoring at Guazhou

1　Wang Anshi (1021 AD−1086 AD) was from Wuzhou of Linchuan, i.e. the now Wuzhou City of Jiangxi. He obtained his official candidature at the age of twenty-two. He had cherished the lofty aspirations to "straighten out the nation and break down the old conventions" since he was young, and when he was appointed twice as Prime Minister he carried out the famous Reforms in spite of the strong opposition of the privileged classes. In time the conservative forces got the upper hand and he was compelled to resign office.

Wang is remembered as a great statesman, an important thinker and one of the "Eight Greatest Essayists of the Tang and the Song Dynasties." He held that literature should be a remedy to society. He was also well established in terms of poetry. His poetic works, which feature a vigorous and refined style, reflect the plight of the people and expose the evils of society.

The present poem expresses the poet's deep feeling towards home: in the course of an official tour the poet anchors at Guazhou (situated on the north bank of the Yangtze River), from which Zhongshan (where his family lives) is near at hand, but he cannot go home in light of the principle "commitment to the nation before concern for the family. " He can only hope that the moon will someday light the way for him on his home-bound trip.

2&3　Jingkou (the now Zhenjiang of Jiangsu) and Zhongshan (the now Nanjing) are situated on the south bank of the Yangtze River.

4　Now that the spring ... the south bank, — This is a fine example of personification. It is said that the poet had been tempted to use some ten other verbs such as "revisited" and "refilled" before he came to terms with "re-greened ", which shows how careful the poet had been with the choice of words.

The verb "re-green" means "cause something to be covered with green grass again." If it is a coined word, let it be as such.

98. 元日　New Year's Day

1　This poem, by depicting the touching sight of New Year's Day, expresses the poet's pretty sentiments in favour of the political reform, which has ushered in a new era of bright prospects and brought about great changes all over the country. The personified spring breeze and the sunshine are symbolic of the reform. Here "New Year's Day" refers to the first day of the lunar year, which marks the beginning of the Spring Festival.

2 In th' midst of firecrackers ... — In bursts of firecrackers ...

It has been a time-honoured tradition for people to burn firecrackers to send off the old year and create a festive atmosphere. Nowadays the burning of firecrackers is forbidden in some places on account of the dangers it may incur.

3 And spring breeze ... Tusu wine — And spring breeze brings such warmth as can be tasted, so to speak, through the Tusu wine — a renowned brand of wine. This line involves a case of synaesthesia.

4 peach-wood charms — peach-wood with magic figures and / or incantations. It was believed that peach-wood charms hung at the door were capable of expelling evil forces and bringing good fortune. With the lapse of time the spring couplets have substituted for peach-wood charms.

99. 桂枝香 Fragrant Is the Cassia Twig

1 This *ci*-poem, which begins with the depiction of the fascinating scenery of the city Jinling, i.e. the now Nanjing, expresses the poet's great concern about the destiny of the nation.

2 All these outshine the painting in terms of beauty.

3 the captured throne's song refers to "Jadeite Trees in the Back Garden", which is said to have been composed by the dissipated emperor of Chen (the last of the Southern Dynasties) for his favourite concubine before the loss of the empire.

100. 饮湖上初晴后雨（其一） Drinking on the West Lake in a Changing Weather (No. 1)

1 The present piece is one of the two poems dedicated to the West Lake. It is simple, compact and expressive. The last two lines are known for the subtle analogy between the lake and the great beauty Xishi.

2 Su Shi (1037 AD−1101 AD), courtesy name Su Dongpo, was from Meishan of Meizhou, i.e. the now Meishan County of Sichuan. He obtained his official candidature in 1057 AD, and thus began an official

Songs of Weal and Woe

career that was haunted by the conflicts between the Reformers and the Conservatives. Politically opposed to the reform, he was demoted from the position of Doctor at the Bureau of Sacrificial Rites to the position of a minor official in the Prefecture of Huangzhou. When Gao the Empress Dowager assumed regency, he became Scholar in charge of Documentation at the Imperial Academy. Owing to his disagreement with the newly-appointed prime minister Sima Guang, he was again relegated. Later he rose to the position of Minister of Protocol and Rites. However, when the reformers regained power, he was once again demoted. What with his beliefs in Daoism, Confucianism and Buddhism, what with his sanguine disposition, he managed to sustain all his setbacks with equanimity. When he worked as Prefect respectively in Dingzhou, Yingzhou, Huizhou and Qiangzhou, he had made attempts to improve irrigation and promote agricultural production.

Su was an artistic and literary genius. He was an accomplished painter, a well-known calligrapher, the soul of Northern Song poetry and one of the "Eight Greatest Essayists of the Tang and the Song Dynasties." In terms of poetry, he had pioneered the Unconstrained School of *ci*-poems and has left behind a legacy of more than four thousand poetic works, which express his sentiments, represent the beauty of nature and reflect the contradictions of society. His style is, on the whole, bold, lively, vigorous, sonorous and easy flowing.

3 Oh, ..., / ... in rain. — These two lines depict the beautiful scene of the West Lake in a varied weather.

4 Xishi — a great beauty from the State of Yue, who helped to bring about the fall of the State of Wu during the Warring States period.

101. 水调歌头 Prelude to Melody of Flowing Waters

1 "Prelude to Water Melody" is the name of the tune to which the present *ci*-poem is set.

The present *ci*-poem was written in the eve of the Mid-Autumn Festival of 1076 AD, when the poet held the position of Prefect of Mizhou. It reflects the poet's inner conflicts — the conflict between emotion and reason and that between the ideas of involvement in and detachment from state affairs; it also expresses the poet's beautiful sentiments about human life.

In the first stanza the poet wanders between reality and fantasy:

he thinks of flying to the celestial palace in the mysterious universe, however, his love of life in the human world prevails and he chooses to stay where he is. In the second stanza, the poet exposes his philosophy by associating life to the moon, which may wax or wane and grow dim or bright; he also expresses his good wishes to his brother and, in a broad sense, to all the human race.

This poem, unrestrained in style, profound in thought and overflowing with enthusiasm, is very popular and has been highly appraised. Hu Zi (1095 AD?−1170 AD), critic of the Song Dynasty, has said: " 'Prelude to Melody of Flowing Waters' by Su Dongpo (i.e. Su Shi) takes the shines off all the other poems on the subject of Mid-Autumn Festival."

2　on high — in the skies

3　Gives me pause — Makes me hesitate. Apart from this expression, we can find other traces of *Hamlet, the Prince of Denmark* in this translation.

4　the crystalline palace — This is a metonymy for the moon. According to Chinese mythology, there's a palace of crystal in the moon.

5　With this regard ... — Taking this into consideration.

6　As the moon ..., /... part or reunite. — The moon may wax or wane and become dim or bright. Similarly, man may prosper or decline, and sometimes he may have to part from his dear ones. Whatever happens in the concurs of nature, man may as well take it easy and remain optimistic.

7　the Beauty's gentle light — The Beauty is a metonymy for the moon.

According to a Chinese myth, the ancient hero Yi had a very beautiful wife named Chang'e who, after swallowing Yi's elixir, flew to the moon and became the reigning goddess therein.

102. 念奴娇·赤壁怀古　Fair Is Niannu — Reflections on Historical Events of the Red Cliff

1　The poet's introductory remark to this master piece makes clear the theme.

2　Washing ... away. —This line involves a case of metaphor.

3　Zhou Yu (175 AD−210 AD), renowned for his resourcefulness, was a general of the Kingdom of Wu.

4　Xiao Qiao, Zhou's wife, whose surname is Qiao. Xiao here means "the younger (of the sisters) ."

103. 江城子·密州出猎　Riverside Town — Hunting in Mizhou Prefecture

1　As an opponent to Sima Guang, the newly-appointed prime minister, the poet was banished to Mizhou as the prefect. This poem, by narrating the hunting and alluding to a political event in the Han Dynasty, expresses the poet's aspiration to serve the nation by bringing his talent into full play.

2　Sun Quan (182 AD−252 AD) was the enterprising King of Wu during the Three Kingdoms period.

3　Feng Tang is the antonomasia for "guardian." This is an allusion to the history of the Han Dynasty. Wei Shang, Prefect of Yunzhong, had been dismissed for a mistake in his report. Feng Tang, who talked Emperor Wen into remitting the punishment, was sent as imperial envoy to the prefecture to reinstate Wei, and thus ensured peace of the region.

4　The Wolf is a star, which symbolizes the invader in Chinese literature.

104. 江城子·乙卯正月十二日夜记梦　Riverside Town — A Record of My Dream

1　The present *ci*-poem is an oft-quoted elegy, in which the poet expresses his keen and sincere love for his deceased wife in a straightforward style.

2　Here "a wretched light" is a case of transferred epithet, in which "wretched" is actually used to reveal the poet's as well as his deceased wife's state of mind.

105. 蝶恋花　The Butterfly Fluttering around the Flowers

1　This *ci*-poem reveals the poet's optimistic attitude towards the elapsing spring. The first stanza pictures the beauty of nature by the end of the season, and the second describes whom the poet as a passer-by sees and how the poet feels about the chance encounter.

2　This line means to say that the poet as the loving can hardly hide his fondness for the maid, who has said nothing.

106. 望江南·超然台作　Yearning for the South — Composed at the Detachment Tower

1　The poet came to Mizhou in 1074 AD, and in the next year he had an old tower renovated, which was renamed Detachment Tower by his brother

Su Zhe. This *ci*-poem, which expresses the poet's homesickness, was written in the third year.

2　the willows trim — the willows pleasingly neat in appearance

3　The Cold Food Day, during which people stop cooking for three days, is observed in honour of Jie Zitui, a sage of Jin in the Warring States period who declined the king's offer of enfeoffment to live a secluded life. To scare him out from the mountains so as to reinstate him, the king had the woods burned, only to find the sage burnt to death. The festival begins two days before Pure Brightness.

4　For wine ... incline. — Because composing poetry and drinking wine suits the happy disposition of young people.

107. 临江仙　Immortals over the River

1　This *ci*-poem, which expresses the poet's disgust with the officialdom and longing for an unconstrained life, sheds light on the poet's loftiness and optimistic broad-mindedness.

2　In ancient times, people divided a night into five periods (which were called watches).

108. 鹧鸪天　Partridges in the Sky

1　This *ci*-poem reflects the poet's optimistic attitude towards the adversities he is confronted with .

2　The employments of metaphor, personification, reduplicated words and the other techniques make the creation of images vividly unique. Here "drifting life" , which denotes a wandering life out of one's control, is a case of metaphor.

109. 定风波　Taming the Waves and Winds

1　The rain and sunshine in this *ci*-poem are respectively symbolic of the seamy and the bright sides of life, in face of which the poet, who has known the ups and downs, remains optimistically self-composed. The poem imparts to the reader the philosophy that one must not lose sight of the sunshine of hope in face of adversities.

2　Howe'er could one ..., / ... life's wind and rain? —This is a rhetorical question, meaning "As an optimistic man, I've experienced many hardships and setbacks in my life. How could I be seized with dread?" In the phrase "his sanguine coir-coat", "sanguine" is a transferred epithet, which in actual fact is intended to modify the poet himself.

110. 清平乐　Celebrating Peace and Order

1　This poem, with the overlapping events and images brought up in a natural graduation to a climax, expresses the poet's amorous thoughts of spring. In the poem the oriole, which usually appears with spring, is symbolic of that season.

2　Huang Tingjian (1045 AD−1105 AD), formally named Huang Luzhi, was the founder of the Jiangxi School. He set store by the source of diction and the organization of composition. He was also a renowned artist and calligrapher.

3　Would anyone ... / ... she should stay? — In these two lines spring is personified.

4　Yet ... / ... th' fowl does fly! — However, the bird's twittering is hardly understandable, and to my disappointment it flies away with a gust of wind!

111. 鹊桥仙　Celestial Beings on the Magpie Bridge

1　The present *ci*-poem, with "Celestial Beings on the Magpie Bridge" as the tune name, is Qin's representative work. It draws inspiration from the myth about the ardent and yet eventful love of the Cowherd (the Chinese name for Altair) and the Girl Weaver (the Chinese name for Vega), who are separated by the Celestial Queen with the Milky Way and allowed to meet only once a year. It eulogizes the sincere and faithful love and the unyielding spirit of the Cowherd and the Girl Weaver, and expresses the poet's entirely new concept of love. The ideas expressed are original, the images created are vivid, and the style of the poem is refined and easy flowing.

　　The earliest poetic composition related to the myth is included in *The Book of Poetry*, which dates back to the Zhou Dynasty.

2　Qin Guan (1049 AD−1100 AD), courtesy name Qin Shaoyou and styled Huaihai in seclusion, had been Collator at the Commission of Classic and Documents and Compiler at the Institute of National History before he was banished to Chenzhou and Leizhou in succession. He was a prominent poet known for his graceful elaboration and moderate richness.

　　Qin is an outstanding representative of the Sentimentalist School.

His lyrics, which mostly deal with love and personal grievances, are characteristics of delicate feelings, refined language, strict metre and exquisite style. Wang Anshi, in a letter to Su Shi, says that Qin's poetry is "fresh and beautiful."

3　Her yearning ... /... th' Cowherd grieves.— The Girl Weaver subtly expresses her yearning for the Cowherd through the patterns and colours of the clouds she weaves, while the Cowherd's feeling of grief is bursting like the shooting stars. These opening lines, which describe the fervent love, display the poet's vivid imagination.

4　Howe'er, no secular love ... /... for a time share. — These two lines extol the lofty sentiments of the lovers and express the poet's concept of ideal love, which sets store by the spiritual aspect of love between man and woman. It sounds somewhat Platonic, doesn't it?

5　th' Magpie Bridge — The myth goes that the magpies are deeply touched by the faithful love of the Cowherd and the Girl Weaver, and that they voluntarily form a bridge across the Milky Way on the seventh day of the seventh month to ensure the meeting of the great lovers. The bridge they have constructed is called the Magpie Bridge.

6　But nay, ..., /... each night and day? — But that is not the case. So long as their love remains steadfast, what matters if they are sometimes torn apart?

　　Here the poet employs a rhetorical question to emphasize the fidelity.

112. 踏莎行 · 郴州旅舍　Walking on Grassland — Composed at the Inn in Chenzhou

1　This *ci*-poem was possibly written in the spring of 1097 AD, when the poet was banished to Chenzhou, a place bleak and desolate at the time. The mist, the assailing chill, the pale moon and the cuckoo's wailing mentioned in the poem are symbolic of setbacks and hopelessness, and the rill flowing elsewhere metaphorically denotes the frustration of the poet's aspiration to render service to the nation.

2　This is an allusion to Tao Yuanming's namesake essay, meaning the ideal land, which is roughly equivalent to Utopia.

3　The silk scrolls ... / ... the flowers sent by post — These lines contain two cases of metonymy denoting "the messages" or "letters."

4　... the Chen Rill ..., / ... to th' Xiao and th' Xiang Rill flow? — In these two lines the poet laments over the wrong course of the political developments.

113. 鹧鸪天　Partridges in the Sky

1　As one of the best elegies in *ci*-poetry, the present poem, written in memory of the poet's deceased wife, ranks as high as Su Shi's "Riverside Town – Hunting in Mizhou Prefecture" in artistry as well as in popularity.

2　He Zhu（1052 AD–1125 AD）, courtesy name He Fanhui, was a versatile poet. His compositions are characteristic of an exquisite diction and a varied style.

3　The Changmen Gate is the west city gate of Suzhou.

4　Since we'd shared life, ... / ... with th' mate lost? —The rhetorical questions, seemingly irrational, serve to give an emphatic effect to the expression of the poet's heart-rending grief; and apt are the cases of simile, which liken the poet to a half-dead parasol and a lone white-haired mandarin duck, which is symbolic of fidelity in Chinese culture.

5　th' old nest: a case of metaphor denoting the home once shared by the poet and his wife.

6　th' half-vacant bed — the bed with the other half of the couple missing.

7　Whoever could mend my coat in the lamplight in your stead? — You are absolutely irreplaceable! Ingenuous is the creation of the image of the poet's wife mending a coat for the poet in the lamplight, for the act is typical of wifely care and the image is, as it were, spotlighted.

114. 行路难　Life's Journey Is Perilous

1　The tune name, unlike those of the other pieces, is suggestive of the theme: the poet's burning indignation over the social reality, in which life's journey is full of perils and a gifted man can find no scope for his rare abilities. In this *ci*-poem allusions (such as that of "no mediocrity" to Li Bai) are aptly employed.

2　This refers to Lei Yi of the Han Dynasty, who was known for his strong sense of justice and readiness to help the weak. He had helped a person get remitted of his punishment but refused to accept his gold gift as a reward. He had declined the offer of an official position by pretending to be mad.

3　According to Chinese mythology, the sun rises from the place where the Fusang Tree stands.

4　The contrast, formed by the conception of time being too fast and that of "a day too long to bear," reveals the poet's inner contradiction, which serves as a foil to the poet's frustration.

115. 苏幕遮　Temple Music

1　Unlike many of the poet's compositions, this *ci*-poem, which features natural ease and simplicity, is free from elaboration. In the first stanza, the overlapping images of twittering birds, the rising sun, the rain drops on the green lotus leaves, etc., present a word picture of a summer morning; while in the second, which involves the employment of rhetorical questions, the poet expresses his homesickness and yearning for the friends in his distant hometown.

2　Zhou Bangyan (1056 AD–1121 AD), formally named Zhou Meicheng and styled Qingzhen in Seclusion, was a prominent figure of the Sentimental School. He had served as an official at the Imperial Institute of Dasheng, which took charge of musical affairs, and had contributed a great deal to the development of *ci*-poetry. His compositions are elegant in diction, meticulous in metre and neat in organization.

116. 好事近　A Blessing at Hand

1　This is one of the six *ci*-poems on the theme of a fisherman's life. In literature the image of the fisherman is suggestive of freedom from the lust for fame, wealth and power.

2　Zhu Dunru (1081 AD–1159 AD), courtesy name Zhu Xizhen and style name Yanhe, had lived a secluded life before he held the post of Proof-Reader at the Imperial Commission of Classics and Documents. Having experienced the ups and downs, he left the court in 1149 AD and lived a retired life in the now Jiaxing of Zhejiang.

3　The image of the wild goose is symbolic of freedom.

117. 病牛　The Sick Farm Cattle

1　The present poem was written in 1132 AD, when the poet had retired from office. By vividly creating the image of a farm cattle, which is the incarnation of the poet's own self, the poet expresses his utter devotion to the nation and willingness to labour for the sake of people's livelihood without the slightest consideration for his personal gain or loss.

2　Li Gang (1083 AD–1140 AD), who was from Shaowu of the now Fujian, obtained his official candidature in 1112 AD. He had held the positions of Deputy Director of the Bureau of Sacrificial Rites, Vice-Minister of War, Senior Aide to the Prime Minister and Prime Minister. As an ardent patriot, Li had adhered to the policy of resistance against the invasions by the Jin Dynasty. He was consequently squeezed out of office by the capitulation clique.

Li's poetry, which is overflowing with zeal, expresses the poet's aspirations to render service to the nation and feelings about the times.

3　I lie ...: /... why should I regret! — Though I'm exhausted after a day's work, I lie at dusk with a tranquil mind: as long as the common people are relieved from the threats of cold and hunger, why then should I regret toiling for them?

These two lines lay bare the poet's outlook on life, especially his altruistic sense of mission rooted from Daoism.

118. 六幺令·次韵和贺方回金陵怀古，鄱阳席上作　Liuyao Melody — Reflections on History Improvised at the Banquet on the Boyang Lake in Reply to He Fanghui with the Same Rhyme Sequence

1　The present *ci*-poem, through reflections on history, expresses the poet's firm belief in the policy of armed resistance, a policy in opposition to the capitulation policy. The other poet present on the occasion was He Zhu, who is mentioned in the introductory remarks as He Fanghui (courtesy name).

2　"Trees of Jade" — short for "Jade Trees and Flowers in the Back Park" (see Note 4 to Poem 77 — "Mooring on the Qinhuai River"）.

3　Against the railing, ..., / ... a fearless angler's seen. — This couplet demonstrates the poet's determination to follow the example of the "fearless angler", a literary image created by Liu Zongyuan in his *The River Permeated with Snow*.

119. 减字木兰花　The Lily Magnolia (A Simplified Version)

1　This *ci*-poem, by drawing a word picture, so to speak, of a naive and lively girl with a lovely spray of flowers, lays bare the inner world of the girl, which is active with ardent love for the soul of her heart.

2　Li Qingzhao (1084 AD‒1151 AD?) was from a scholar's family in what was to be the now Jinan of Shandong. She had lived happily with her husband Zhao Mingcheng before the north of the country was seized by the Jin aggressor. She was compelled to move to the south when her husband died of illness, and began to lead the woeful life of a lonely refugee.

Though a representative of the Sentimental School, she sometimes sounds powerful and free, especially when she touches such themes as of patriotism, courage and the significance of life. As the most distinguished Chinese poetesses, she is adept in the creation of singular artistic images and she writes in a lively, succinct and original style. Her literary career may be divided into two periods, with the fall of the Northern Song Dynasty as the demarcation line. Her poems of the early period mainly deal with love and the beauty of nature, while those of the later period express the poetess's deep grief over personal sufferings and great concern over the destiny of the nation.

3 It beams ..., / ... and morning dew. — Here "it" refers to the spray, which is personified.

120. 一剪梅 A Spray of Plum Flowers

1 This *ci*-poem expresses the poetess's keen yearning for her husband by narrating the loneliness of separation and likening the affections to something alive and visible.

2 In Chinese literature the wild goose is an image suggestive of "message" or "messenger" in Chinese literature. It is derived from a story about the rescue of Su Wu (140 BC–60 BC), an envoy from the Han Empire who had been detained by the Huns for ten years.

3 Here the feelings, which seem to move about (from the knitted brows to the yearning heart), are personified.

121. 声声慢 Beats Slowing Down

1 As it is of slow beats and sounds plaintive, the tune suits such themes as departure, loneliness, misfortunes, etc. The present *ci*-poem, being a case in point, expresses the poetess's deep sorrow over the adversities inflicted by the invading Jin forces. The repetition of "at a loss", and the device of climax — the moodiness built up in intensity by the expressions "at a loss" and "in such lonely melancholy and plaintive solitude as seem unreal," etc., make the poem touching.

2 In Chinese literature, the rain, the parasol and the dusk are images symbolic of sadness.

122. 醉花阴　Tipsy in the Shade of Flowers

1　In the present *ci*-poem, the poetess expresses her yearning for her husband Zhao Mingcheng, an epigraphist. The style is simple and natural.

2　a drop — (understatement for) some wine

3　This rhetorical question means that love-sickness is undoubtedly consuming.

4　When it ... / ... th' yellow flower of th' day. — In this couplet the wind is personified, and "a soul" refers to the poetess herself, who is supposed to have grown thinner owing to cares and grief.

123. 武陵春　Spring in Wuling

1　In 1127 AD, the Jin forces swooped south. To escape from the flames of war, the poetess and her husband fled to the south. After her husband died of illness in Jiankang, i.e. the now Nanjing, she was reduced to a wandering life. The present *ci*-poem, composed during the poetess's stay in Wuzhou, i.e. the present-day Jinhua City, is a record of what mental sufferings she had to sustain.

2　Here what's abstract (sorrow and despair) is objectified (given shape or weight), which constitutes a case of synecdoche.

124. 夏日绝句　Four-Line Poem Composed in Summer

1　The present poem was written after the Song rulers moved the capital to the south. By expressing her principle of life and respect for Xiang Yu, the poetess directs a scathing satire at the capitulation-oriented Song ruling clique, who are content with temporary ease in Lin'an (the now Hangzhou). Unlike most of her poems, which feature delicate feelings, this piece is impassioned and vigorous.

2　Be a man of men ..., / ... even if doomed to die! — One should be a courageous and righteous person with mettle while living, and die a heroic death if circumstances should require so.

These lines imply that one should fight to the last drop of his blood for the just cause of resistance against aggression at the time. They express the poetess's patriotism and philosophy of life, in addition, they contain a bitter condemnation against the fatuous Song rules, who lack moral integrity.

3　Xiang Yu, ... / By crossing th' River, — This is an allusion to the history

咏
情
言
志

474

of the late Qin Dynasty, when uprisings shattered the country and Xiang Yu rose with eight thousand men from the south of the Yangtze River. After the Qin Empire was toppled down, Xiang Yu and Liu Bang, who represented two major forces, began to contend for state power. As a result, Xiang was defeated and cornered to the brink of the Wujiang River. He could have survived by crossing the river, but he preferred to take his own life rather than live in humiliation. People of later generations love Xiang Yu for his sense of dignity regardless of his defeat.

By eulogizing the heroic spirit of Xiang Yu, the poetess brings out an implied contrast between the hero and the ruling clique of the Southern Song Dynasty, and satirizes the latter for their lack of moral courage.

125. 渔家傲·题玄真子图　Pride of the Fisherman — An Inscription on the Portrait of Genuine Meta-Physician

1　This *ci*-poem expresses the poet's love for freedom and independence in addition to disgust with worldliness through picturing the unfettered life of Master of Genuine Metaphysics, i.e. Zhang Zhihe (c.732 AD⁻744 AD), a famous poet and painter of the Tang Dynasty, who lived a secluded life after his resignation.

2　Zhang Yuangan (1091 AD⁻c.1161 AD), courtesy name Zhang Zhongzong, was a pioneer of the Xin School. He had served under General Li Gang as a non-military clerk.

3　Yutong and Qiaoqing were to be matched by Zhang as a couple.

4　a thorn — metaphor for something that causes pain, trouble, irritation or annoyance.

126. 满江红　The River All Red

1　Yue Fei (1103 AD⁻1142 AD) was a resourceful general from Xiangzhou of Tangyin, which was in the now Henan. He had held such positions as Commander in Chief of the Henan and Hebei Expeditionary Armies and Vice-Minister of War, etc. The army under his command — the mainstay of resistance against the Jin aggression — had won sensational victories and recovered vast areas of lost territory before he was recalled from the front to be framed up and killed by the capitulation-oriented clique headed by Qin Hui.

Yue is an immortal national hero. His poetry, full of power and grandeur, expresses his ardent love for and lofty aspirations to render service to the nation. He also excels in calligraphy.

The present poem, which has attained a perfect unity of ideological content and artistic form, is an eternal classic of patriotic poetry. In a vigorous and sonorous style it expresses the poet's unwavering loyalty to his motherland and strong will to avenge the national humiliation upon the enemy and to immense. From generation to the security and prosperity of their motherland.

"The River All Red" is the tune name of the present *ci*-poem.

2　I make light of ..., /... in the flames of war! — These two lines narrate that nothing, be it merit or honor, shall hold the poet back (from his pursuit of territorial integrity through resistance against the aggressors).

3　Waste not ... / ... would my heart gnaw. — These three lines express the poet's eagerness to perform meritorious deeds in his youth.

4　th' Humiliation / Of Jingkang — In the year 1127 AD during the Reign of Jingkang, the Jin aggressors captured the capital Bianjing (the now Kaifeng City), when Emperor Qinzong and Ex-Emperor Huizong were taken prisoners. This event, which marked the fall of the Northern Song Dynasty, is known as the Humiliation of Jingkang.

5　Howe'er can we ... /... burning indignation appease? — This rhetorical question means that, as the emperor's subjects, we can never appease our burning indignation unless we put out the flames of war.

127. 游山西村　Visiting the Shanxi Village

1　The present metrical poem was written in Shanyin in 1167 AD, a year after the poet was relegated from the position of Co-Governor of Longxing because of his support of the Northern Expedition, which had ended in defeat. By depicting the scene of and describing the custom in the country, it expresses the poet's love of nature and of the simplicity of country life.

2　Lu You (1125 AD−1210 AD), style name Lu Fangweng, was from Shanyin of Yuezhou (the now Shaoxing of Zhejiang). He had cherished the lofty aspiration to resist the Jin aggression since he was young. "On horseback th' savage Hu invaders I will fight; / Dismounting th' steed letters of challenge I'll indite", he writes. He had held positions in both civil and military services. As he had adhered to the stand of resistance, he had been hated and suppressed by the capitulation-oriented clique.

Lu is a famous patriotic poet. With a prodigy of more than nine thousand and four hundred poems, he ranks first among the Four Eminent Poets of Resurgence (the other three being Fan Chengda, Yang Wanli and You Mao). His works, which are marked with the beauty of vigour and succinctness, express his ardent patriotism, reflect people's plight and expose the impudence of the capitulation-oriented Southern Song rulers. He flies his own colours in versification and has made a remarkable impact on Chinese literature.

3　Facing ...; / ... vista will appear. —This couplet, owing to its optimistic element, has become a celebrated dictum. It is often quoted to describe a new world that's unfolding its mystery, or to narrate the unexpected solution of a very complicated problem. The noun "村", formerly rendered into "village", is now put into "vista" to embrace the connotations proliferated in circulation.

4　The simple clothing ..., /... Spring Offering's drawing near. — The farmers' simple clothing shows that they still keep up the traditional values; and the rehearsal of the village band heralds the approaching of Spring Offering (a traditional festival in spring, during which people make offerings to the God of Land and pray for a prosperous new year).

128. 鹧鸪天　Partridges in the Sky

1　The present *ci*-poem expresses the poet's indignation over the reality and enjoyment of an unfettered life and pride of being a fisherman free of worldly cares and desires.

2　Amuse myself here and there as well I may. — This is an inverted sentence meaning " I may as well amuse myself here and there."

3　Creator ..., / ... decay. — Here the poet satirizes the throne, who fails to allow the talented any play.

129. 鹧鸪天　Partridges in the Sky

1　This *ci*-poem expresses the poet's pride of being a vanity-free fisherman.

2　The melon grower ... / To copy?　— This sentence involves a case of allusion. It means to say "I don't care the least to follow the example of Shao Ping of the Han Dynasty, who made a name by growing melons outside the Green Gate of the capital."

130. 钗头凤　Phoenix Hairpin

1　The present *ci*-poem constitutes a strong protest against the feudal

Songs of Weal and Woe

convention. Though they lived happily after their marriage owing to their mutual love, the poet and Tang Wan were compelled to separate because of Lu's mother's strong grudge against Tang Wan. A few years later, when they met at the Shen's Compound, the poet improvised this poem to express his deep sorrow. The first stanza recalls the happiness and sorrow, and the second, which turns back to the sorry reality, reinforces the poet's emotions.

2　The east wind is symbolic of the feudal forces, which have rid the tree of marriage of its happy flowers.

3　The repetition of "grief", as is the case with "wrong" in the next stanza, gives emphasis to the statement in question.

4　th' bars — the obstacles preventing exchanges.

131. 诉衷情　Relating Heartfelt Sentiments

1　In the present poem, the poet laments over the reality, which allows him no chance to render service to his nation in times of danger or crisis.

2　Tianshan and Cangzhou are place names employed as cases of metonymy respectively for the frontier and the rear area.

132. 鹊桥仙　Immortals on the Magpie Bridge

1　In the Reign of Xiaozong, the poet had served in the armed forces in the command of General Wang Yan. The forces had won one victory after another when Wang's staff office was dismissed, and consequently the poet was compelled to leave the front line. This *ci*-poem, written on the way from Nanzheng (where the army's headquarters had been located) to Chengdu, expresses the poet's loneliness and disappointment.

2　The cuckoo is associated with sorrow and / or nostalgia in Chinese literature.

133. 鹊桥仙　Immortals on the Magpie Bridge

1　This *ci*-poem pictures the leisurely life of the poet as a fisherman, who makes light of gain and fame.

2　In this line the coir-coat is personified, and so is the case with the fishing-rod in the previous line.

3　The Fishing Terrace, where Yan Guang had angled, is located in the now Zhejiang.

4　Yan Guang (39 BC–41 AD), who had once and again rejected the emperor's offers of high-ranking positions, was a distinguished hermit of the Eastern Han Dynasty.

5   When — whereas

134. 鹊桥仙   Immortals on the Magpie Bridge

1   The first stanza of this *ci*-poem describes the poet's military service and expresses the poet's indignation over the reality, in which the foolish are promoted while the wise and meritorious ignored; the second stanza demonstrates the proud poet's enjoyment of an unconstrained life.

2   The throne denotes the royalty.

135. 卜算子·咏梅   The Diviner — Ode to the Plum Flower

1   This is a classic in symbolism. "The Diviner" is the name of the tune to which the present poem is set, and "Ode to the Plum Flower" is the title.

    In this *ci*-poem, the poet extols the fine qualities of the plum tree: its noble loftiness in nature, its undaunted spirit in face of adversities and frustrations, and its unchangeable aspiration to better the world.

    The first stanza describes the many adversities the plum flower is confronted with: solitude, anxiety, the remote location and the hostile elements (winds and rains). The second stanza eulogizes the beauty of the plum flower's inner world (her fine qualities and lofty sentiments). The personified plum flower, dignified, dauntless, void of vanity and steadfast to truth, is in fact the embodiment of the poet, who had suffered repeated setbacks for upholding the policy of resistance against aggression, which piqued the hatred of the pacifists.

2   the post — A post was a place of duty where couriers changed horses or rested in ancient times.

3   ... expecting none to flatter. — ... without expecting that someone would ever come to enjoy your beauty.

4   the favoured — the favoured flowers, metaphor for those crafty officials (or men of letters) who have won the favour of the ruling clique.

5   your fragrance — your true worth, i. e. your fine qualities.

136. 示儿   Will to My Sons

1   The present poem, was written in the spring of 1210 AD, expresses the poet's undying patriotic passion in a simple and succinct style.

2   ... when life's sands run out — ... when life comes to an end.

3 Except the savage invasion of the enemy, which will still make me sad even after death.

4 while offering sacrifice — It was, and still is in some places, customary to commemorate the ancestors during important festivals by offering sacrifices.

5 The Central Plain is usually a synecdoche for the nation, here it refers to the enemy-occupied territories in the north.

137. 四时田园杂兴（其三十一） **Idyllic Life of the Four Seasons (No. 31)**

1 Fan Chengda (1126 AD−1193 AD), who was from Wu (the now Suzhou), obtained his official candidature in 1154 AD. He displayed an unyielding moral integrity on a diplomatic mission to the Jin Dynasty in 1170 AD, which won him extensive popularity. Later he was respectively appointed Magistrate of Jingjiang — the now Guilin, Magistrate of Mingzhou (the now Ningbo), Governor Plenipotentiary of Sichuan, and Vice-Premier. He retired at fifty seven because of poor health.

Fan was one of the Four Eminent Poets of Resurgence, who had transcended the influence of the Jiangxi School and ushered in a new era of poetic creation. His style is fresh, beautiful and realistic. His seventy-two short poems, which were composed during his mission to Jin, express the longing for unification of the people living in the enemy-occupied areas, and his collection "Idyllic Life of the Four Seasons" presents a vast panorama of country life, reflecting the industry, simplicity and the sufferings of the farmers under exploitation and oppression.

"Idyllic Life of the Four Seasons" includes 60 poems, of which the present is the thirty-first. By capturing the distinctive characteristics of the country, the poet vividly depicts the busy life of the farmers.

2 ... has got a role to play — ... has his or her own duty to perform.

3 ... to actual work know — ... to know actual work, i.e. to be well prepared for doing practical work.

4 to pumpkins grow — to grow pumpkins.

138. 念奴娇 · 和徐尉游口湖 **Fair Is Niannu — Composed at the Kouhu Lake in the Same Rhyme Sequence with Xu Wei's Poem**

1 In 1166 AD, after he was removed from office as Deputy Prefect of

Longxing, the poet began to lead a secluded life on the Jinghu Lake (in other words the Mirror Lake), where the present poem was written.

The present poem pictures a secluded life and a lofty detachment from the social reality, to which the poet appears to be inclined, however, the last two lines reveal the poet's actual state of mind — Not that the poet is cynical, but that he is indignant, for he could find no room to bring his talent into full play.

2　A dream of three years ... — (elliptical sentence) A dream of three years have passed ...

3　None of the seekers of fame and wealth, as a rule, are of good repute.

139. 鹧鸪天　Partridges in the Sky

1　This *ci*-poem, by drawing a picture of country life, reflects the poet's love for nature, which is mixed up with a touch of sadness over the wandering life.

2　The masterly use of the verbal phrase "buzz and hum", a device of onomatopoeia, adds pastoral charm to the artistic realm.

140. 眼儿媚　Charming Eyes

1　Through the description of spring-induced grief, which seems to permeate the premises, the poem reflects the poetess's sorrow caused by her unfortunate marriage. The vividness might be attributed to such devices as personification and parallelism.

2　Zhu Shuzhen (1135 AD−1180 AD), style name The Secluded, was a poetess whose talent is popularly regarded as only next to that of Li Qingzhao.

3　The melodious voices, ... / And from th' begonias beside the shed. — This stanza, by employing the devices of simile and climax, creates a subtle conceptual realm.

141. 浣溪沙　Rinsing Yarn in the Brook

1　By depicting the frontier life, this *ci*-poem condemns the crime committed by the aggressors and expresses the poet's deep sorrow over lost territories.

2　Zhang Xiaoxiang (1137 AD−1169 AD), courtesy name Zhang Anguo, had held official positions at the Imperial Secretariat and in some local governments as magistrate. As he advocated the recovering of lost territories, he had once and again received attacks and had twice been dismissed from office. He was a pioneer of the Patriotic School. His poetry features a free and vigorous style.

3   sad — a transferred epithet here.

142. 生查子·独游雨岩　Hawthorns in the Wilderness — Touring Yuyan the Dripping Cliff Alone

1   This *ci*-poem eulogizes the beauty of Nature, which seems to be animated by the poet's rich imagination embodied in the the subtle employment of such devices as metaphor and personification (of the stream and trees).

2   Xin Qiji (1140 AD—1207 AD) was from the now Jinan of Shandong. At the age of twenty-one he rose in resistance against the Jin aggressors with two thousand men, who in time joined forces with the army of volunteers operating in enemy-occupied areas. When Geng Jing, commander of the army, was murdered by the traitor Zhang Anguo, Xin attacked the barracks of the Jin army with a light cavalry, captured the traitor and went to the Southern Song Empire, where he successively held the positions of Prefect of Chuzhou, Governor Plenipotentiary of several regions, i.e. Hunan, Jiangxi, Fujian and Zhedong. Firmly upholding the policy of resistance against aggression, he organized military training and encouraged agricultural production wherever he went. He was taken as a target for attack by the capitulation clique and was twice compelled to leave office.

　　Xin, one of the greatest patriotic poets, had not only carried forward the vigorous style of the Unconstrained School represented by Su Shi and the patriotic tradition built up by Fan Zhongyan, Zhang Yuangan and Zhang Xiaoxiang, but he also created and led the Patriotic School—the most powerful school of poetry in the middle of the Southern Song Dynasty. He had revolutionized *ci*-poetry by diversifying its form, broadening its realm of content, and by making it more capable of expressing rich imagination and embracing the quintessence of prose. Apart from his essays, which excel in form and content, he has left us a legacy of some seven hundred and fifty poetic works (mostly *ci*-poems). His style is lively, compact, vigorous and natural. A poet of rare artistic attainments, he has produced a tremendous impact on Chinese literature.

3   Is it th' ghost, or th' fairy? — Is it the ghost or the fairy that is singing in reply?

143. 青玉案·元夕　The Desk of Green Jade — The Lantern Festival

1　This *ci*-poem draws a picture of the Lantern Festival, which takes place on the fifteenth of the first lunar month. It manifests that the poet is a master in word painting. Such rhetorical devices as onomatopoeia (e.g. "crack and boom"), zeugma (e.g. "shedding smile and perfume"), simile (e.g. "like hosts of shooting stars"), etc., together with the surprise ending, make the description of the festival vivid.

2　"Fish" and "dragons" — lanterns made in the shapes of fish and dragons.

3　why — an exclamation of surprised pleasure.

144. 西江月·夜行黄沙道中　The Moon over the West River — A Night Trip through the Yellow Sand Hills

1　"The Moon over the West River" and " A Night Trip through the Yellow Sand Hills" are respectively the tune name and the brief introduction which functions as the sub-title. The Yellow Sand Hills are located to the southwest of Shangrao City, Jiangxi Province.

　　Xin Qiji writes in a variety of artistic styles, and his works are sometimes breezy, picturesque and beautiful. A good case in point is the present poem, which expresses the poet's love of nature and great joy over the signs of a favourable year by dramatizing the peculiar beauty of the stars, the shower and the unexpected sight of the familiar inn.

2　in the minor light — in the moon

3　Here the frogs are personified.

4　And ... two or three raindrops ... down steal — And a few raindrops come down stealthily on this side of the hill.

　　The visibility of stars and the fall of raindrops may seem paradoxical, and yet it's typical of the southern weather, in which the sky is sometimes partly clear and partly overcast with rain clouds.

5　I make a turn ... /... temple comes in sight! — Before the impending shower I am at a loss as to where to find shelter, and what I can do is to hurry along the winding path and across the bridge. Suddenly an inn near the village temple comes in sight, and it turns out to be the one I had stayed in (or seen) before. How delighted I feel!

145. 清平乐·村居　Celebrating Peace and Order — Country Life

1　The typical activities, related in a refreshingly simple style, imbue the present poem with a strong smack of country life. The poem flows with natural ease.

2 ... verges on ... — is near to ...

3 Lotus seeds can be eaten raw.

146. 菩萨蛮·书江西造口壁 The Buddhist Dancers — An Inscription on the Cliff of Zaokou in Jiangxi

1 The present *ci*-poem was composed in 1176 AD, when the poet visited the Yugu Terrace (situated in the southwest of Ganzhou in Jiangxi) in the capacity of Magistrate of Justice of the Peace of Jiangxi. Forty-seven years before (in 1129 AD), the Jin aggressors came past the above-mentioned terrace in their hot pursuit of Longyu the Ex-Empress Dowager, looting and killing all the way. Inspired by that historical event, the poet wrote the poem to express his feelings.

As a classic of the Xin School, it expresses the poet's great sympathy with the refugees, deep sorrow over the lost territories and resolution to defeat the invaders. The first stanza vividly associates the river water to the immeasurable sufferings inflicted upon the people by the invaders, expressing the poet's deep sorrow over the lost territory; the second stanza likens the strong will of the people to the irresistible Clear River and lays bare the poet's concern about his nation's destiny. The poet conveys his sentiments by creating metaphoric and symbolic images, for instance, the gushing water is a metaphor for tears as well as for the poet's unwavering determination; and the moaning partridges are symbolic of sorrow.

2 th' Clear River — a river in Jiangxi Province.

3 Chang'an — Chang'an, which had respectively been the capital of the Han and the Tang Dynasties, euphemistically stands for Bianjing, capital of the Northern Song Dynasty.

4 The river ..., /... ne'er be ceas'd. — The river is a symbol for the strong will of the people to drive away the invaders, and the mountains are symbolic of all sorts of obstacles to the struggle against aggression, especially those placed by the capitulation clique.

5 My heart ..., /... in the hills. — The dusky river makes me feel sad, what's more, the plaintive chuckling of the partridge is heard from the deep mountains. As the chuckling of the partridge sounds somewhat like "It won't do, brother" to the Chinese ear, the bird is symbolic of hardships and perils ahead.

147. 永遇乐·京口北固亭怀古 The Joy of Lasting Acquaintance-
ship — Reflecting on Historical Events at Beigu Pavilion in Jingkou

1 The present *ci*-poem was written in 1205 AD, when the poet had
been appointed Prefect of Zhenjiang (in the now Jiangsu). The Beigu
Pavilion was located in the Beigu Mountain in Jingkou (the now City of
Zhenjiang). This poem expresses in a vigorous style the poet's patriotic
sentiments by alluding to historical events.

　　In the first stanza, the poet cherishes the memory of the ancient heroes,
showing his esteem for their heroic spirit. In the second, he alludes to the
hasty expedition in the Reign of Yuanjia, recalls the devastation of the
Jin aggression, and expresses his grief over lost territory, his strong will
to resist aggression and his indignation against the Southern Song rulers,
who grudge talented people any free play.

2 Sun Quan (182 AD−252 AD), founder of the Kingdom of Wu, had once
made Jingkou the capital. He had defeated Cao Cao's expedition to his
kingdom during his reign.

3 In command of ..., / ... in his reign. — Jinu was the childhood name of
Liu Yu. He had initiated an armed struggle from Jingkou, overthrown
the Eastern Jin Dynasty and founded the Song Dynasty, the first of
the Southern Dynasties. On an expedition to the north, his tiger-like
army swept across the Central Plains (comprising the middle and lower
reaches of the Yellow River), toppling down the Southern Yan and the
Later Qin Dynasties and recovering vast areas, including Luoyang and
Chang'an.

4 The hasty expedition ... / ... remorseful sore. — In 450 AD, the adventurous
Wang Xuanmo was appointed by the unscrupulous Emperor Wen of
Song (i.e. Liu Yilong) as commander of an expedition to the north.
Consequently Wang's army was defeated and chased to the brink of the
Yangtze River. When the emperor turned north and saw the turbulent
pursuit troops of Later Wei, he was seized with terror and remorse.

　　The poet's allusion to the frustrated expedition in Yuanjia is an implied
warning to the rulers: a military operation without full preparations is
doomed to failure. True enough, the Southern Song rulers, eager for a
quick success, paid no heed to such correct opinions and organized an
expedition to the north in 1206 AD, which resulted in defeat.

5 Fresh in my mind ... / ... th' flames of war. — Forty-three years before, the
poet came from Shandong to the Southern Song Empire via Yangzhou.

On the way he witnessed the burring, looting and killing of the Jin aggressors.

In these two lines the poet condemns the crimes of aggression and expresses his determination to revenge himself on the enemy for the devastation.

6　Whoe'er can ... /... any more? — Nobody can ever bear to see the invaders riding roughshod over the vast areas under their occupation.

The Foli Temple was located on the Guabu Hill in the Lihe County of Jiangsu. Foli (childhood name of Emperor Taiwu of Later Wei) had a resort constructed when he chased Wang Xuanmo's army there. It's strange to the poet that people of the Southern Song Dynasty should have regarded the resort as a place for worship, totally ignoring its past. Here Foli Temple is symbolic of the invaders' conquest.

These two lines express the poet's hatred for the enemy, with an implied indignation at the Southern Song rulers who, content with temporary ease and resigned to circumstances, have no ambition to recover lost territory.

7　Alas, but ...: /... as good as before?" — Lian Po, a famous general of the State of Zhao during the Warring States period, was ensnared and compelled to leave Zhao in his later years. When the state was under the attack of Qin, the king of Zhao thought about reinstating him and thus sent an emissary to see whether he was physically qualified. To show that he was in sound condition, Lian Po demonstrated an exceptionally good appetite and feats of horsemanship in face of the emissary. However, the king didn't reinstate him because of the emissary's false report.

These two lines, put in the form of a rhetorical question, mean to say that the Southern Song rulers would not even deign to enquire after talented people like Lian Po, let alone to allow them a full play. The poet expresses his indignation by making an implied contrast between the Southern Song rulers and the king of Zhao and by comparing himself to Lian Po, who aspired to rendering service to his motherland.

148. 摸鱼儿　Fumbling for Fish

1　As he was ensnared by crafty sycophants and dismissed from office in 1181 AD, the poet began to live a country life in Shangrao. The present poem, by mirroring part of that life, vent the poet's indignation at being unfairly treated by the disappointing ruling clique.

咏
情
言
志

2   Here spring is personified.

3   This alludes to an event of the Han Dynasty. The empress, being out of the emperor's favour, had stayed in the Changmen Palace in confinement. She had sought the help of Sima Xiangru in order to regain the emperor's favour.

4   Oh, ... / ... to dust turned? — Yang Yuhuan of the Tang Dynasty and Zhao Feiyan of the Han Dynasty were favoured concubines of the monarchs. In this couplet the poet shows his contempt for the crafty officials by likening them to those so-called "belles."

149. 破阵子·为陈同甫赋壮词以寄之 Undermining the Battle Array — To Chen Tongfu as an Encouragement

1   This poem reflects the conflict between the poet's soaring aspiration to defend the nation and the indifferent reality, which are respectively signified by the grand spectacle of frontier life in the poet's mind and the grey hair.

About the poet's close friend Chen Tongfu please refer to Note 2 to Poem 150.

2   The horses of the Dilu breed was known for their physical capacity.

150. 水调歌头·送章德茂大卿使虏 Prelude to Melody of Flowing Waters — To Zhang Demao, Out-Going Deputy Minister of Justice in the Capacity of Envoy to the Enemy State

1   Bursting with ardent love for the nation, great pride of the cultural heritage and full confidence in the final victory, the present poem stands out as a patriotic classic.

2   Chen Liang (1143 AD−1194 AD), courtesy name Chen Tongfu and style name Longchuan, was a prominent thinker, writer and poet of the Free and Powerful School. Extant are his Collections of *Longchuan's Writings* and *Longchuan's Ci-Poems*.

3   This line alludes to Han Yu's writing, which praises Bole for his wise judgements on horses, saying that when Bole went through Northern Ji, the place was skimmed off its steeds.

4   The nomads used to dwell in yurts. Here the yurt is a metonymy referring to the ruling centre (or imperial palace) of the Huns.

5   This is an allusion to the history of the Han Dynasty. The grappling of five chieftains after the split of the Empire of the Huns around 60 BC

evolved into the continuous confrontation of the Northern Huns and Southern Huns. The bloodthirsty monarch (呼屠吾斯 , ?−36 BC) of the Northern Huns had once and again attacked the State of Wusun (located in the now Kyrgyzstan), extorted tributes from such city states as Dawan (located in the now Kyrgyzstan), detained and killed the envoys from the Han Empire. Supported by some friendly states, Chen Tang (?− 6 BC), in the position of Deputy Commander of the troops subject to the Commission of West Regional Affairs, launched an expedition and subdued the Northern Huns, whose monarch died of serious wounds received in the campaign. In light of Chen Tang's proposal, the event was make public on the Gao Street, where foreign envoys' residences were located at that time, so as "To manifest the policy that he who violates the sovereignty of the powerful Hans, no matter how far he flees, will find no escape from the penalty of death."

151. 念奴娇　Fair Is Niannu

1　The present *ci*-poem expresses the poet's reflections on history and aspiration to recover lost territories. Allusions to historical events are employed to manifest the points.

2　my strategy sound — my feasible strategy (of armed resistance).

3　Zu Ti (266 AD−321 AD), a famous general of the Eastern Jin Dynasty, who is known for his valiant attempt to recover the territory.

152. 扬州慢　Song of Yangzhou with a Slow Rhythm

1　*The Millet*, which is mentioned in the introductory remarks, refers to a poem from *The Book of Poetry*.

　　In 1161 AD, the Jin aggressors swooped upon the south, looting and killing all the way. In 1176 AD, when the poet travelled via Weiyang (i.e. the present-day Yangzhou), he was shocked by the rueful sight of the place, hence the composition of the present *ci*-poem. By making a sharp contrast between the pre-war prosperity and the post-war desolation, the poet condemns the crimes committed by the aggressors. The rhetorical devices, such as personification, metaphor, contrast, rhetorical question, etc., are employed.

2　Jiang Kui (c.1155 AD−c.1221 AD), formally named Jiang Yaozhang, was at the same time a poet, calligrapher, and musician. His poetry is marked with candidness and originality.

3　The word "steeds" denotes the cavalry of the Jins.

4　Du Mu — a famous poet of the Tang Dynasty.

153. 清平乐　Celebrating Peace and Order

1　This *ci*-poem conveys, in a way, a sense of detachment from worldliness. The rich imagination brings the poet to the moon, which presents a peculiar vista of the earth.

2　Liu Kezhuang (1187 AD–1269 AD), courtesy name Liu Qianfu, had held the position of Minister of Industry and Agriculture. His poetry features a free, powerful and romantic style.

3　The three-legged toad is a metonymy denoting the moon in Chinese mythology.

4　Chang'e is the Goddess of the Moon in Chinese mythology.

154. 题临安邸　An Inscription at a Lin'an Hotel

1　Lin Sheng (?–?) was believed to be an intellectual who, in light of "Anecdotes of and Notes to Song Poetry", lived in the later half of the twelfth century.

The Southern Song rulers had led a dissipated life ever since they crossed the Yangtze River and made Hangzhou the capital. Emperor Caozong (i.e. Zhao Gao, 1107 AD–1187 AD) had gone in for a large-scale construction of palaces, parks and flower gardens. To cater to the need of aristocrats and bureaucrats, wine-shops, brothels and luxury workshops had been set up. Indulging in sensual pleasures, the upper class had cast to the winds the issues concerning the recovery of lost territory and revenge upon the invaders for the Jingkang Humiliation.

The present poem, which first appeared in the form of an inscription at a hotel in Lin'an (i.e. Hangzhou), is a famous satire directed at the high society, especially the rulers. It is succinct, vigorous and implicit in style.

2　Mountains ... in proud array — Hangzhou had been famous for its beautiful scenery, which centers around the West Lake, and the places of amusement — including more than forty parks and flower gardens built by Zhao Gao — might have added much to the physical charm of the city. However, the poet assumes a sarcastic tone here, for he is disgusted with the mental attitude of the city.

3   Whether song and dance ... who should know? — This rhetorical question boils down to saying that there's no telling whether people would ever give up their pleasure-seeking attitude and face squarely the stern reality of aggression and a latent social crisis.

4   th' drowsy breezes — The poet is punning on this ambiguous phrase, which literally means a gentle spring wind capable of making people sleepy and figuratively means the sensual pleasures by which people's willpower is sapped.

5   ... that they /... th' fallen capital — Bianzhou! — The sightseers are so intoxicated by the will-sapping pleasures that they have forgotten all about the Jin aggression, about the suffering of the conquered people and the fall of the former capital Bianzhou (i.e. the now Kaifeng) !

490

155. 游园不值   Shut without the Garden

1   Ye Shaoweng(?−?) was from Longquan of the now Zhejiang. He lived in the middle and the latter half of the Southern Song Dynasty.

The present poem expresses the poet's aesthetic appreciation of spring. The first couplet narrates the poet's being kept outside the garden, and the second couplet subtly turns to the witty comment about and vivid description of spring, as is embodied in the twig of flowers flaming out of the fence. This poem, which has attained the figurative meaning that the true, the good and the beautiful will sooner or later find a way to express themselves despite any means of suppression, has enjoyed an unbroken popularity for its artistic attainments — the vivid images, the unusual conception and the profound philosophy therein.

2   My clog-prints ...: /... after all. — I knock at the gate, but nobody comes to answer. Is it because the garden's owner bears me a spite on account of my defacing the beauty of the mossy path with clog-prints?

3   A gardenful of spring ... /... out o'er th' wall! — "A gardenful of spring", which stands for "a gardenful of spring-time grandeur", is a case of synecdoche, and the twig of flowers as the symbol of spring time is personified.

156. 过零丁洋   Crossing the Lonely Bay

1   In 1278 AD, the poet, as a prisoner of war, was forced to go with the Yuan troops which were in pursuit of the Song emperor Zhao Bing. In the course of crossing the Lonely Bay early the next year, the traitor

Zhang Hongfan, who then served as commander in the Yuan army, tried to elicit from him a letter inducing the Song general Zhang Shijie to give up resistance. In response the poet composed the present poem, which narrates his eventful life, expresses his grief over the ill fate of his nation and manifests the will that he would rather die than submit to the invaders. It is concise, vigorous, and analogical. The great ideological worth, matched with a high artistic attainment, entitles this poem to shine with eternal glory. It has inspired many to fight for just causes and to devote their lives to their nation's security, stability and prosperity.

2   Wen Tianxiang (1236 AD−1283 AD), a great national hero, was from Jishui of Jiangxi.

In 1256 AD, he came first in the highest imperial examination and, in the course of nature, was entitled Number One Scholar. As Governor-Plenipotentiary of Jiangxi, he organized an army of volunteers in 1275 AD to resist the Yuan invading forces and in time to defend the capital Lin'an. The next year, he was sent on a peace-negotiation mission in the capacity of Prime Minister, only to be taken into custody by the Yuan side. After he managed to escape from detention he carried on strenuous armed struggles against the aggressors successively in Zhejiang, Fujian and Jiangxi. In 1278 AD, he was defeated in an engagement and taken prisoner in what is the now Haifeng County of Guangdong. A man of moral integrity, he remained unyielding in face of threats and inducements during his four years of imprisonment in Dadu (i.e. the now Beijing). He accepted death with perfect equanimity at the age of forty-seven.

Wen's posthumous twenty-volume book — *The Complete Works of Sir Wen Shan* — expresses the author's elevated sentiments and reflects the grim reality as well as the author's heroic deeds, which may move people to song and tears. Wen's style is refined and vigorous.

3   resistance — the armed struggle against the Yuan aggression.

4   Like the catkin ...; /... by the rain. — This couplet vividly narrates the land's adversities and the poet's eventful life by likening them respectively to the helpless catkin in the wind and the vulnerable duckweed under the ruthless assaults of rains.

5   On the Panic Shoal ...; /... I now lament. — In this couplet the poet subtly puns on coincidental place names to recount his feelings and experiences. The Panic Shoal is one of the eighteen shoals in the Ganjiang River. In

1277 AD the poet was defeated by the Yuan forces and compelled to retreat from Jiangxi to Fujian via the above-mentioned shoal. The Lonely Bay is within the bounds of the now Zhongshan County of Guangdong.

6 Death befalls all ..., /... in th' tablets of bamboo! — The "tablets of bamboo" is a metonymy for "history" or "book of history" — In very ancient times dehydrated bamboo tablets had been used as material to write on. Hence the original may be liberally rendered into "One's life can be long or short, and death befalls all from of old; / At any cost loyalty that shines in history I'll uphold !"

This couplet highlights the central idea of the poem — the poet's outlook on life and death, and his resolution to maintain his moral integrity and loyalty to his nation. It has become a celebrated maxim.

157. 酹江月 · 和友驿中言别　Libation to the Moon over the Rill — In Reply to Deng Guangjian in the Same Rhyme Sequence

1 In Chinese folklore, the dragon is symbolic of sovereignty, magical power, or auspiciousness.

2 The dragon's dauntless spirit is an encouragement to the poet, who is confronted with adversities.

3 Oh, ... like snow! — Those three lines contain two cases of antonomasia, which shed light on the the truth that high aspirations might be frustrated. Cao Cao was king of the Kingdom of Wei who, full of hope, launched an expedition against the Kingdom of Wu, during which he composed "A Short Song" on deck of his warship before he was defeated in the famous Campaign of the Red Cliff (Chibi), and Wang Can, distressed, wrote his *fu*-poem "Ascending the Tower" to express his homesickness and feelings about the sufferings inflicted upon by war and social upheavals while staying in Jiangzhou as a refugee at the fall of the Han Dynasty. As regards the poet himself, he had been confident in the resistance, but to his disappointment all the efforts have come to naught.

4 In Chinese literature, the image of the cuckoo is symbolic of faithful resolution.

Chapter Six　Poetry of the Liao, the Jin and the Yuan Dynasties

Introductory Remarks

From the tenth century to the fourteenth, three dynasties had sooner or later emerged in the north — the Liao (916 AD–1125 AD), the Jin (1115 AD–1234 AD) and the Yuan (1271 AD–1368 AD), which eventually conquered the whole nation. Literature of these dynasties gradually made its way into recognition chiefly by bringing to maturity of the drama and the songs — including the dramatic songs and the *song*-poems (i.e. non-dramatic songs).

The song is a product of the fusion of the music of the northern nationalities, the *ci*-poetry, and the ditties and melodies of the north and of the south. Though similar to the *ci*-poetry in form, it has a higher rhyme frequency, admits more colloquialisms and covers a wider range of subjects than the *ci*-poetry does. It also allows more freedom in tonal patterns and in the number of words (extra words, esp. functional words, can be added to what is required of a particular song). As a rule dramatic songs make up the lyrical part of a drama, while the narrative part is written in prose. It follows that a good dramatist is at the same time a good poet. The dramatic songs are to be performed on the stage, whereas the song-poems are only meant to be sung. In case a complicated subject is involved, a number of songs will be joined together according to certain rules to form a suite.

The brilliant artistic attainments of the Yuan Dynasty in dramatic and non-dramatic songs can fairly compare with those of the Tang and the Song Dynasties in classical and metrical verse and in *ci*-poetry. Some dramas, such as *Salvation of the Abducted* (《救风尘》), *The Injustice to Lady Dou* (《窦娥冤》), and *The Romance of the Western Bower* (《西厢记》), have held the stage for some six hundred years, and quite a number of song-poems are still on the lips of millions today. Among the great poet-dramatists and song-poets are Guan Hanqing, Wang Shifu, Wang Heqing, Baipu (1226 AD–?), Zheng Guangzu, Ma Zhiyuan, Li Zhi (1235 AD–1300 AD), Zhang Kejiu (1270 AD?–1329 AD), Liu Shizhong (1305 AD?–1370 AD?), Guan Yunshi (1286 AD–1324 AD) and others.

As to poetry in its narrow sense, the Jin and the Yuan Dynasties had produced such important poets as Yuan Haowen, Liu Yin, Sa Dula and Wang Mian (1287 AD–1359 AD) despite the hindrance of the formalist tendency in artistry.

158. 北渡三首

元好问

其一
道旁僵卧满累囚，
过去旃车似水流；
红粉哭随回鹘马，
为谁一步一回头。

其二
随营木佛贱于柴，
大乐编钟满市排。
虏掠几何君莫问，
大船浑载汴京来。

其三
白骨纵横似乱麻，
几年桑梓变龙沙。
只知河朔生灵尽，
破屋疏烟却数家。

A Trilogy Composed on My North-Ward Journey[1]

Yuan Haowen[2]

No. 1

The felt-hooded wagons[3] are rumbling northward like a
  stream;

Still bound up are the captives on the roadside lying dead.

Dragging on behind the Huihu steeds, th' rouges screech and
  scream.[4]

Lo, what makes every one of them frequently turn her head?

No. 2

As wood th' Buddhist statues in th' market are as cheap,

And so are th' chime-bells from th' Office of Music sold.

What's the deed to size up the booty heap by heap?

Lo, on board the ships is Bianjing, th' city of old! [5]

No. 3

Scattered are the victims' grayish bones here and there;[6]

Into desert th' cultivated fields have been turned.

Th' depopulated north is a sight of despair,

Gasping with smoke are just a few homes not yet burned.[7]

159. 南吕·一枝花
不伏老（尾）

关汉卿

我是个蒸不烂、煮不熟、
捶不匾、炒不爆、响珰珰一粒铜豌豆。
恁子弟每谁教你钻入他锄不断、斫不下、
解不开、顿不脱、慢腾腾千层锦套头。
我玩的是梁园月，饮的是东京酒，
赏的是洛阳花，攀的是章台柳。
我也会围棋、会蹴蹋、会打围、会插科、
会歌舞、会吹弹、会咽作、会吟诗、会双陆。

I Defy My Old Age —
To the Tune of "A Spray of Flowers"[1]

Guan Hanqing[2]

Denouement

I'm resistant to steaming, cooking, crushing

And frying, being a sonorous bronze pea.[3]

I've jumped into the soft brocade noose,

Following th' advice my fellow actors have given me.[4]

In the multiplex noose, which can't be cut off, loosened,

Severed, removed or shaken off, I stay with glee.

The Eastern-Capital wine I regard as a treat,

And the moon over the Park of Liang delights me;

'Tis fun to embrace Willows of the Zhangtai Street[5],

And the peonies of Luoyang amuse me.

I can give a kick to the foot-ball,

And the game of go is my hobby;

I'm good at dancing, hunting and jesting,

And 'tis my line to do vocal mimicry,

To play on musical instruments, to have

A game of double-six[6] and to compose poetry.

Since Creator has endowed me with such a habit[7],

你便是落了我牙、歪了我嘴、瘸了我腿、折了我手，
天赐与我这几般儿歹症候，尚兀自不肯休！
则除是阎王亲自唤，神鬼自来勾。
三魂归地府，七魄丧冥幽。
天哪！那其间才不向烟花路儿上走！

I'll not give up the spree

E'en if my teeth have fallen, e'en if my mouth

has been deformed, e'en if my foot's been crippled

Any my arm broken. And so,

Before the King of Hell personally calls for me

Or the Ghosts of Fate comes to arrest me;

Before my trio-soul returns to the nether world[8]

And my septa-spirit travels to the undiscovered country,

I shall never shun the homes of flowers[9]and the spree!

503

160. 天净沙·秋思

马致远

枯藤老树昏鸦，
小桥流水人家，
古道西风瘦马。
夕阳西下，
断肠人在天涯。

The Moods of a Traveller in Autumn —
To the Tune of "Desert under the Clear Skies"[1]

Ma Zhiyuan[2]

A little bridge lies across th' stream, which past houses flows;

A withered vine still clings to th' old tree, in which crows rest.

A lanky horse crawls along th' ancient road, and th' west wind
blows.

The dusky sun sinking down th' west,

Earth's remotest corner witnesses a stranger much distressed.

505

161. 西厢记诗曲
三首

王实甫

（一）张君瑞吟诗探幽

月色溶溶夜，

花阴寂寂春；

如何临皓魄，

不见月中人？

（二）崔莺莺寄简待月

待月西厢下，

迎风户半开。

隔墙花影动，

疑是玉人来。

（三）崔莺莺听琴知重

其声壮，

似铁骑刀枪冗冗；

其声幽，

似落花流水溶溶；

其声高，

Extracts from *The Romance of the Western Bower*[1]

Wang Shifu[2]

Poem 1: Zhang Junrui's Tentative Recitation

The luminary crystallizes th' air of th' night,

While th' charm of spring flowers th' nocturnal shades impair[3].

In search of th' Beauty I gaze up at th' minor light[4]:

Alas, invisible still is the Goddess Fair[5]!

Poem 2: Cui Yingying's Implicit Invitation[6]

The moon in expectancy rises o'er th' west-wing room;

To let in breezes th' door is left half open in th' gloom.

A rustle through the flowers is heard from yon the wall:

Could it signify th' soul of my heart has come to call?

Poem 3: The Appeal of Music to Cui Yingying

— To the Tune of "The Shaven-Headed Servant"[7]

'Tis majestic, like the clanking

Of th' armoured steeds and weapons of contending foes;

'Tis melodious, like the floating

Of fallen petals in a stream which gently flows.

When tinkling at a pitch that's high,

似风清月朗鹤唳空；
其声低，
似听儿女语，小窗中，
　喁喁。

It makes the thrilling note of cranes flying across a moonlit sky;

When falling to a lower key,

It suggests two lovers whispering behind the window with glee.

162. 念奴娇·登石头城

萨都拉

石头城上，
望天低吴楚，
眼空无物。
指点六朝形胜地，
惟有青山如壁。
蔽日旌旗，
连云樯橹，
白骨纷如雪。
一江南北，
消磨多少豪杰。

寂寞避暑离宫，
东风辇路，
芳草年年发。
落日无人松径里，
鬼火高低明灭。
歌舞尊前，
繁华镜里，

Fair Is Niannu —
An Ascent of the Gate Tower of the Rocky City[1]

Sa Dula[2]

Atop the Rocky City I gaze

As far as where Wu and Chu[3] merge with th' skies.

The world, seeming devoid of content, comes in sight.

Of the Six Dynasties what's still left?

Only wall-like green mountains remain on the historical site.

The masts of warships, which might have touched the clouds,

And the banners, which might have hidden th' sun,

Have only left behind bones snow-white.

Oh, how many talents, north and south of th' River,

Had been ruined or reduced to a hopeless plight?

Each year in spring, when the grasses grow lush

On its corridors, the royal summer palace,

Now deserted, presents a sorry sight.

After sunset, along th' abandoned paths below the pines,

Will-o'-the-wisp ghastly rolls on, now dim, now bright.

Ere exquisite wine cups the youth of men of th' hour

Had faded away, and in th' mirrors th' raven locks

暗换青青发。
伤心千古，
秦淮一片明月！

Of princely souls, sapped by song and dance, had turned white.

Forever gone is the heart-rending past, but lo,

O'er the Qinhuai River the moon is forever shining bright.

163. 正宫·醉太平

无名氏

堂堂大元，
奸佞专权。
开河变钞祸根源，
惹红巾万千。
官法滥，刑法重，
黎民怨。
人吃人，钞买钞，
何曾见。
贼做官，官做贼，
混贤愚。
哀哉可怜！

Toasting to Stability — To the Tune of Zhenggong[1]

Anonymous

What an imposing Empire of Yuan,

In which crafty sycophants in power gain!

Thousands upon thousands of Red Kerchiefs

Have risen in revolt, flooding banknotes being the bane[2].

Laws being exorbitant, penal codes severe,

Common people groan and complain.

Men are feeding on men, bills can only buy bills —

Such state of affairs is never seen.

Thieves secure office, and officials commit thefts;

Confounded indeed the wise and the stupid have been.

Alas, what a lamentable scene!

515

Songs of Weal and Woe

注释　**Notes and Commentary**

158. 北渡三首　**A Trilogy Composed on My North-Ward Journey**

1　Early in 1233 AD, the Jin Emperor Aizong fled to Guide (the now Shangqiu of Henan) after suffering repeated defeats, and the Jin's Southern Capital Bianjing (the now Kaifeng) was besieged by the Mongolian army. In the fourth lunar month that year, the mutinous former Jin Marshal Cui Li sent the Jin royalty under escort to the Mongolian army headquarters in Qingcheng, where the Mongolians killed some male members (including two princes) and sent the rest northward to Hepu (in the now Republic of Mongolia). As an ex-official of the conquered Jin Empire, the poet was taken prisoner and sent to Liaocheng (in the now Shandong) via Qingcheng. He composed the present group of three poems to express his feelings about what he had witnessed on the way. They expose the crimes committed by the invaders and expresses the poet's sympathy with the people under the cruel hooves of the invaders.

2　Yuan Haowen (1190 AD–1257 AD), alias Yuan Yishan, was of the Xianbei Ethnic Group (鲜卑族). He had served in the Jin Empire successively as magistrate of Neixiang County, magistrate of Nanyang County and Assistant Director the General Affairs Department of the Cabinet. When the Jin Empire was annexed by the Yuan Empire, he abandoned his official career and took pleasure in writing. His works include *Chronicle of the Jin Dynasty*, *An Anthology of the Central Plains* and the posthumous *Selected Works of Yishan*.

　　Yuan's poetry, rich in content and vigorous in style, reflects the social upheaval and expresses the poet's great sympathy with the suffering people. In his thirty short poems, influential in the history of literary criticism, he puts forward the ideas of originality and naturalness on the one hand, and on the other expounds his strong opposition to affection and meretriciousness. His attainments has entitled him the literary giant around the turn of the Jin and the Yuan Dynasties.

3　The felt-hooded wagons are typical of the nomads' way of life.

4　In this line, the Huihu steeds and the rouges, respectively used to denote the Mongolian cavalry and the young ladies, are cases of antonomasia and metaphor.

5　Bianjing had been the capital of the Jin Empire. Here "Bianjing" is used

as a synecdoche referring to the fortunes of the city, which are loaded on
board the ships and taken away.

6 Historical records reveal that city-wide massacres had been committed
   by the Yuan invaders in Suzhou (肅 州 , the now Jiuquan), Zhongxing
   Prefecture (中兴府 , the now Yinchuan) and Yangzhou (洋州 , the now
   Xiyang County).

7 In this line "homes" are personified.

159. 南吕 · 一枝花 不伏老（尾） I Defy My Old Age — To the Tune of "A Spray of Flowers"

1 The present song-poem is an excerpt from "I Defy My Old Age" — a
   suite of four self-mocking monologues. It successfully creates the image
   of a playwright, who is funny, daring, versatile and anti-conventional
   but assumes a hedonistic attitude towards life (which is exaggerated in
   the last eleven lines). This poem is marked with a wealth of humour and
   rhetorical devices. It is anti-feudalistic; on the other hand it reveals the
   poet's dissolute life style.

2 Guan Hanqing (1220 AD?−1300 AD?) was from Dadu (the now Beijing).
   He had once held the position of director of the Imperial Hospital, but
   most of his life he lived among people of the lower stratum.

   Guan is one of the most original dramatic geniuses that China has
   ever produced. He has written more than sixty plays, *Salvation of the
   Abducted* (a comedy) and *The Injustice to Lady Dou the Widow* (a
   tragedy) being his masterpieces. In his many plays he vividly creates the
   images of people who dare to revolt against the vicious and powerful,
   warmly eulogizes the wisdom and virtues of the downtrodden and
   ruthlessly castigates the cannibalistic feudal society. Xiong Zide (writer
   of the Yuan Dynasty), in his *Biographical Sketches of Renowned
   Officials*, pictures him as "a witty, erudite and resourceful man of
   unconventional grace, who excels in writing."

   Guan is also known as a successful poet. Those of his poems which
   have been handed down aggregate seventy-two pieces. His style, in
   drama as well as in verse, is vivid, witty and romantic.

3 ... being a sonorous bronze pea. — Here lies the punch line, which
   induces the sense of humour. The pun "bronze pea" is ambiguous: it may
   metaphorically stand for "a luster" or "a man of strong character."

4   To jump into a brocade noose means to become addicted to whoring. The brocade noose is the metaphor for the artifice employed by a whorehouse for attracting whore-mongers. When the narrator says he's "Following th' advice ... have given me", he is just shifting the blame for his bad conduct onto others — the actors who are said to have given him the advice.

5   And the ... the Zhangtai Street — In these lines "the Park of Liang" refers to a famous place of amusements in ancient times, and "Willows of the Zhangtai Street" is an euphemism for women living on the street.

6   double-six — a form of gambling in ancient times.

7   Since Creator ... such a habit — Here the monologist once again is trying to shirk responsibility for his misconduct, this time by throwing the blame upon the Creator. To call whoring "a habit" is a case of understatement.

8   Before the King of Hell ... to the nether world — It was believed that a person dies when his trio-soul and septa-spirit return to the nether world, and that the nether world is ruled over by the King of Hell.

518

9   the homes of flowers — (euphemism for) the whorehouses

160. 天净沙 · 秋思   The Moods of a Traveller in Autumn — To the Tune of "Desert under the Clear Skies"

1   As is true of the poet's many works, the present song-poem (set to the tune of the *Yue Melody*) bears with it a tragic element in the expression of a roamer's distress by portraying a dusky scene. It comprises twelve images: a withered vine, an old tree, ... and a remotest corner of the world, all of which, well chosen and vividly portrayed, are subtly integrated to form an intricate artistic realm. Succinct, sonorous and touching, it has enjoyed a high place in the history of Chinese literature.

2   Ma Zhiyuan (1250 AD?−1324 AD?), a famous poet and gifted dramatist, was from Dadu, i.e. the now Beijing. He had held public office in the Jiangsu-Zhejiang Administrative Division before he began to lead a secluded life at about fifty. He had written fifteen dramas and a large number of poems, among which have been handed down seven dramas, one hundred and fifteen lyrics and twenty-three suites of songs. His works cover a wide range of subjects and feature a varied and elegant style.

161. 西厢记诗曲三首   Extracts from *The Romance of the Western Bower*

1   *The Romance of the Western Bower*, a five-act play, relates the love story

of Zhang Junrui (a young scholar) and Cui Yingying (daughter of the deceased prime minister), who dare to break the fetters of feudalism. The synopsis of the play is as follows:

The hero and the heroine chance to lodge at the same temple and in due course fall in love with each other. With the loyal and efficient help of the witty and audacious handmaiden Hongniang (or: Maiden Red), they manage to exchange poems and carry out secret rendezvous under the nose of the rigorous Mme. Cui (the heroine's mother). As luck would have it, the temple is besieged by a gang of mutinous soldiers, whose ringleader claims to marry the heroine by force. In this emergency Mme. Cui summons all the monks and lodgers to her presence and pronounces that she will marry her daughter to whoever obviates the impending danger. However, when the hero has successfully performed the task (by sending a letter to his friend — a general, who comes to their rescue), the lady goes back on her promise. This notwithstanding, the lovers persist in their struggle and are eventually united.

The play is partly written in verse. The extracts here include two poems and one dramatic song. Poem 1 is the hero's recitation intended to sound out the heroine's mind, which finds a ready echo in the heroine's heart, the other is the heroine's letter of implicit invitation to the hero. As to the dramatic song, it is the heroine's expression of admiration for the hero's musical talent.

The subtitles the dramatic song and poems are given by the author of the present book. By the way, the authorship of Poem 2 might be attributed to Yuan Zhen of the Tang Dynasty, whose short story (i.e. *The True Story of Yingying*) had served as the prototype of the play.

2 Wang Shifu (1260 AD?–1336 AD?), an important dramatist of the Yuan Dynasty, was from Dadu (the now Beijing). He had written fourteen plays, the most famous being *The Romance of the Western Bower*, which has held the stage for some six hundred years. Of his song-poems only three have been handed down. His style is beautiful, humorous and in some cases vernacular.

3 While th' charm of spring flowers th' nocturnal shades impair — while the nocturnal shades impair the charm of spring flowers.

4 The minor light, as is the case with "the luminary", are cases of euphemism denoting the moon.

5 "Th' beauty" and "the Goddess Fair" refer to the heroine.

6 This poem, forwarded to Zhang by Hongniang, hints that Zhang may come for the rendezvous by surmounting the partition when the moon rises and that the heroine will be expecting his arrival with her door half open.

7 This is a dramatic song, of which "The Shaven-Headed Servant" is the tune of music. In this song, "it" refers to the music performed by Zhang Junrui on the instrument *Qin*.

162. 念奴娇·登石头城 Fair Is Niannu — An Ascent of the Gate Tower of the Rocky City

1 The present *ci*-poem expresses the poet's critical review of the past and outlook on life and history. Atop the Rocky City the poet is lost in contemplation: The glory of victories in war have faded away, and desolation has become a substitute for the splendour of the empires; Neither power nor natural barriers can ever ensure its permanence. Eternity embraces nothing but nature.

The Rocky City, which had been the capital of the Kingdom of Wu, the Eastern Jin, the Song, the Qi, the Liang and the Chen Dynasties, was located in the limits of the present-day Nanjing.

On the one hand the poem might bear a sobering effect on those obsessed with the insatiable desire for power, fame and gains; on the other it smacks somewhat of nihilism. As long as everyone does his own bit for the peace and betterment of the world, a bright future will surely come within Man's reach.

2 Sa Dula (1272 AD–c.1355 AD), a poet, calligrapher and painter of the Hui ethnic group, was from Yanmen (the now Daixian County of Shanxi). Since his possession of official candidature in 1327 AD, he had been appointed to several positions, the highest being that of Deputy Director of the Supervisory Commission of Hebei Administrative Division. As he had a strong inclination for nature, many of his poems are devoted to the portrayal of landscapes.

3 Wu and Chu — areas which used to be the Kingdoms of Wu and Chu.

163. 正宫·醉太平 Toasting to Stability — To the Tune of Zhenggong

1 This is a song-poem set to the tune of "Toasting to Stability". A series of figures of speech, such as antithesis, orthodox, are employed to exposes the corruption of the ruling clique.

2 ... flooding banknotes being the bane — ... inflation being the root cause.

Chapter Seven   Poetry of the Ming Dynasty

Introductory Remarks

The peasants' uprisings ended the rule of the Yuan Dynasty and, as a result, the Ming Dynasty (1368 AD−1644 AD) was established. After some hundred years of reconstruction and recuperation the nation presented a scene of economic prosperity. Capitalist relations of production, which were in the embryonic stage, began to develop slowly under the heavy yoke of feudalism. An incontestable indication of the nation's comprehensive strength was the fact that Chinese fleets, under the command of Zheng He (1371 AD?−1433 AD?), had visited more than thirty regions and countries from 1405 AD to 1433 AD, the farthest places they had called being the eastern coast of Africa and some of the Red Sea ports. Prompted by the cultural needs of townspeople, whose numbers were large in places more developed in handicraft and commerce, the drama, the novel and the popular tunes flourished vigorously, whereas the "serious poetry" and the essay as "orthodox literature" of feudal China gradually declined.

Neo-Confucianism, which never ceased to advance, had contributed much to ontology, naturally-based philosophy, psychological ethics and morality-oriented philosophy. As far as verse is concerned, its development had been hampered by the tendency towards divorce from the reality. The Officialese School, represented by the Three Yangs (i.e. Yang Shiqi, Yang Rong and Yang Pu), beautified the times and extolled the achievements of the rulers; the Chaling School assumed

Songs of Weal and Woe

a critical attitude towards the Officialese style but was not able to throw off its shackles; the Seven Early Talents (Li Mengyang, He Jingming and the others) and the Seven Later Talents (Li Panlong, Wang Shizhen and the others) opposed themselves to the Officialese School under the banner of classicism, only to fall into the quagmire of artistic imitation; the poets of the Gong'an School, headed by the Yuan brothers (i.e. Yuan Zongdao, Yuan Hongdao and Yuan Zhongdao), rose in opposition to the imitative classicism by advocating that the very role of verse is "to express individuality without formality," and thus inevitably turned poetry into an instrument for self-amusement; and the poets of the Jingling School (such as Zhong Xing and Tan Yuanchun), who held similar opinions to those of the Gong'an School, had resort to the works of the ancients for inspiration and consequently found themselves trapped in the blind lane of literary creation. In sum, the verse of the dynasty in question pales beside the other forms of literature.

It doesn't follow, though, that the fine traditions of Chinese verse had discontinued. Poets of the above-mentioned schools had written some good poems; Gao Qi had formed a romanticist style of his own; moreover, many progressive thinkers, statesmen and people with lofty ideals had created excellent poetic works, which have profound social substance, express noble sentiments and reflect people's dauntless spirit to combat evil forces, Yu Qian, Qi Jiguang, Chen Zilong and Xia Wanchun being the most prominent poets of this group.

The folk songs and song-poems had prospered in the Ming Dynasty. Some of them reflect the dark reality in a vivid and militant style. Feng Weimin, whose song-poem *Needless to Say* is included in the present book, ranks with the most important song-poets.

164. 越歌

宋濂

恋郎思郎非一朝，
好似并州花剪刀。
一股在南一股北，
几时裁得合欢袍？

A Yue Song[1]

Song Lian[2]

Day in and day out 'tis for you I yearn and care,

For we're just like Bingzhou scissors[3] which make a pair.

If one scissor stays in th' north and th' other in th' south,

When could th' happy gowns be tailored for us to share?[4]

Songs of Weal and Woe

165. 旱

施耐庵

赤日炎炎似火烧，
野田禾稻半枯焦。
农夫心内如汤煮，
公子王孙把扇摇！

The Drought[1]

Shi Nai'an[2]

The sun is scorching like a devastating fire[3];

The crops for want of water languish and expire.

The farmers' hearts ache as if being boiled in pans;

The scions, howe'er, just at leisure flirt their fans!

❀

166. 岳王墓

高启

大树无枝向北风，
千年遗恨泣英雄。
班师诏已来三殿，
射虏书犹说二宫。
每忆上方谁请剑，
空磋高庙自藏弓。
栖霞岭上今回首，
不见诸陵白露中。

The Tomb of Yue Fei

Gao Qi[1]

No branch of the trees at the tomb does slant towards the
 north[2];

O 'er the wrong done to th' hero, I weep in eternal wrath.[3]

Though imperial edicts had been issued for retreat[4],

He still petitioned to avenge th' throne and th' foe to defeat[5].

Who else had e'er got the spine to plead for th' Sword Supreme[6]?

'Tis shameful that th' throne had invented arrows for the
 scheme![7]

Atop the Rosy Cloud Ridge, where th' hero lies, in White Dew[8],   531

I look back, only to find the Song Tombs cast out of view[9]!

167. 石灰吟

于谦

千锤万凿出深山，
烈火焚烧若等闲。
粉身碎骨全不怕，
要留清白在人间。

532

Ode to the Limestone[1]

Yu Qian[2]

Having suffer'd countless strikes you've come from th' mounts
deep,

And you're fearless of the flames which around you leap.

Though doom'd to pulverize you show no sign of fright,

For 'tis your wish to leave to th' world what's pure and white![3]

168. 双调·清江引

冯惟敏

乌纱帽，
满京城日日抢，
全不在贤愚上。
新人换旧人，
后浪推前浪，
谁是谁非不用讲。

Needless to Say — To the Double Tune of "The Limpid Stream"[1]

Feng Weimin[2]

Alas, the black-gauze hats[3]

Are scrambled for in th' capital every day!

Just as some waves push the others aside,

So the newly-appointed kick th' old timers out of th' way.

Wise or dense, he wins who snatches one by means fair or foul.

Whether one's honest or cunning 'tis needless to say.

169. 登盘山绝顶

戚继光

霜角一声草木哀，
云头对起石门开。
朔风边酒不成醉，
落叶归鸦无数来。
但使雕戈销杀气，
未妨白发老边才。
勒名峰上吾谁与，
故李将军舞剑台。

An Ascent to the Summit of Mount Pan

Qi Jiguang[1]

In th' frosty morn bugles come to th' trees and grass as a
   shock[2],

Fleecy clouds hanging high up above the opened door of rock.

Frontier wine's invalidated by th' north winds[3], which fiercely
   howl;

Countless home-bound crows, accompanied by drifting leaves,
   growl.

To dispel the clouds of war with th' halberd 'tis my delight[4];

What matters if I should guard th' borders till my hair turns
   white?[5]

For me to follow who has yet set an example fine?

'Tis Li Jing, whose deeds embodied by th' Sword-Dance
   Terrace shine![6]

170. 京师人为
严嵩语

无名氏

可笑严介溪，
金银如山积，
刀锯信手施。
尝将冷眼观螃蟹，
看你横行得几时？

A Satire Circulating in the Capital on Yan Song[1]

Anonymous

Though his gold and silver pile up like a hill,

And his knife and saw[2] he brandishes at will,

Ludicrous is Yan Jiexi in public view.

We coldly watch the fierce crab that crawls askew[3]

And question: "Can there be much time left for you?"

171. 赞花瓦氏
征倭语

无名氏

花瓦家，
能杀倭；
腊而啖之有如蛇。

Song in Praise of Madame Huawa[1]

Anonymous

Huawa's men are staunch and stout!

Like eagles swooping on snakes[2]

They wipe the Looting Dwarfs out!

172. 五人墓

林云凤

五人埋骨处，
客过每停舟。
姓氏闻鹓阙，
精灵傍虎丘。
宦官应敛迹，
缇骑尚含愁。
若不锋端死，
空成侠少游。

The Tomb of the Heroic Five[1]

Lin Yunfeng[2]

To pay tribute, people go out of th' way to come ashore,[3]

And in front of the reverent tomb they will stand in awe.

Although on the Tiger Hill their remains have been interred,

Even in th' imperial palaces their names are heard.

Their deeds have made th' ferocity of the eunuchs abate,

Ere the innocent th' fierce agents will henceforth hesitate.

Glory goes to those who'd rather confront the evil knife

Than linger o'er a conformist's insignificant life!

543

173. 秋日杂感

陈子龙

行吟坐啸独悲秋，
海雾江云引暮愁。
不信有天常似醉，
最怜无地可埋忧！
荒荒葵井多新鬼，
寂寂瓜田识故侯。
见说五湖供饮马，
沧浪何处着渔舟？

Reflections in Autumn[1]

Chen Zilong[2]

Wherever I am, th' only theme I drone is autumn gloom;

Th' saddening mist and haze over the sea and river loom.

Could Providence remain crazy and go on with th' mischief?[3]

I lament that Earth offers no places to bury grief[4].

Deserted wells have witnessed slaughter victims all around;

In melon patches ousted marquises are to be found.[5]

Th' lakes turned to mangers for th' foe's steeds, th' fisherman

    doe wail:

"There are no unconquered waters for people to set sail!" 545

174. 别云间

夏完淳

三年羁旅客，
今日又南冠。
无限河山泪，
谁言天地宽。
已知泉路近，
欲别故乡难。
毅魄归来日，
灵旗空际看。

Farewell, Yunjian!

Xia Wanchun[1]

I have been tramping 'bout for three good years,[2]
And now the Southern Hat I'm doomed to wear.[3]
For the lost domains I shed boundless tears,
And mourn the world reduced to the beasts' lair.[4]
I'm conscious that the Yellow Spring is near,[5]
And 'tis hard to take leave of home for me;[6]
But then my dauntless soul shall re-appear
To see the sacred banners in high glee![7]

164. 越歌　A Yue Song

1　This love song, which reflects the girl's courage in pursuing her happiness, is written in the style of the Yue songs. The language is simple but expressive, and the style features a natural ease.

　　The simile likening a couple of young people in love to a pair of scissors is apt, for a pair of scissors won't function properly if taken apart, besides, young girls are in general familiar with scissors.

2　Song Lian (1310 AD−1381 AD) was an important statesman and renowned scholar of the Ming Dynasty.

3　Bingzhou is the now Taiyuan of Shanxi Province. The Bingzhou scissors boast of a famous brand with a long-standing history.

4　This is a rhetorical question, which expresses the girl's strong wish for the happy union.

165. 旱　The Drought

1　The present poem is taken from Chapter XVI in *Outlaws of the Marsh*, which recounts how the rebels tactfully intercept the precious birthday gifts which Governor Liang of Daming Prefecture has prepared for his father-in-law — Cai the Premier. Bai Sheng, one of the rebels who has disguised himself as a wine vendor, hums the poem when he approaches the convoy of birthday gifts. By bringing out a striking contrast between the attitude of the farmers and that of the scions towards the serious drought, the poem reflects the sharp class contradiction of the time.

　　Some researchers believe that *Outlaws of the Marsh* was written by Shi Nai'an in collaboration with Luo Guanzhong, another famous writer of the early Ming Dynasty.

2　Shi Nai'an (1296 AD?−1370 AD?) was an important writer of the early Ming Dynasty. In light of the epitaph written by Wang Daosheng of the Ming Dynasty, which is recorded in *The Sequel of General Records of Xinghua County*, Shi was from Suzhou. Since he obtained his official candidature at the age of thirty-five, he had held an official position in Qiantang (the now Hangzhou) for two years and then abdicated the post to engage himself in writing in his hometown. He moved to Xinghua County in his later years.

Shi's representative work is *Outlaws of the Marsh*, a classic in rebellion literature. It tells how one hundred and eight heroes and heroines lead the outlaw army in the courageous and resourceful struggle against the tyrants. It presents a vivid picture of Chinese society in the Reign of Emperor Huizong of the Song Dynasty, with all the characters coming across "as distinct personalities, convincingly and in depth" (Sidney Shapiro: Translator's Note to *Outlaws of the Marsh*). In terms of its ideological content, it is a direct challenge to the feudal concepts that the monarch is the Son of Heaven and that people should give an unquestioning obedience to his authority no matter how he may take his own course.

3　The sun is scorching like a devastating fire — This short poem features specification and figures of speech. In this line, for example, "scorching" is a specific word, and "like a devastating fire" is a case of simile.

166. 岳王墓　The Tomb of Yue Fei

1　Gao Qi (1336 AD—1374 AD) was from Changzhou, i.e. the now Suzhou. In 1369 AD he was called on to compile *History of the Yuan Dynasty* and in the next year he received the title of National Historian at the Imperial Academy. He was killed by the emperor for the writing of a satiric poem.

　　Learned and talented, Gao is reputed as one of the Four Talents of Wu (the other three being Yang Ji, Zhang Yu and Xu Ben). He is one of the prominent poets of the Ming Dynasty. Some of his poetry reflects people's sufferings and eulogizes the unification of the Ming Empire in a fresh, vigorous and beautiful style.

　　In the present poem, Gao expresses his conception of history and his standards of love and hate by cherishing the memory of the national hero — Yue Fei.

2　No branch ... towards the north — Trees in general tend to slant slightly towards the southeast for sunlight. Here the poet aptly employs this phenomenon and makes the trees at the tomb an embodiment of Yue Fei's unyielding spirit in face of the ferocious invaders from the north and utter devotion to his nation.

3　Here "eternal wrath" denotes great righteous anger of the populace through the ages, which is induced by the injustice done to the hero.

4　Though imperial edicts ... for retreat — In 1140 AD, the army under Yue

Fei's command won sensational victories over the Jin invaders, which stimulated the morale of the nation. The capitulation-oriented Emperor Gaozong and his prime minister Qin Hui, however, ordered Yue to withdraw. They issued twelve edicts for that purpose within a day's time.

5　to avenge th' throne and th' foe to defeat — to avenge the two emperors (who had been captured by the invaders) and to defeat the foe.

6　th' Supreme Sword — In ancient times, the Supreme Sword (or Sword of State) was the token of absolute power authorized by the throne. Here the Sword is the metonymy for military power to resist invasion.

7　'Tis shameful ... scheme! — It is shameful that the emperor had prepared invented charges against the meritorious hero.

8　White Dew — one of the twenty-four solar terms.

9　... only to find the Song Tombs cast out of view —... only to find that the Song Tombs, in which emperors of the Song Dynasty lie, have sunk into obscurity.

Sima Qian (135 BC?–?) says: "Though death befalls all men alike, it may be weightier than Mount Tai or lighter than a feather." In people's mind's eye, Yue Fei's death is certainly weightier than Mount Tai, whereas that of the fatuous emperors' is lighter than a feather.

167. 石灰吟　Ode to the Limestone

1　The present poem was written in 1414 AD, when the poet was seventeen. By eulogizing the fine qualities embodied in the limestone, the poet expresses his outlook on life and his noble sentiments of self-sacrifice, dauntlessness and devotion to the pursuit of what's true, good and beautiful. It is allegoric: the limestone is personified, and the mining, burning and pulverizing symbolize the ordeal he has to go through in the course of realizing his ideal — as far as the poet is concerned the betterment of the world.

Laocius says, "The zenith of benevolence may be likened to water, which purports to favour all life without vying for self-interest." The poet's life is the earnest practice of that benevolence.

2　Yu Qian (1398 AD–1457 AD) was from Qiantang (the now Hangzhou). He obtained his official candidature in 1421 AD, after which he was successively appointed Official Supervisor in the Official Supervisory Bureau, Vice Minister of War. He had taken measures to relieve the people of stricken areas, redressed mishandled cases, led the armed

550

forces and civilians of the capital in the successful campaign against the Mongol aggression and carried out military reforms to enhance the combat effectiveness of the army. When Emperor Yingzong was captured by the Mongolian invaders, Yu, who was opposed to the proposition of moving the capital to the south, had supported the crowning of Emperor Jingdi. In 1457 AD, when the dethroned Yingzong restored his authority by means of a coup d'etat, Yu was given the bad name of treason and killed.

Yu is better known as an honest and capable statesman than as a poet. However, his poetry is highly commendable for its content and conception. In contrast with the "Courtly" poems, which tends to present a false picture of prosperity and stability, Yu's poetry expresses the poet's lofty and beautiful sentiments and reflects the rulers' cruel oppression and exploitation of the people.

3 For 'tis your wish ... pure and white! — For it is your aspirations to contribute to the human world by adding to it something pure and valuable! The colour white symbolizes moral goodness, i.e. noble-mindedness.

168. 双调·清江引　Needless to Say — To the Double Tune of "The Limpid Stream"

1 The present song-poem satirizes the filthiness of the officialdom. The language is vivid and vernacular.

2 Feng Weimin (c.1511 AD–c.1580 AD) was from Lingqu of Qingzhou, i.e. Lingqu of the now Shandong. By and large his poems, which cover a wide range of subjects, expose the corrupt government, satirize the ways of the world and reflect the plight of farmers. They are vivid, forcible and colloquial.

3 The black-gauze hat is the metonymy for an official position.

169. 登盘山绝顶　An Ascent to the Summit of Mount Pan

1 Qi Jiguang (1528 AD–1587 AD), a famous patriotic general of the middle Ming Dynasty, was from Dengzhou (the now Penglai County of Shandong). He started his military career from the hereditary position of commander of the Dengzhou garrison. For his unusual talent he was successively promoted to the position of commander of a military subarea in Zhejiang, commander plenipotentiary of Fujian, and

commander in chief of the army stationed in Jizhou (with the concurrent authority over the troop training affairs of Jizhou, Changzhou, Liaozhou and Baozhou). He had led his army in the successful battles against the pirates known as Looting Dwarfs in the coastal provinces.

Qi is remembered not only for his military exploits, but also for his literary attainments. He has left us some valuable works.

The present poem was written in 1568 AD, when the poet had held authority over the troop training affairs of the four military areas. In it the poet expresses his lofty aspirations to guard the borders so as to maintain the security and stability of the nation. The first four lines describe the rugged frontier life, and the last four lines convey the poet's lofty sentiments.

The Looting Dwarfs refer to the invaders of the 13th−16th centuries who, unlike the Vikings and pirates in Europe, infested the seaside cities of China (such as those in Shandong, Southern Zhili, Zhejiang, Fujian and Guangdong) and Korea in stead of snatching vessels at sea, constituting a serious threat to the local people. So far as Jiangsu and Zhejiang are concerned, tens of thousands had died in the bloody hands of the Looting Dwarfs during that period of time. At the early stage, the looters were mainly from Japan. As they were short in stature, people called them Looting Dwafts.

2　In th' frosty morn ... a shock — The plants are, so to speak, shocked by the thrilling sound of the bugle in such a frosty morning.

　　The thrilling effect of the bugle is exaggerated.

3　Frontier wine's ... north winds — At the frontier the effect of wine is greatly diminished by the cold north winds.

4　To dispel ...'tis my delight — It is my delight to help dispel the cloud of war with my weapon.

　　Here the poet expresses the idea that unjust war can be avoided or eliminated by means of arms. "Halberd" is a synecdoche for "arms".

5　What matters if ... turns white? — This is a rhetorical question, meaning: "It doesn't matter at all if I should guard the borders till I am very very old."

6　For me to follow ... ? / ... by th' Sword-Dance Terrace shine! — This couplet means the poet is to follow the shining example set by General Li, for whose heroic deeds people have constructed the platform on the summit of Mount Pan.

170. 京师人为严嵩语　A Satire Circulating in the Capital on Yan Song

1　The people, who can few be hoodwinked for long, have a natural inclination to expressing their thoughts. They'll air their opinions in secret if not allowed the freedom of speech, and the undercurrent of jokes and satirical poems is capable of undermining any skyscrapers of power.

　　The present rhyme, which circulated in the capital of the Ming Dynasty during the Reign of Jiajing (1522 AD–1567 AD), is a good case in point. Directed at the then tyrant prime minister Yan Song (1480 AD–1567 AD), it accuses Yan's crimes by using the technique of caricature. "One who sows evil will evil reap." Sure enough, Yan was dismissed from office and his properties were confiscated in 1564 AD.

2　knife and saw — metonymy standing for cruel persecutions.

3　The crab is the metaphor for Yan. In Chinese, "to craw / move askew" means "to run rough shod over (somebody)" or "to play the tyrant."

171. 赞花瓦氏征倭语　Song in Praise of Madame Huawa

1　This folk song is taken from *The Encyclopedia of Verse of the Ming Dynasty* (《名诗综》). It sings out people's praises of Madame Huawa (花瓦夫人，1496 AD–1555 AD), whose surname was Qin (岑) in actual fact，for her heroic deeds in fighting the Looting Dwarfs. The style is straightforward and the language is expressively succinct.

　　Madame Huawa was an accomplished Governor of Tianzhou, Guangxi Province, as well as a famous woman general of the Zhuang Nationality (壮族). In answer to the call of the imperial court of the Ming Dynasty, she led an army of 6,800 men to the Jinshan Post of Zhejiang to resist the invasions in 1554 AD (i.e. the 34th year in the Reign of Jiajing). In the battles the forces under her command had wiped out more than 4,000 invaders.

2　This is a case of simile, which likens the men under the lady's command to eagles and the Looting Dwarfs to snakes.

172. 五人墓　The Tomb of the Heroic Five

1　This poem is related to a notorious event, of which a brief account is as follows:

　　In 1626 AD, when the powerful eunuch Wei Zhongxian sent his secret agents to arrest Zhou Shunchang, member of the Donglin Party that was opposed to the eunuchs' tyranny, the citizens of Wuxian in Jiangsu

Province rose up in struggle against the perverse act. The struggle was cruelly suppressed, and consequently Zhou was tortured to death in jail, and five participants laid down their lives. The next year, Wei was sentenced to death for his heinous crimes and the name of Zhou and the heroic five rehabilitated, thus people tore down the temple built as a tribute to Wei and buried the remains of the heroic five in its place.

The present poem warmly extols the worth of the martyrs' lives in a concise and vigorous style.

2　The poet was from Changzhou, i.e. the present Suzhou. According to *The Encyclopedia of Verse of the Ming Dynasty*, Lin's "poetic works had been numerous, unfortunately only a few remain extant."

3　People come ashore specially to pay tribute.

173. 秋日杂感　Reflections in Autumn

1　In the present poem, the poet condemns the conquerors for the devastation and mourns the fall of the Ming Empire in a solemn and compassionate style.

2　Chen Zilong (1608 AD−1647 AD) was from Huating of Songjiang, now the Songjiang District of Shanghai. After he obtained official candidature in 1637 AD he was appointed as a staff member of the Supervisory Department under the Ministry of War. To remedy the crisis — ridden Ming Empire he founded the Hope Society, which in time merged into the Renaissance Society. After the fall of Nanjing he organized armed struggles against the Qing Conquerors first in Songjiang and later in the Taihu region. He took his own life when defeated.

Chen was a prominent poet of the late Ming Dynasty. His poems, "elegant and vigorous, excels the other contemporary compositions," as is pointed out by Wu Weiye (1609 AD−1671 AD), important writer of the early Qing Dynasty.

3　This line alludes to Zhang Heng's *Fu-Poem of the Western Capital*, which relates that in His tipsiness Providence bestows the territory of Chunshou（鹑首）on the State of Qin.

4　to bury grief — a metaphoric expression

5　This line alludes to the historical event that, after the fall of the Qin Empire, the Marquis of Dongling（东陵侯）was reduced to the status of a gourd grower. Here "marquises" is used as an antonomasia denoting high-ranking ex-officials of the Ming Dynasty.

174. 别云间　Farewell, Yunjian!

1　Xia Wanchun (1631 AD−1647 AD) was from Huating of Songjiang, the now Songjiang District of Shanghai. At the age of fourteen he followed the lead of his teacher Chen Zilong, who advocated and initiated armed resistance against the Qing conquerors. When the resistance was suppressed, he carried on his anti-Qing activities in the lower reaches of the Yangtze River. He was arrested and killed by the conquerors.

Mencius says: "He is a true man of moral integrity who's not to be corrupted by wealth and rank, not to be swayed by poverty and humbleness and not to be subdued by force and power." Xia, who has composed a stirring song of beautiful personality with his short but brilliant life, is entitled to the honour of such a man.

Xia's poems, included in *The Complete Works of Xia Wanchun*, express the beautiful sentiments of an ardent patriot in a vigorous style.

The present piece is taken from the poet's *Drafts of a Prisoner*, a collection of poems written after his arrest. Like the other poems of his later period it is filled with grief, indignation and militancy.

2　I have been ... years — The resistant forces sustained an irretrievable defeat around the year 1645 AD, since which the poet had lived a wanderer's life before he was arrested in his hometown in 1647 AD.

3　And now ... wear. — And now I've been taken prisoner.

To wear the Southern Hat, which means to be a prisoner, is a case of metonymy derived from an anecdote of the Warring States period. When Zhong Yi of the State of Chu was taken prisoner and brought before his presence, the Marquis of Jin asked: "Who is the man tied up and wearing a southern hat?" The official in charge answered that he was a prisoner. From then on the "Southern Hat" has become a metonymy for "prisoner".

4　And mourn ... lair. — And I'm deeply grieved that the world has been dominated by the enemies, who are as savage as beasts.

5　I'm conscious ... near, — I know that I'll be put to death soon.

The Yellow Spring is a euphemism for death or hell.

6　And 'tis hard ... me; — And I can't bear to bid farewell to my hometown.

7　But then ... /... in high glee!　— But I'm confident that, when my soul returns to this world, I'll be able to see with great delight the sacred banners of resistance fluttering in the air!

This concluding couplet actually means that the poet is convinced that the just cause of resistance will be victorious after his death.

Chapter Eight   Poetry of the Qing Dynasty

Introductory Remarks

The Qing Dynasty (1644 AD–1911 AD) marked the last phase of feudalism. The ruling clique of the Man nationality, who had snatched the throne by force, now began to exact submissive obedience by savage cruelty. Emperor Shunzhi decreed in 1645 AD that people of the other nationalities should abide by the Man custom of wearing plaits within the time limits, otherwise would be decapitated without mercy. They had executed the notorious literary persecution known afterwards as "Jail for Men of Letters" from the beginning to the end. It's estimated that over 10,000,000 files, archives and documents of the Ming Dynasty have been destroyed, that apart from those censored, 13,600 classic totalling 150,000 copies had been burned up merely in the Reign of Qianglong, and that there had been over 200 accusations and lawsuits brought about by literary offensives, in which many were sent to jail or killed.

The 3,503 classics totalling 79,337 volumes, which had passed the censorship, were put into *The Complete Library of Four Categories*. As luck would have it, a small number of extinct classics (such as *Call to Arms against the Man Conquest*, *Sketches about the Yangzhou Massacres*, and *Brief Accounts of the Massacres in Jiading*) were found extant in other countries (e.g. Japan) later.

The perversity of the Qing Dynasty had invited the foreign powers to share Chinese territory, incurred the signing of unfair treaties, and at the same time paved the way for the bourgeois democratic revolution, which put an end to the semi-colonial feudal society.

Notwithstanding, Neo-Confucianism and cosmology continued to develop, and in their reflections and criticisms of the past, such famous thinkers as Gu Yanwu (1613 AD–1682 AD), Huang Zongxi and Wang Fuzhi (1619 AD−1692 AD) had put forth their own ideas, thoughts and theories and established their own logical systems, of whom some showed concern over the ultimate significance of life. Meanwhile textology, which came into being in the Ming Dynasty, had reached its prime owing to the pains-taking efforts of such erudite and prolific scholars as Dai Zhen (1724 AD−1777 AD), Zhang Xuecheng (1738 AD−1801 AD) and others.

In the early Qing Dynasty, the nationalists who found it hard to accept the reality of the Qing Conquest, wrote stirring poems to mourn the fall of the Ming Empire and to express their ardent love for their nation. The most important among them were Gu Yanwu, Wang Fuzhi and Qu Dajun (1630 AD−1696 AD). In the field of poetic theory, Wang Shizhen (1634 AD−1711 AD) advanced the idea of implicit charm, which had produced a far-reaching influence on the development of Qing poetry. Living across the Ming and the Qing Dynasties, the ignored but prolific Li Yu, whose poetry amount to 838 pieces, flied his own colours.

In the middle of the dynasty, Shen Deqian (1673 AD−1769 AD) and Yuan Mei (1716 AD−1797 AD) respectively advocated the theories of regular and phonological beauty and of vitality and individuality. They tended to be divorced from reality, though their works were not without originality. On the other hand, such poets as Zheng Xie (1693 AD−1765 AD), Zhao Yi, Jiang Shiquan (1725 AD−1785 AD), Huang Jingren (1749 AD−1783 AD) and Shu Wei (1765 AD−1815 AD), who remained unconstrained by the theoretical trammels, gave their works a deep social significance. Since the Opium War broke out, new and startling developments have taken place. Gong Zizhen, early thinker of the bourgeois reformist movement, successfully reconciled the realities of social and political life with the dreams of romanticist poetry. His poems not only lay bare the social contradiction, but they also express the poet's fervent wish for reforms. Gong's contemporaries, such as Wei Yuan, Lin Zexu, Zhang Weiping (1780 AD−1859 AD) and Bei Qingqiao (1810 AD−1863 AD), also wrote very good poems to expose the evils of the rulers and of the foreign aggressors.

The so-called "Poetic Revolution," i.e. the reform movement of verse, constituted a component part of the bourgeois reform movement. Huang Zunxian was the first important poet who had blazed the trail for the poetic reform movement in theory as well as in practice. His poetic creations, which describe national events, depict exotic scenes and reflect the latest cultural developments in foreign countries, represent the highest attainment of the poetic reform movement. Among the important poets of the time were Kang Youwei, Liang Qichao (1873 AD−1929 AD), Tan Sitong, Yan Fu (1853 AD−1921 AD), Jiang Zhiyou (1865 AD−1929 AD) and others.

During the Bourgeois Democratic Revolution, progressive poets emerged in large numbers and verse became an effective weapon against feudalism. Representatives of those poets (and poetesses) were Qiu Jin, Zhang Binglin (1869 AD−1936 AD), Liu Yazi (1887 AD−1958 AD) and others. Their poems expose the corruption of the Qing Dynasty, advocate revolution and express their beautiful sentiments in varied and effective styles.

It would be a shame not to acquaint the reader with the *fu*-poetry — an important genre in Chinese literature derived from *The Verse of Chu,* which had reached its zenith in the Han and the Tang Dynasties, hence a few pieces are included in this anthology.

The brilliant developments of verse in the Qing Dynasty once again bespeak the infinite vitality of Chinese poetry.

Songs of Weal and Woe

175.天仙子·示儿辈

李渔

少小行文休自阻，
便是牛羊须学虎。
一同儿女避娇羞，
神气沮，
才情腐，
奋到头来终类鼠。

莫道班门难弄斧，
正是雷门堪击鼓。
小巫欲窃大巫灵，
须耐苦，
神前舞，
人笑人嘲皆是谱。

Song of Immortals — To My Children[1]

Li Yu[2]

About learning to write why should you hesitate?

E'en if born cattle th' tiger you should imitate.

Once timid and shy you in your childhood become,

You will just grow up to find

Yourselves dull in taste and dumb.

Your spirits ebbing, with th' rats you'll be of a kind.

In applying your ax 'fore Lu Ban[3] there's nothing wrong;

At th' door of th' Thunder God just beat the drum and th' gong.

To learn from th' wizard no pains should you ever spare.

Just keep on dancing ere th' shrine

And observe th' tricks with great care:

In what evokes cheers and sneers lies what makes you shine.

176. 鸡鸣赋

李渔

鸟之以声事人者众矣！要皆进谀献媚之口，非震聋启聩、助勤警怠之音也；惟鸡则不然。前人之于禽鸟，自凤鸾之大以及燕雀之微，莫不有赋，独鸡不及焉。惟浩虚舟有《木鸡赋》，是赋不鸣之鸡，非鸣鸡也；宋言有《鸡鸣度关赋》，亦匪赋鸡，赋人而鸡者也；皇甫湜有《鹤处鸡群赋》，是欲尊鹤而抑鸡，意不在鸡而在鹤也。予欲特书其功，以补前人之未逮，或曰："贱物耳！焉用赋之？"予曰："匪贱也，为多屈耳。使天能爱宝，偶然一生，则在外必贡于朝，在内必献中国，能使神鹤失灵而凤凰不得称瑞者，必是物也。贱云乎哉！"赋曰：

Ode to the Dawn Announcer[1]

Li Yu

Most birds incline to cater to the needs of men, cooing and twittering merely for the sake of favour, without the slightest intention to hint, to warn or to advise. The only exception is perhaps the rooster. However, unlike the other fowls — from the gigantic phoenix to the petty swallow, it remains snubbed, deprived of any claim to a song of praise.

Undeniably, there are *Ode to the Wooden Rooster* written by Hao Xuzhou, *Ode to the Escapees from the Pass by Mimicking Crowing* composed by Song Yan, and *The Crane amid a Host of Chickens* intoned by Huangpu Ti; but equally undeniably, what the first lauds is the rooster that cannot crow, what the second extols is the men who imitated the crowing of the rooster, and what the third praises is the crane rather than the rooster, which is conventionally to be tarnished beside the former.

Therefore, I feel compelled to compliment the rooster on its merits and thus make up for the sorry ignorance. People may ask, "What sense would it make to speak for such an unworthy thing as the rooster?" My answer will be: "Not that it is unworthy, but that it is unjustly treated. If the world had cherished what is really valuable, it would have for sure

咏
情
言
志

566

鸟名近百，
羽族盈千。
或以瑞者，
或以灵传；
或贵形体，
或珍羽翰；
或以好音饰听，
或以美色娱观。
以色事人者，
无足论矣；
以音悦众者，
试取衡焉。
鸦善鸣凶，
人憎饶舌；
鹊能报喜，
情同附热。
雀肺争闹以喧呼，

become the very gift that foreign delegates may present, or the very treasure that the subjects may dedicate to the monarchs, when they pay tribute to the throne. No creature but the rooster can outshine the propitious phoenix and the immortal crane! How can we deem it unworthy?" Hence here goes the ode:

In th' world live a thousand kinds
Of fowls with many a name.
Some are known for their smartness;
Some for auspice gain their fame;
Others for their pretty shapes,
Or for their good-looking plumes.
If void of a silver tongue,
Dazzling looks a bird assumes.
Th' creatures which win favour with appearance
Are beneath our dignity to mention,
And thus on those standing out for their looks
We'll for th' moment focus our attention.

The crow, which chatters to report sad news[2],
Being too talkative, incurs man's hate;
The time serving magpie, which tends to herald
Glad tidings, does ofttimes nauseate.
To make a fuss out of nothing th' sparrow does vie,

蝉不悲伤而哽咽；
莺求人识其巧，
鸠徒自鸣其拙。
深秋畅饮，
何劳鸿雁挑愁；
半夜酣眠，
焉用子规啼血。
画眉以一身兼众口，
多能无补于民；
鹦鹉以禽语作人声，
如簧终难代说。
鹤声嘹亮兮，
亦可有而可无；
燕语呢喃兮，
非难少而难缺。
之数虫者，
空矢好音于听闻，
尽是无功之啁哳。

有功无誉，
谁克当之？
惟鸡为然，
百无一疵。
智能烛夜，

Just like the cicada which, though not sad, inclines to cry.

Th' warbler flaunts its feat in every possible way;

Th' turtledove cries loud, just its dullness to betray.

When men drink to their hearts' content,

Why should th' wild goose choose to pick up plaintive strains?

And while people are sound asleep,

Why does the cuckoo wail to tell bygone pains?

Well, the thrush is melodious,

Yet, what good for the folk does it make?

The parrot's apt at imitation,

Howe'er, it's useless for expression's sake.

Although resonant, no difference

Does th' crane's voice make;

As to the swallow, with too much

Of twittering people it sickens.

To display their tongues, all th' above-mentioned coo and wail,

But th' efforts they make are to no avail!

What bird then, are meritorious

But have never been given praise?

'Tis th' modest rooster, who is flawless

E'en if assessed in all the ways:

Smartly conscious of night's elapse,

The rooster announces th' break of day

信不失时。
一唱百唱，
义无参差。
恋母惟孝，
哺卵惟慈。
克正夫纲，
戒鸣伏雌。
见食呼群，
仁者无私。
遇敌辄斗，
勇始不辞。
食人之食，
司其所司。
有餐非素，
有位弗尸。
守一主兮弗变，
视九四兮如归。
此诚羽族之冠，
而堪为百鸟之师者也。

至其养锐蓄精，
戒之在斗。
致力于宵，
息机在昼。

In a sonorous voice, which is

To be echoed without delay.

Touched by his husband-like way,

She hatches eggs with care and love;

Th' offspring return her with the same.

Th' refrained hen remains soft and tame.

She hatches eggs with care and love;

Th' offspring return her with the same.

Kind, when food is found he invites

His friends to share it in one breath;

And in face of th' foe's invasion,

He will fight without fear of death!

As he lives on man's provision,

In his duty he's never slack.

And for what he had consumed,

He'll for sure handsomely pay back.

Firmly devoted to his sole master he is just great!

Oh, he is really worthy champion and teacher of the fowls!

Moreover, he accommodates himself to his own fate.

As to his conservation of energy,

He must get prepared in case of a fight.

He reconstructs his vitality by day,

And remains vigilant and watchful at night.

Not that he declines th' benefit of sleep,

岂不爱眠，
虑难辞咎。
未醒其躯，
先寤乃味。
振羽待鸣兮若惊，
试音待发兮如嗽。
尔乃形同鹤立，
貌似鹰扬。
一声初起，
万吻齐张。
不军令以严肃，
无国法而纪纲。
初鸣忌促，
利在悠扬；
再鸣忌缓，
韵短声长；
三唱则无烦律吕，
乱鸣而人始彷徨。
惟事万作齐兴，
三农尽起；
朝臣搢笏以趋，
估客束装而徒。
织素缝裳之女，
先盥栉以待明；

But that his sense of duty is strong.

Although not yet fully awake, he tries

His tongue and flaps his wings for th' morning song.

No sooner has he made the starting note

Than his fellows in chorus coo and caw.

Lo, he assumes a posture near to that of th' crane

And th' air of an eagle that is ready to soar!

Caw — cuckoo — coo!

Caw — cuckoo — coo!

The whole world is activated all at once

As soon as he utters the very first strain,

Discipline is carried out without orders,

And without a statute law peace we obtain.

As the first movement is slow in nature,

He's never found hasty in any case;.

Aware that the second movement is quick,

After th' transition he picks up his pace;

And at last, unconstrained in his style,

He stimulates with an easy grace.

He just wants to ensure that all walks of life

Are animated. At his voice people prepare

For farming, animal husbandry and fishing;

Th' courtiers for morn audience hold th' tablets with care;

凿壁囊萤之士，
复焚膏而继晷。
听之起舞者，
史笔特书；
闻以戒旦者，
风人所美。
孳孳为善者舜之徒，
既侧耳以待兴；
孳孳为利者跖之徒，
亦潜踪而避悔。

设天未明，
不由此声；
人将五夜，
视作三更。
举国皆梦，
谁其独醒。
君由之而度失，
臣以此而祸萌。
贾者失其早利，
农夫薄于秋成。
士慵女惰，
蚕死蛊生。

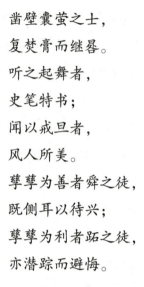

For th' day's mobile trade the peddlers set out early;

Th' women weavers and spinners wash and comb their hair,

And students, kindling their lamps, for reading prepare.

Well, those who at the crowing rise to fence

Have left in history a glorious page,

And th' early birds are by the folk praised.

Like King Shun[3] many a kind-hearted sage

Can't wait to start a new day, and robbers

Such as Zhi[4] flee to avoid the law's rage.

Just fancy what would happen if his position

Th' rooster should fail to maintain!

Men would likely take dawn for mid-night,

And in the dreamland they might remain.

The subjects might thus invite trouble,

And th' monarch lose control of th' domain.

The merchant might miss the chance for profit,

And meager harvests farmers may sustain.

The ladies for sure would grow lazy.

And th' intellectuals become slack.

Consequently silkworms would starve,

And clothes moths would roam pack by pack.

Oh, but for th' rooster there's no way to know when we should

    wake,

世何由而卜昼，
治焉能以励精？

是此一禽者，
为羲和氏之功臣，
神农氏之良吏。
暗司日月之光，
而人不知；
明归造物之功，
而身不与者也。
奈何怒之如贼，
叱之若奴；
偕豕作队，
与犬同呼；
既利其生而致其死，
复食其卵而断其雏也哉！

Still less to encourage th' diligent for the nation's sake!

And thus, it goes without saying that, like the wise Minister Xihe[5]

And the sagacious magistrate to God of Agriculture,

The rooster ingeniously measures the elapse of night and day,

And devotes himself to creation without asking for any pay!

I would at this point venture to question:

What right do we have against him to rave

As if he were a thief? Howe'er can we

Hush him, as if he were merely a slave?

Why should we address him like a poor dead dog,

And even worse, rank him with the foolish swine?

Moreover, how can we kill him at random,

When we should regard him as a creature fine?

And above all, how can we bear to consume

The eggs, which are his offspring in th' direct line?

Shouldn't we to this bird of birds take a shine?

177. 龙灯赋

李渔

何物神龙,
化为祝融。
逃乎水族,
宅于火中。
忽过疑电,
远眺犹虹。
明月失照,
晴霞敛烘。

尔乃笙歌队里,
游群济济。
突如其来,
天矫莫比。
或蟠或伸,
倏行倏止。
群手批其鳞而不怒,
万炬煎其心而不死。

若夫目嗔嗔兮明珠,
尾曳曳兮珊瑚。

Ode to the Dragon Lantern[1]

Li Yu

Oh, you miraculous holy dragon!

How come you turn into Zhurong[2], my sire?

Leaving behind th' other creatures in th' sea,

You have now come to inhabit in fire.

You flash along as swift as lightening,

And th' form of a rainbow you show.

Beside you the bright moon looks bedimmed,

And much more tarnished is the morning glow!

You dance through clusters of men and ladies

In a grand parade of music and song.

With such an energetic grace as is

Incomparable you ramble along.

Now coiling, now stretching, you meander

On in a way without a binding girt.

A thousand hands touching your scales, you are not offended;

A myriad torches burning inside, you won't feel hurt.

Oh, your eyes shine like diamonds and pearls,

And your coral-like tail gracefully sways.

Songs of Weal and Woe

肤寸寸兮冰雪，
甲片片兮琉璃。
行将飞而上天兮，
旦宇宙而不夜；
不则潜而入海兮，
照水国以夺犀。

我将乘其背而周观八
　　荒兮，
虽夜游而无须秉烛；
抑将训扰于石渠、天
　　禄兮，
纵晚较而奚事吹藜。
于时鼓吹雷发，
士女云随。
乐事浓于万姓，
欢声塞乎九逵。
斯游观之最胜，
称人巧之极奇。

重曰：
龙为灵兮灯有明，
明可照兮灵乃祯。
明不察察兮，

Your complexion's as transparent as ice,

And your glass-like scales look like tiles with glaze.

To light up th' cosmos and make it e'er bright,

You take trouble to soar high up to th' skies;

Once you dive into th' ocean, you outshine

Th' rhino's horn[3] and make men open their eyes.

Oh, how I wish I could ride on you and exhaust

The universe, when there's no need for candlelight!

And if I read with you at th' Shiqu and th' Tianlu[4],

There will be no need for a lamp or torch at night.

Oho, the trumpets and drums resound like thunder;

And th' folk, men and women alike, walk in th' band's wake.

Millions intoxicated in the spirit

Of th' festival, earth and skies the hails and cheers shake!

Oh, of amusements this is the most miraculous;

Of inventions this is the most ingenious!

Finale:

The dragon is divine, and the lantern is bright;

'Tis in brightness that divinity gains its might.[5]

Brightness without the slightest excoriation,

灵不矜矜。
斯万物无遁形兮，
四海有休征。
吾愿在天在田之大人兮，
胥体此以加民。

And divinity without the least dictation,

On everything in th' world these will surely shed light,

Which may assure a clear line between wrong and right.

To the mighty on earth and on high I appeal:

Please treat lives in th' spirit that th' lantern does reveal! [6]

178. 好了歌解注

曹雪芹

陋室空堂，
当年笏满床；
衰草枯杨，
曾为歌舞场。
蛛丝儿结满雕梁，
绿纱今又糊在蓬窗上。
说什么脂正浓，
粉正香，
如何两鬓又成霜？
昨日黄土陇头送白骨，
今宵红灯帐底卧鸳鸯。
金满箱，
银满箱，
转眼乞丐人皆谤。
正叹他人命不长，
那知自己归来丧！
训有方，
保不定日后作强梁；
择膏粱，

Explication to *The Song of Rise and Fall*[1]

Cao Xueqin[2]

Incredibly, the humble rooms and shabby hall

Had once been filled with audience tablets and all[3],

And where poplars wither and grasses rankly grow

There had been held many a pompous show.

Covered with spider's webs the painted beams are now seen;[4]

But what used to be a shabby window is hung with curtains

   green.

Didn't the woman oft boast of her buoyant youth with delight?

Alas, her temple hair has so soon turned frost-white!

When he buried the dead yesterday, what sorrowful tears the

   man shed,

And yet tonight he's embracing his bride in the luxurious bed!

Why! In a twinkling one becomes a beggar people scold,

Whose suitcases had been crammed with silver and gold.

O'er th' untimely death of others one had sighed,

Who could imagine that, when he got home, he himself died?

Many a good father finds himself stricken with grief,

For his well-bred son's become a thief;

And one who chooses to marry his daughter above[5]

Ne'er anticipates that she is to be reduced to a soiled dove[6].

谁承望流落在烟花巷!
因嫌纱帽小,
致使锁枷扛;
昨怜破袄寒,
今嫌紫蟒长。
乱哄哄你方唱罢我登场,
反认他乡是故乡。
甚荒唐,
到头来都是为他人作
　嫁衣裳!

Listen, there are still those officials who have spared no pains

To seek higher ranks and who are now in chains.[7]

Yesterday they loathed their ragged coats for their lack of
strength,

Today they dislike their purple python robes for their length.[8]

In chaotic contention they crazily themselves engage;

Hardly have they played their parts when others step onto th'
stage.[9]

How absurd 'tis that the others should, in the final last, use
and wear

The trousseaux which they have exerted themselves to
prepare![10]

587

Songs of Weal and Woe

179. 论诗（其二）

赵翼

李杜诗篇万口传，
至今已觉不新鲜。
江山代有才人出，
各领风骚数百年。

咏情言志

588

On Poetry (No. 2)[1]

Zhao Yi[2]

The poems of Li and Du[3] have long since been in public favour;

Howe'er they have nowadays seemed to lack a novel flavour.

Unusual talents, who appear in every generation,

Will for hundreds of years enjoy their share of reputation.[4]

589

180. 赴戍登程口占示家人（其二）

林则徐

力微任重久神疲，
再竭衰庸定不支。
苟利国家生死以，
岂因祸福避趋之？
谪居正是君恩厚，
养拙刚于戍卒宜。
戏与山妻谈故事，
试吟断送老头皮。

Oral Improvisations to My Family
upon Leaving for the Garrison (No. 2)[1]

Lin Zexu[2]

Sure enough, the vital posts I can no longer sustain,

The posts which, beyond my ability, have tired me out.[3]

What's in the interest of the state I'll do with might and main,

And personal weal or woe is not to be cared about.[4]

Demotion only shows His Majesty's favour[5], and life

In the' frontier will perfectly suit my mortal dim and dull.[6]

Let me, on leaving, retell a story to my dear wife

And read aloud the poem therein 'bout "forfeiting th' old

    skull"[7].

181. 己亥杂诗
（其一百二十五首）

龚自珍

九州生气恃风雷，
万马齐喑究可哀。
我劝天公重抖擞，
不拘一格降人才。

592

Miscellaneous Poems (No. 125)

Gong Zizhen[1]

'Tis lamentable when millions of horses never neigh[2]:

For in th' winds and thunder national vitality lies.[3]

May you, my Providence, exert yourself once more, I pray,

And send down talent of diversified types from the skies!

182. 江南吟十章（效白香山体）（其八）

魏源

阿芙蓉，阿芙蓉，
产海西，来海东。
不知何国香风过，
醉我士女如醇醲。
夜不见月与星兮，
昼不见白日，
自成长夜逍遥国。
长夜国，莫愁湖，
销金锅里乾坤无。
涸六合，迷九有，
上朱邸，下黔首，
彼昏自瘤何足言，
藩决膏殚付谁守？
语君勿咎阿芙蓉，
有形无形瘾则同：

Intonations in the South — In the Style of Bai Xiangshan's Namesake (No. 8)[1]

Wei Yuan [2]

Opium, opium! What a product of the west!

Across the ocean to the east it comes;

Like an intoxicating wind sweeping over

The land, our men and women alike it benumbs.

Indulging in th' kingdom of hallucination,

For nothing else at all will the addicted care.

Their eyes bedimmed cannot see the constellations

At night, and by day e'en of th' sun they aren't aware.

During their endless night,

On shore of th' Careless Lake[3],

O'er th' gold-consuming pot[4],

The whole world they'd forsake.

Not a few, from the nobles down to th' common folk,

Have fallen victim to the atrocious drug's lure.

Moreo'er, when th' state's vigour and treasury are sapped,

However can the Nine Domains remain secure?

Of course, opium's by no means the only thing to blame,

For there are still invisible drugs whose effect is th' same:

边臣之瘾曰养痈，
枢臣之瘾曰中庸，
儒臣鹦鹉巧学舌，
库臣阳虎能窃弓。
中朝但断大官瘾，
阿芙蓉烟可立尽！

Influential officials' faith in th' doctrine of the mean [5],

Frontier commanders' appeasements to the ferocious foe,

Pedantic officials' awful practice of parroting

And treasurers' likeness to Yang Hu [6], who stole th' state-

   owned bow.

Provided those "addictions" on the top are relinquished,

Pretty soon will opium be easily extinguished!

183. 述志诗

洪秀全

手握乾坤杀伐权，
斩邪留正解民悬。
眼通西北江山外，
声振东南日月边。
展爪似嫌云路小，
腾身何怕汉程偏。
风雷鼓舞三千浪，
易象飞龙定在天。

Intonation of My Aspiration

Hong Xiuquan[1]

Predominating power once I hold over the state,[2]

I'll cherish virtue, purge vice[3] and change people's adverse
   fate.

The northwest beyond mounts and streams cannot escape my
   eyes;[4]

My roar will shake the southeast where the sun and th' moon
   arise.

The sky will be too narrow if my limbs are in full play[5],

When soaring I'll defy the twists and turns of th' Milky Way[6].

The dragon, as foretold by *th' Book of Changes*, will in th' vault

Of heaven appear, calling forth storms, waves and thunderbolt![7]

184. 书愤（其一）

黄遵宪

一自珠崖弃，
纷纷各效尤。
瓜分惟客听，
薪尽向予求。
秦楚纵横日，
幽燕十六州。
未闻南北海，
处处扼咽喉。

Indignation Written Down (No.1)[1]

Huang Zunxian[2]

Ever since the abandonment of the "Pearl Bluff,"[3]

The other powers[4] swarm east in th' fore-goer's wake.

With an insatiable desire for concessions,

Our territory they carve up at will and take.

Chaos of th' Warring States Period there had been;

Sixteen You-Yan regions' cession history's seen.[5]

Howe'er, ne'er have there been so many cut-throat posts

Stationed by aliens along our homeland's coasts!

185. 过虎门

康有为

粤海重关二虎尊，
万龙轰斗事何存？
至今遗垒余残石，
白浪如山过虎门。

Crossing the Tiger Gate[1]

Kang Youwei[2]

At the coastal post the Tigers[3] still with dignity stand,

But what remains of the sight where once boomed the "dragons

grand?"[4]

Resonating with the mountainous waves I find my thoughts

When crossing th' Tiger Gate: the ruins used to be the forts![5]

186. 狱中题壁

谭嗣同

望门投止思张俭，
忍死须臾待杜根。
我自横刀向天笑，
去留肝胆两昆仑。

An Inscription on the Wall of the Jail[1]

Tan Sitong[2]

Some seek asylum like Zhang Jian[3] within many a gate;
While others bear th' ordeal like Du Gen[4] and for a chance
   wait.
Holding my sword crosswise I laugh to the skies, inspir'd that,
Like th' Kunlun Mounts, th' two types of comrades are equally
   great!

187. 黄海舟中日人索句并见日俄战争地图

秋瑾

万里乘风去复来，
只身东海挟春雷。
忍看图画移颜色，
肯使江山付劫灰！
浊酒不销忧国泪，
救时应仗出群才。
拼将十万头颅血，
须把乾坤力挽回！

A Poem Composed on Board the Ship[1]

Qiu Jin[2]

After a brief stay, ere th' wind I now come anew;
At sea I hear th' fervour in me like thunders roar.
Who could bear to see th' map change its natural hue[3]
And the land burnt to ashes by the flames of war?
Turbid wine ne'er drowns sad tears for our nation shed;
'Tis on rare talents that salvation should depend.
Even at th' cost of ten million heroic heads[4],
We shall resolutely reverse the adverse trend!

607

Songs of Weal and Woe

注释　Notes and Commentary

175. 天仙子·示儿辈　Song of Immortals — To My Children

1　"Song of Immortals" is the tune name of the *ci*-poem, while "To My Children" denotes the actual theme.

　　For the healthy mental and physical growth of their offspring, ancient people, especially those of the illustrious families, set store by family education, which is embodied in their clan advice, family instructions or guideline for the younger generation. Of the many examples Zhuge Liang's *Letter of Advice for My Sons*（《诸葛亮戒子书》）, *Family Instructions of the Mao's*（《毛氏家训》）, and *Family Instructions of Zhu the Scholar*（《朱子家训》）are the most popular.

　　The present poem by Li Yu, in which are advocated aspiration, courage, diligence, perseverance, and observance, may be regarded as a mini-letter of advice for his sons and daughters. Here metaphor and analogy are the major means of persuasion.

2　Li Yu (1611 AD−1680 AD), style name Li Liweng, was a literary genius from Lanxi of Zhejiang. He was at the same time a great dramatist, short-fiction writer, essayist, architect, publisher and poet. In addition to his *Random Sketches Written at Leisure* and theatrical theory embodied in a collection of essays, he has left us a handsome legacy of sixteen plays, two collections of short stories, together with eight hundred and thirty-eight poems and over one hundred and eighty couplets, which are included in *The Complete Works of Li Yu*. As part of the cultural heritage of the world, Li Yu's works have spread far and wide.

3　Lu Ban, i.e. Gongshu Ban (c.507 BC−444 BC), a famous inventor who lived from the Spring and Autumn to the Warring States periods. According to *Mozi* (《墨子》), he is worshiped as the Pioneering Master of Carpenters. He is said to have conducted experiments in manufacturing the aircraft.

　　"Applying the ax on the doorway of Lu Ban" is a proverb warning people against showing off in face of the expertise. The anti-conventional poet here encourages his children to learn by laying bare their own weaknesses through practice so that they can get advice or nudges from those who know the business better.

咏
情
言
志

608

176. 鸡鸣赋　Ode to the Dawn Announcer

1　The *fu*-poetry features figures of speech, parallelism and antithesis (the matching of both sound and sense in two lines, sentences, etc., usually with the matching words sharing the same parts of speech) and the juxtaposition of prose and verse; in style, it is characteristic of rhyming, allusion, and extravagant description. It may fall into four variations: the grand *fu*-poetry, the antithetical *fu*-poetry, the metrical *fu*-poetry and the literary *fu*-poetry.

　　Li Yu's *fu*-poetry, as is included in *The Complete Works of Li Yu*, amount to fourteen pieces. Characteristic of humour, naturalness and fluency, they reflect the poet's personality and convey the poet's profound thoughts.

　　In this humorous work, the rooster symbolizes the labourer, who contributes much to the development of human civilization without acknowledgement. The poet, by vividly portraying the image of the rooster, eulogizes such fine qualities as devotion, altruism, the sense of fellowship, and the sense of responsibility, etc., and calls for love and respect for those of low social strata. The poet employs such rhetorical devices as personification (e.g. the personified rooster), and allusion (to Xihe, King Shun, Zhi), etc., to make his creation vivid. As for the onomatopoeia (caw — cuckoo — coo), it is the translator's little trick to make the discourse alive with sound without adding superfluous information to the theme.

2　In Chinese folklore, the crow is a symbol of bad luck.

3　Shun was a wise king in ancient Chinese history.

4　Zhi was a notorious robber in Chinese legend.

5　In light of Chinese legend, Xihe is Chariot Driver to God of the Sun.

177. 龙灯赋　Ode to the Dragon Lantern

1　The Dragon Lantern, a lantern manufactured in the shape of the dragon, is indispensable in the Dragon Dance, and smart men chosen to perform various parts working in harmony to simulate the soaring, diving, plunging or meandering of the legendary animal. The Dragon Dance, as a traditional Chinese entertainment of the Lantern Festival (the fifteenth day of the first lunar month), has originated from the ancient rite to pray for rain, which had come into practice as early as in the Shang Dynasty.

In the present *fu*-poem, the poet not only gives a vivid description of the dragon dance, but he also metaphorically expresses his political ideal in the Finale, i.e., government in the spirit of humanitarianism.

2　Zhurong is God of Fire in the Chinese legend.

3　A legend goes that with a torch of the rhino's horn one could reveal the ghastly looks of all sorts of vampires and demons which were usually invisible, and that Wen Qiao (温峤) of the Eastern Jin Dynasty died from the ghosts' retaliation against him for that matter.

4　The Shiqu and the Tianlu are names of ancient libraries.

5　In other words, the mightiness of anything divine lies in righteousness and justice. According to the poet, divinity and justice should be properly measured and handled so that people can live at ease, and order will reign only when there's a clear distinction between right and wrong.

6　The last two lines embody the poet's social ideal that those in power should show concern for people's livelihood.

178. 好了歌解注　Explication to *The Song of Rise and Fall*

1　The present song is taken from the novel *A Dream of Red Mansions*. It is the explication by Zhen Shiyin (one of the characters) of the lame Daoist's *Song of Rise and Fall*. Through the mouth of Zhen the author expresses his philosophy of life, which is based on the idea of CHANGE, and his attitude towards the reality of the last autocracy of feudalism, in which the conventional morality is collapsing and the conflicts arising from the redistribution of power and wealth are intensifying. In this song profound thoughts are expounded by means of simple terms and typical images. The perfect unity of the refined and the popular demonstrates the author's wonderful mastery of the language.

2　Cao Xueqin (1715 AD?−1763 AD?), courtesy name Cao Mengruan, had an involved family history: his ancestors had been Hans, but later became banner-men of the Man nationality. One of his ancestors came south of the Great Wall with the Qing conquerors and settled down in Hebei. Favoured by the royalty, Cao's forefathers had consecutively held the position of Textiles Commissioner of Jiangning (a prefecture which included the now Nanjing and six contiguous counties). When Yongzheng rose to power in the fierce struggle among the royalty for the claim to the throne, the Cao family began to take a turn for the worse. In 1727 AD, it was charged with the crime of embezzling public funds and consequently Cao Xueqin's father was removed from office and the estated of the family were confiscated. Then the family moved to Beijing, began to show some signs of revival after Emperor Qianlong was crowned but declined again not long afterwards. Later, when he commenced to write the world-famous novel *A Dream of Red Mansions*, Cao Xueqin was reduced to living in poverty-stricken circumstances.

It is beyond the necessity and capacity of this book to give a comprehensive appraisal of Cao's *A Dream of Red Mansions*, a social-political-psychological classic which has survived the times. What can be said here is, it is an encyclopedia of feudal China and a manifestation of human knowledge and intellect. Its meaning is profound and manifold. By recounting the rise and fall of an illustrious family it truthfully reflects the social contradictions of the time, penetratingly exposing the evils of the feudal system and of man himself.

In the novel the author's immense knowledge — his knowledge of medicine, architecture, horticulture, culinary art, and of man and society, etc. — is brought into full play. As far as verse is concerned, the author has achieved such a height of thought and artistry as few other poets of the Qing Dynasty have attained to.

3   audience tablets and all — audience tablets and everything. The audience tablet, required of an important official who was allowed an audience by the emperor, was a symbol of power and social status.

4   Covered with ... are now seen; — The painted beams are now seen covered with spider's webs.

5   And one ... above — And one who chooses to marry his daughter to a man wealthier and/or more powerful than he himself.

6   a soiled dove — a prostitute

7   ... who are now in chains. — ...who are now chained up as prisoners.

8   Yesterday ..., /... for their length. — People are insatiable: When they were poor in the past, they hated their ragged coats for the fact that it couldn't keep them warm enough; now that they've worked their way up from the bottom and become high-ranking officials, they dislike their purple robes embroidered with the image of a python simply because they are too long!

This couplet mocks at the insatiability of officials in the narrow sense, and of men in the broad sense.

9   In chaotic contention ...; /... stage. — This couplet vividly describes the

internal strife of the ruling class.

The " stage" is a pun meaning "theatrical stage" literally and "political arena" figuratively.

10 How absurd 'tis that ... /... to prepare! — These two lines imply that what one does in pursuit of wealth, power and position will be futile and meaningless in the final analysis and that one will only find himself taken advantage of.

179. 论诗（其二） On Poetry (No. 2)

1 The present piece is taken from a group of five poems entitled "On Poetry". It expresses the poet's critical view of the past and optimistic outlook to the future, moreover, it advocates the significance of innovation, on which not only liberal arts but also sciences and civilization depend. Its style is succinct.

2 Zhao Yi (1727 AD–1814 AD) was from Huyang, the present-day Wujin County of Jiangsu. He was an Official Candidate of 1761 AD. The highest position he had held was that of Commissioner of Defence Affairs of Guixi Administrative Region. In his later years he abandoned his official career and engaged himself in teaching and writing.

Zhao was a famous poet and historian. He advocated the theory of originality and evolution in terms of versification.

3 Li and Du — Li Bai and Du Fu

4 Unusual talents ..., /... reputation. — This couplet means that unusual talents, who emerge in an endless stream, will outshine those of the past in freshness and thus are entitled to their share of fame and recognition for their literary excellence.

This couplet has become a celebrated dictum usually quoted to praise or encourage new talent.

180. 赴戍登程口占示家人（其二） Oral Improvisations to My Family Upon Leaving for the Garrison (No. 2)

1 Since the Opium War broke out, Lin Zexu, as a statesman of vision, had written some good poems, which express his lofty patriotic sentiments in a neatly vigorous style. The poet composed some poems impromptu as parting words in Xi'an in 1842 AD, when he, relegated, was leaving for Xinjiang to garrison the frontier, the present poem being the second. It manifests the poet's optimistic outlook on life and noble idea of putting

咏
情
言
志

612

the interests of the nation before anything else. It features a witty style.

2   Lin Zexu (1785 AD−1850 AD) was from Houguan (the now Fuzhou) of Fujian. He entered upon an official career in the Reign of Jiaqing (1796 AD−1821 AD), during which he became an official candidate. He was farsighted, wisely practical and seriously concerned with the nation's destiny and people's livelihood. He initiated significant irrigation and water conservancy projects respectively in Jiangsu, Xinjiang and in the lower reaches of the Yellow River. In the capacity of Governor-General of Hunan and Guangdong he took effective measures to ban opium smoking and trafficking in 1838 AD. In the next year, when he was sent to Guangdong as Imperial Envoy, he ordered the confiscation and destruction over one million kilograms of opium owned by British and American traders; and in the meantime he did what he could to strengthen the coastal defence of Guangdong. In January 1840 AD, he assumed the office of Governor-General of Guangdong and Guangxi. Under his leadership the army and civilians had made Guangdong impregnable to the British aggressors at the early stage of the Opium War (1840 AD−1842 AD). He was dismissed from office in October 1840 AD by the Qing rulers, who were frightened out of their wits and were eager to sue for peace when the aggressors sailed north, capturing Dinghai and threatening Dagu. He was reinstated as Imperial Envoy in 1850 AD, when he was sent on an expedition to suppress the peasant's uprising in Guangxi but died of illness on the way.

    June 26th, the day on which the destruction of opium at the Tiger Gate reached its conclusion, has been designated by the UNGA as International Day Against Drug Abuse and Illicit Trafficking.

3   Sure enough ..., / ... tired me out. — The poet is trying to console his family for his demotion. The couplet means: " I couldn't, even if I had not been relegated, have been able to sustain the important posts, which has made me exhausted." Note that in ancient times the Chinese used to belittle themselves in communication to show modesty.

4   What's in the interest ..., /... about. — I'll do with might and main whatever is beneficial to the state, no matter what may happen to my own person.

5   Demotion only shows His Majesty's favour — The fact that the emperor hasn't imposed a more severe punishment than demotion upon me only shows that His Majesty is lenient enough to me.

Here the poet's tone is subtly sarcastic.

6 ... and life /... dull. — ... and frontier life will suit me well, as I'm bodily weak and mentally unintelligent.

This clause shows the poet's optimism and modesty.

7 And read ... skull" — And read aloud the poem in the story, which is about "forfeiting th' old skull" (i.e. losing one's life).

This is an allusion to the anecdote about the recluse Yang Pu, which goes as follows: When Emperor Zhenzong summoned him to his presence to test his ability in versification and asked: "Has anybody presented you with a poem recently?" Yang answered: "Yes, my wife gave me one upon my leaving home. It reads:

'You won't be able to indulge in wine,
And your fascination with poems will lull:
Now that you are arrested by the crown,
You will for certain forfeit your old skull.'"

Upon hearing this the emperor burst out laughing and let him go.

The poet alludes to the anecdote to cheer his family up and to dispel the sadness is in the atmosphere, which demonstrates the poet's good sense of humour and broad-mindedness.

181. 己亥杂诗（其一百二十五首） Miscellaneous Poems (No. 125)

1 Gong Zizhen (1792 AD–1841 AD) was from Renhe (the now Hangzhou) of Zhejiang. As an official candidate he had respectively been appointed Junior Staff Member of the Sacrifice Rites Department and Senior Member of the Reception Department of the Protocol Ministry. He was one of the pioneers in the reformist movement, who advocated reforms in order to solve internal problems and to resist foreign invasions.

Gong was a man of substantial literary achievement. Overflowing with romantic fervour his poetry by and large expresses his aspiration to pursue the ideal and lashes out at the evils social and political.

The present piece is taken from a group of 315 poems written in the course of the poet's round journey between Beijing and Hangzhou. The poem was composed in Zhenjiang upon the request of the Daoist priests on the occasion of a parading ceremony in honour of the Jade Emperor (the supreme deity of Daoism), of the God of Winds and the God of Thunder. It expresses the idea that the salvation of China lies in a drastic social Change and "talent of diversified types", which and who can

bring renewed vitality to the ancient country.

2   ... when millions of horses never neigh — ... when honest and capable
personnel are suppressed and denied the opportunity to play their role so
that whole nation remains in a state of dead silence.

The "horses" is a case of metaphor for "capable personnel".

3   For in th' winds ... lies. — The vitality of China depends upon social changes.

The "winds and thunder" constitutes a case of metaphor for the
dynamic social forces.

182. 江南吟十章（效白香山体）（其八） Intonations in the South-In the Style of Bai Xiangshan's Namesake (No. 8)

1   This is the eighth piece from a sequence, which was composed in 1831
AD to express the poet's thoughts ad feelings about the state of affairs.
It describes the calamities resulting from opium trade and exposes the
corruption of the officialdom as the root cause of the evil.

2   Wei Yuan (1794 AD−1857 AD) was from Shaoyang of what was to be the
now Hunan. Since he obtained his official candidature in 1844 AD, he had
held several positions, including that of the Prefect of Gaoyou. Wei was a
thinker and poet of remarkable attainments. So far as poetry is concerned,
he ranks with the famous poet Gong Zizhen. Marked with vigour and
distinct imagery, his poems reflect exposes the political evils and eulogize
the people's struggles of resistance against foreign aggression.

3   The Careless Lake, a famous scenic spot, is located in the city of
Nanjing. Here the name is used as a pun.

4   The pot, referring to the apparatus for opium consumption, is a case of
synecdoche.

5   Generally speaking, the doctrine of the mean (which approximately
means neutrality in opposition to radicalism and conservatism) is one of
the basic moral qualities for the pacific harmony advocated by Confucius
and elaborated by Zisi. In the present context it means "inaction for
dodging responsibility."

6   Yang Hu (?−?) was a powerful official of the State of Lu, who stole the
big bow (a treasury bestowed by the Zhou royalty) from the palace.

183. 述志诗 Intonation of My Aspiration

1   Hong Xiuquan (1814 AD−1864 AD) was from Huaxian County of
Guangdong. He had taught in an old-style private school. Inspired

by the bourgeois ideology of the west and the Christian concept of equality, he set up in 1843 AD an association of Christianity through which he enlightened the peasants. In 1851 AD, he launched the Taiping Revolution — the largest of peasant uprisings in China's history — and founded the Heavenly Kingdom (1851 AD–1864 AD) in Guiping County of Guangxi. In 1853 AD, the Taiping army captured Nanjing and made it Capital of the Heavenly Kingdom. The revolution had extended its influence over eighteen provinces, shaking the rule of the Qing Empire to its very foundations. Hong took his own life when Nanjing fell in 1864 AD.

By and large Hong's poems disseminate revolutionary ideas and express the poet's soaring aspirations to salvage the nation. In the present poem Hong likens himself to the dragon, expressing his firm resolution to topple down the Qing Empire and to deliver the Chinese people from the abyss of misery.

咏
情
言
志

616

2　Predominating power ... state, — Once I lay hold of the predominating power over the state.

3　I'll cherish virtue, purge vice — I'll cherish virtuous people and wipe out the vicious elements.

The abstract nouns "virtue" and "vice", which respectively stand for "people of virtue" and "vicious persons", form two cases of synecdoche.

4　The northwest ... eyes; — (Being a dragon) I can see as far as the northwest despite the barrier of countless mountains and rivers.

5　... if my limbs are in full play — ... when I as a dragon bring my limbs into full play.

6　... I'll defy the twists and turns of th' Milky Way — ... I'll make light of the corrupt autocracy of the Qing Dynasty.

It was the belief of a school of astrology of the Han Dynasty that the Milky Way would appear as straight as a stretched string when the land was ruled over by a good and wise monarch. Conversely the monarch was bad and fatuous when there twists and turns in the Milky Way.

7　The dragon ... /... thunderbolt! — As prophesied by *The Book of Changes*, the dragon will surely appear in the skies and bring about drastic changes in the world!

Generally speaking the dragon has a good connotation. It is a symbol for the throne or good luck.

184. 书愤（其一） Indignation Written Down (No. 1)

1 In 1998 AD, Germany forced the Qing Empire into "leasing" to it the Jiaozhou Bay, some other powers followed suit and clawed hold of some important bays and seaports. Those events roused great indignation in the poet, who was inspired to compose five poems, the present being the first.

2 Huang Zunxian (1848 AD–1905 AD) was from Jiaying Prefecture, i.e. the now Meizhou City of Guangdong. He had succesively held the positions of attache at the Chinese embassies to Japan and to Britain, and consul-general first to San Francisco and then to Singapore. After his return from abroad he was appointed Chief-Procurator of Hunan. He took an active part in the abortive Reform Movement of 1898 AD, after which he was relegated to his hometown.

As a representative of the Poetic Revolution, he opened up new realm of conception and wrote in an unconstrained style. His poems reflect the misery of the people, expose the corruption and incompetence of the Qing rulers and condemn the aggression of imperialist powers.

3 This line implies the concession of the Jiaozhou Bay to Germany in the name of a lease. It involves an allusion to an event of the Han Dynasty. Emperor Yuandi intended to send an expedition to the Pearl Bluff to suppress an uprising, but was persuaded into abandoning the scheme. Henceforth the term "Pearl Bluff" has become an antonomasia for "abandoned territory."

4 According to the poet's note to this line, the other powers refer to Russia, Britain, and France, which respectively gripped hold of Lushun, Dalian, Weihai and the Port of Guangzhou as "leased territories."

5 Chaos ...; /... history's seen. — This couplet implies that, as the Qing rulers are by far more incompetent than those of the previous dynasties, the situation confronted with is the most desperate in history. It alludes to:

    1) the chaotic Warring States Period, during which the rivals between the States of Qin and Chu, which respectively adopted the strategies of Breadth-wise Union and Length-wise Alliance; and

    2) the cession of sixteen prefectures to the Empire of Liao in the year 938 AD by the puppet Emperor Shi Jingtang, who, propped up by the forces of the Qidan Ethnic Group, had overthrown the Later Tang Dynasty (923 AD–936 AD) and established the Later Jin Dynasty (936

AD−946 AD).

185. 过虎门　Crossing the Tiger Gate

1　Unlike those written in his later period, Kang's early poems, which are imbued with the spirit of Romanticism, reflect the corruption of the Qing government and the intensification of national crisis, express the poet's political zeal for reforms and condemn imperialist aggression. In the present poem Kang cherishes the memory of the heroic struggle of the Chinese people against the British aggressors, and expresses his indignation at the national traitors. It is written in a crisp, succinct and passionate style.

2　Kang Youwei (1858 AD−1927 AD) was from Nanhai County of Guangdong. He obtained his official candidature in the Reign of Guangxu. Fully aware of the national crisis he petitioned the imperial court for reformation in 1889 AD but was paid no heed to. After the Sino-Japanese War of 1894 AD−1895 AD, he once again submitted a letter to the court proposing reforms, and he established the Association for National Strength in Beijing and a branch of that association in Shanghai. He had a great and growing influence in politics. Later he was recommended to Emperor Guangxu, with whose support the Reform Movement was inaugurated. When the movement was crushed, he fled abroad, to be opposed in due time to the bourgeois democratic revolution led by Dr. Sun Yixian (1866 AD−1925 AD) from the standpoint of a royalist.

3　the Tigers — The Senior Tiger Hill and the Junior Tiger Hill, which form the Tiger Gate.

4　the dragons grand — (a case of metaphor for) the powerful cannons.

To guard against possible British retaliation for the banning of opium, Lin Zexu had taken measures to strengthen the coastal defence, including the equipment of the key posts with guns. When the capitulation-oriented Qishan took over Lin Zexu's position, he ordered the withdrawal of garrisons and the dismantlement of some fortes. Most of the cannons were later destroyed by the British aggressors.

5　Resonating ... / ... forts! — The ruins, which used to be defensive works, evoke my thoughts, which are resonating with the mountainous waves.

186. 狱中题壁　An Inscription on the Wall of the Jail

1　The present poem was written in 1898 AD, when the Reform Movement

was crushed by the diehard conservatives headed by Empress Dowager Cixi. Tan's friends had tried to talk him into fleeing Beijing, but Tan made up his mind to die for the cause he had pursued and was consequently arrested. This poem extols the devotion of the poet's fellow reformists and expresses the poet's lofty sentiments — his optimism about the future and his spirit of devotion. It is rich in allusion.

2   Tan Sitong (1865 AD−1898 AD) was from Liuyang of Hunan. He had a sturdy and self-sacrificing character. After China's defeat in the China-Japan War, he set up the Southerners' Association in Hunan, aspiring to making China strong by means of reform. A radical participant in the Reform Movement led by Kang Youwei and Liang Qichao (1873 AD− 1929 AD), he scathingly criticized monarchism and feudal ethics while advocating the ideals of equality and democracy. He died a heroic death after the movement was suppressed.

Tan's poems are mostly imbued with enthusiasm and patriotism.

3   Zhang Jian — Zhang was an official of the Eastern Han Dynasty. He had impeached the powerful eunuch Hou Lan with the crime of oppressing the populace, for which he was reduced to living a refugee's life. As people respected him for his noble character, they offered him asylum at all risks. Later Hou was sentenced to death for his crime.

4   Du Gen — Du was an official of the Eastern Han Dynasty. He had offended Empress Dowager Deng for petitioning her to hand over her power to the emperor. As a result the empress dowager ordered that he be put in a bag and killed by knocking him against the ground. However, the executioners sympathized with him and didn't actually take his life. When the empress dowager's men came to verify the prosecution, Du pretended to be dead. Later, when the empress dowager was put to death, Du was promoted to the position of Senior Official Supervisor.

187. 黄海舟中日人索句并见日俄战争地图 A Poem Composed on Board the Ship

1   It had so happened that Japan and Russia warred within Chinese territories in 1904 AD for the control of Northeast China, when to the wrath of the people the rotten Qing Empire declared "neutrality." The poetess returned from Japan for a visit with her relatives in the winter of that year, and left for that country again early the next year. As the poetess describes in the note to the title, on the voyage across the Yellow

Sea some Japanese passengers requested that she write a poem. Just then she caught sight of the Map of the Russo-Japanese War, which gave her inspiration for the composition.

2   The poetess Qiu Jin (1875 AD−1907 AD), a well-known heroine of the bourgeois democratic revolution and pioneer of feminism, was from Shaoxing of Zhejiang. Having witnessed the devastation committed by the Eight-Power Allied Forces in Beijing and painfully aware of the gravity of national crisis, she aspired to topple down the feudal system by means of revolution. She went to Japan to pursue her studies in 1904 AD and took an active part in progressive movements. The next year when she returned from Japan, she joined the Society for National Resurrection. In 1907 AD, She was arrested and killed for organizing an abortive uprising.

3   As a rule, when a nation's territory is "leased" or snatched by foreign forces, the colour of the territory in a map will be changed.

4   heads — (synecdoche for) lives

参考文献
References

1. 侯健等：《中国诗歌大辞典》，作家出版社，1990 年版．

2. 季镇淮等：《历代诗歌选》，中国青年出版社，1980 年版．

3. 金启华等：《诗经鉴赏辞典》，安徽文艺出版社，1990 年版．

4. 王　力：《楚辞韵读・王力文集》，山东教育出版社，1984 年版：451-565.

5. 吴祥林：《英诗格律及自由诗》，商务印书馆，1979 年版．

6. 萧涤非等：《唐诗鉴赏辞典》，上海辞书出版社，1983 年版．

7. 周汝昌等：《唐宋词鉴赏辞典》，上海辞书出版社，1988 年版．

8. 卓振英：《华夏情怀——历代名诗英译及探微》，中山大学出版社，1996 年版．

9. 卓振英：《大中华文库・楚辞》，湖南人民出版社，2006 年版．

10. 卓振英：《汉诗英译论纲》，浙江大学出版社，2011 年版．

11. 卓振英：《李渔诗赋楹联赏析》，外语研究出版社，2011 年版．

12. 卓振英：《古今越歌英译与评注》，商务印书馆，2018 年版．

13. 卓振英：《中国经典文化走向世界丛书・诗歌卷五》，外语教育出版社，2018 年版．

14. 包彩霞：《汉诗英译中的互文参照》，《湘潭大学学报》，2010 年第 2 期．

15. 王芳、卓振英：《有关诗词外译的若干探讨——卓振英教授访谈录》，《中国外语研究》2019 年第 1 期．

16. 卓振英：《"官仓鼠"英译》，《大学英语》1991 年第 4 期．

17. 卓振英、刘少华：《论文学翻译中的总体审度》，《韩山师专学报》1993 年第 2 期．

18. 卓振英：《诗歌的模糊性及翻译的标准和方法》，《福建外语》1997

年第 3 期.

19. 卓振英:《汉诗英译的总体审度与诗化》,《外语与外语教学》1997
   年第 4 期.

20. 卓振英:《汉诗英译中的"炼词"》,《外语与外语教学》1998 年第
   12 期.

21. 卓振英:《汉诗英译中的"借形传神"及变通》,《福建外语》2002
   年第 1 期.

22. 卓振英:《楚辞新考五十例》,《新国学研究》, 2006 年第 4 期.

23. 卓振英:《失之东隅, 收之桑榆——对仗英译研究》,《中国翻译》
   2013 年第 5 期.

24. 卓振英:《典籍英译中的形制研究——以〈九歌〉为例》,《翻译论
   坛》2015 年第 2 期.

25. Poirier, Richard & Mark Richardson. (ed.) Robert Frost: *Collected
   Poems, Prose, and Plays*. Literary Classics of the United States, Inc.,
   1995.

26. 李清照"声声慢"英文翻译, 百度文库, 2012-12-30.https://wenku.
   baidu.com/view/79e757e75ef7ba0d4a733b79.html.

27. 中国诗文外译·李清照"夏日绝句", 中诗网·中诗翻译 (9), 2019-
   07-07.http://m.yzs.com/e/action/ShowInfo.php?classid=396&id=6630.

咏情言志

Afterword
Up Hill and down Dale for the
Beauty I Shall Quest

Having staggered on and on for years, my *Songs of Weal and Woe* is now rushing into print, which adds much to the pleasure stemming from the sonorous cracks of academic hard nuts alongside the unhurried footsteps of a freelance programme.

In the first place, I wish to extend my heartfelt thanks to my friends and colleagues for their advice, support and encouragement. I also feel obliged to all those who have in their own ways shielded me from the trap of fame, the lure of fortunes, the shackle of positions, and the acid of privilege, so that I could have had the right mindset, freedom and energy for the endeavour.

In the second, I would consider it the mission of all the sinless people to resist various forms of evil forces so that the co-existence of all the nations and the continuation of civilization are unshakably ensured. As the booklet is dedicated to the sacred cause of world peace, I would like to avail myself of this opportunity to appeal to peoples of the world to stay on the alert for novel corona-virus and racism-based national terrorism, whose phantoms are looming large.

In the third, Prof. Yang Zijian, renowned for his moral integrity and academic attainments, once hinted to me that "A responsible author might write an afterword to brief the readers what he does in addition to why and how he conducts the task." As I've never before offered any afterword, this one might in a sense serve as a delayed response to Prof. Yang's kindness and at the same time make up for my sorry negligence.

"Knowledge is certainly indispensable to an intellectual, and yet morality must be put in command," says Mozi (c.476 BC– c.390 BC) in "Self-Cultivation" (《墨子·修身》). "Of all the virtues of an intellectual, moral integrity comes first," Chen Shou (233 AD–297 AD) agrees in "Biographies of the Xiahous and the Caos" in his *History of the Three Kingdoms* (陈寿,《三国志·诸夏侯曹传》). In light of the teachings of our ancients I have once and again told my students at the first meetings: " Many people come into being to make this world of ours better than ever, others to take some insatiable bites and sucks at the earth and go, and some few, to wage brutal kicks and cuts on the shrine of humanitarianism, leaving behind a stink. I sincerely hope that, for the sake of life's meaning, we shall strive hand in hand to join the first kind." As a teacher one must certainly be true to himself, and thus I've engaged myself in both E-C and C-E translation for nearly half a century, willingly and happily. Why not if one could more or less conduce to the cultural exchanges and mutual understanding among the nations by expanding the living space of cultural heritage?

The summit of Mount Qomolangma lavishes the excitement and sense of accomplishment which the top of a small mound fails to give. In the pursuit of what's true, good and beautiful, one is supposed to " Aim higher and up th' tower take another flight / To hold a vision broader than one thousand *li*," (Wang Zhihuan) and at the same time get prepared for potential hazards and obstacles ahead. "He is in identity with the Ultimate Truth of the universe who remains intact in face of either offence or reverence," Zhuangzi teaches us. Once "The Daphne and Lily Magnolia die / Where weeds and thorny plants grow thick and high," (Qu Yuan), it would be advisable for one to stay firm and optimistic, for the pendulum will yet swing back. It matters not if the hapless birth of a worthy work to a humble pen may sometimes give birth to sneers and smears. Free from the smog of pride and prejudice, the intrinsic natures of either the snubbed or the flattered will come to light.

It is my goal of self-cultivation to attain the qualities required of an honest and competent translator of classics. (Zhuo Zhenying, 2011: 16-23) In this respect, Qu Yuan, who remained unwavering and unyielding in his pursuit of the Beauty despite scorn, ostracism and frustrations, is a paragon. "Unwavering despite the trend, You stand upright in fine array," he sings the praise of the orange tree, and lays bare his strong will to pursue the truth in the oft-quoted couplet " Long long is th' way, but my efforts nothing'll arrest; / Up hill and down dale for the Beauty I shall quest." The great poet's dicta have become a constant encouragement. Ever since I set up the Research Centre for Studies on Classics Translation, two decades have flashed past, and so far the mere steps towards the goal have turned out to be quite rewarding.

As regards the translation of classical poetry, the way is not only long, but it's also bumpy and tricky, which explains why even famous scholars sometimes stumble. For instance, the original clause "遍地黄花堆砌" possesses quite a few English versions, of which some go as follows:

"Gold chrysanthemums, litter / The ground, piled up, faded, dead," (tr. Kenneth Rexroth)

"The ground is covered with yellow flowers, / Faded and fallen in showers," (tr. Xu Yuanzhong)

"The yard piled up all over with yellow blossoms, / Withered and ruined," (tr. Ren Zhiji & Yu Zheng)

"Fallen chrysanthemums piled up on the ground, so withered," (tr. Yang Xianyi & Gladys Yang)

"The ground is strewn with staid / And withered petals." (tr. Lin Yutang)

(ref. https://wenku.baidu.com/view/79e757e75ef7ba0d4a733b79.

html)

As a matter of fact, chrysanthemums, even if withered, do not fall, and the Chinese character "摘" (pluck) in the context implies that the flowers are still on the plants. Just as Du Fu sheds tears "at the sight of flowers fair," so Li Qingzhao is in no mood for the yellow flowers, which serve as a foil to her sadness in the poem. The translators erred, not that they were short of knowledge, but that common sense and logical thinking were absent in the course of translation. In this regard, I myself had stumbled from time to time. For example, unaware of the polyphonic characteristic of "宓", I had wrongly put "宓妃" into "*Mifei* the Nymph" when the correct translation should be "*Fufei* the Nymph" in the context of "Tales of Woe".

In "Conversations on the Craft of Poetry", Robert Lee Frost, who lays emphasis on "sound of sense" and "sentence-sound," defines poetry as "that which is lost out of both verse and prose in translation." (Poirier & Richardson, 1995: 856) On the one hand, as the advances of translation studies have made it possible to reconstruct or compensate for what might have been lost in Frost's times, (Zhuo Zhenying, 2011b: 151-162; 2013: 97-99) I would regard the definition as a warning against the perils and hardships in the job rather than a pretext for inaction or shoddy workmanship; On the other, I believe what Frost says is still true today if the job is done by careless poor translators, but not when conducted by meticulous gifted ones.

In light of the adopted theory, the reconstruction of the structural, aesthetic and ideological entity involves the synergy of the various factors, concepts and methods, specifically speaking, the selection of subject matter, the overall survey, the formulation of the criteria, principle and strategy governing translation, the adaptive employment of English poetics, the choice of words (diction), the logical adaptation, the exploitation of empathy, the application of methods and techniques of versification, the reconstruction of the imagery and stylistic system, the textual, contextual, historical and philological researches, etc. One can't be too careful in handling those issues. As we all know, in industrial production, the more complex the process is, the more value is added. Likewise, the more time and energy are invested in the translation of classics, the better quality the intellectual product will achieve.

As subsystems (components) of the semiotic system of a poem, the metrical factors (e.g. tonal pattern and rhyme scheme, etc.) have their artistic implications, therefore their absence in a translated text will inevitably lead to the collapse of the entirety. (Zhuo Zhenying, 1997: 45-50; Wang Fang & Zhuo Zhenying, 2019: 129-130) It is worth mentioning that without exception classical Chinese poems are rhymed, and it goes without saying that they must be treated as such in translation. Prose paraphrasing, if necessary, is merely a step towards, but far away from, the destination of versified translation. (Zhuo Zhenying, 1997b: 44-46)

The present booklet comprises the bilingual poems and the English para-texts, including the introductory remarks, notes and commentary, which make up the better part. Tough as nails having been the tasks of gleaning historical knowledge, collecting relevant data, translating the poems, analyzing the artistic features, conducting the exegeses, and organizing them into English texts, it's no surprise if a single piece of work should have emerged from piles of repeated revisions and so-called "final" manuscripts.

At any rate, the theory has guided the programme through thick and thin, which in turn testifies the practicality and explanatory power of the theory. In the course of fumbling in the dark, a small torch makes all the difference (Wang Fang/Zhuo Zhenying, 2019 (1) : 128-131) Here are a few cases in point:

a. I previously took it for granted that "枯鱼" should be "a dried fish," just as others still do (https://baike.so.com/doc/5809428-6022229.html). Nevertheless, the concept regarding textual, contextual, philological researches and logical thinking (Zhuo Zhenying, 2006: 104-134) told me that "枯鱼" is ambiguous (in the context "枯鱼竟得攸然逝", it means a fish landed or caught, while in that of "枯鱼之膳", an edible dried fish), and that it would be ridiculous to fancy a dried fish (which is dead and dehydrated) thinking aloud, shedding tears (which is a kind of liquid), taking a move or articulating a sound, thereupon I decided to adopt the substitute "a landed fish," which can still be alive.

b. My previous version for "山重水复疑无路，柳暗花明

又一村" ("I'm at a loss ere chains of mounts and water courses, / When midst willows and flowers a new village does appear") obviously pales beside the present one in terms of diction — at least the substitution of "vista" for "village", which has resulted from the concept related to ambiguous rendering, makes it possible for the translated text to embrace the connotation proliferated in circulation. (Zhuo Zhenying, 1997a: 45-50)

    c. The word "weight", which signifies the objectification of what's abstract (sorrow and despair) in the version for "只恐双溪舴艋舟，载不动、许多愁" is the result of repeated smelting and tempering in light of the concepts concerning diction, empathy and ambiguous rendering, and so are the adoption of the derivative "en-frames" in the line "The window en-frames the age-old snow-clad West Ridge," which makes the scene more picturesque, and the employment of the word "flame" conversed in its part of speech in the line "A twig of apricot flowers is flaming out o'er th' wall," which lends dynamic and chromatic charm to the flowers. (Zhuo Zhenying, 1998: 3-5.)

    d. The reproduction of the deep-level meaning in "生当作人杰，死亦为鬼雄" was the hardest nut to crack in translating Li Qingzhao's "A Four-line Poem Composed in Summer," and I had balked for fear that such words as "ghost" or "demon" might send cold shivers down the reader's spine, and that the poetess's idea might otherwise be distorted. It was the notion of ambiguous rendering (Zhuo Zhenying, 1997: 45-50) that had elicited the originality in the couplet "Be a man of men with mettle while alive, / And a soul of souls even if doom'd to die." (Zhuo Zhenying, 1996: 232) The version might have won the acceptance of Prof. Xu Yuanchong, whose own version appeared in 2000, reading: "Be man of men while you're alive, / Be soul of souls e'en if you're dead! ...." (http://m.yzs.com/e/action/ShowInfo.php?classid=396&id=6630)

e. The previous version of "西江贾客珠百斛，船中养犬长食肉" ("In striking contrast merchants on the west River are worth / One hundred hu of pearls, their dogs assur'd of meat from birth") has been turned into the present one, which is better in that it is more vivid and colloquial, the phrase "silver spoon" being suggestive of the English idiom "a silver spoon in one's mouth."

English proverbs, maxims, idioms, classics and set collocations constitute a treasure house for Chinese-English translation. The reader may easily find out the traces of *Hamlet's Soliloquy* in the English for Su Shi's *ci*-poem "Prelude to Melody of Flowing Waters" in terms of wording and phrasing.

f. As a result of logical adaptation (Zhuo Zhenying, 2011b: 91-99), the coordinate clauses "雀肺争闹以喧呼，蝉不悲伤而哽咽" are rendered into the compound sentence "To make a fuss out of nothing th' sparrow does vie, / Just like the cicada which, though not sad, inclines to cry."

g. "The Voyage" as the title for 《涉江》in *The Verse of Chu* does not bedim beside *Crossing the Rivers* (tr. Xu Yuanchong) or

Crossing the River (tr. David Hawkes; Yang Xianyi & Dai Naidie). Firstly, the poet tells us that his journey covers travelling both by water and on land ("My horses at the foot of th' hill walk at a sluggish pace, / My carriage, howe'er, arrives at Fanglin at last"), rather than crossing just one river or crossing one river after another, and that when travelling by water, the poet sails *along* rather than *across* the rivers; Secondly, as a derivative from the Old French voiage, the noun "voyage" (meaning "journey" in Middle English) tally happily with the deep-level meaning of the title and the text proper. All in all, the version is verified by reasoning, textual and historical researches. (Zhuo Zhenying, 2011: 196-198)

632

h. Studies on the formative factors have prevented me from mistaking "Eulogy on the Martyrs of the State" (Qu Yuan) for a monologue, (Zhuo Zhenying, 2015: 1-6) and "A Dialogue with the Fisherman" for a piece of prose. Moreover, guided by the new findings I have avoided the misinterpretations or distortions of the poet's ideas which might otherwise be committed. (Zhuo Zhenying, 2006: 104-134)

i. "The Rats in State-Owned Granaries" first appeared in *College English* (Zhuo Zhenying, 1991: 78). In the present version, the replacement of "dippers" by "cats" as the vehicle for the tenor (target domain) "rats" not only makes the simile more vivid and suitable, but also creates an internal rhyme; meanwhile the added quotation marks together with the supplemented "I quiz aloud" make the version logical and coherent.

j. *The Verse of Chu* presents a rich and varied literary style corresponding to that of the original, rather than the style of blank verse or that which features a monotonous repetition of a quatrain pattern from the beginning to the end. (Zhuo Zhenying, 2006: 104-134)

Examples as such can be found elsewhere.

Anyhow, efforts have been made so as to see that the tonal pattern and rhyme scheme, or "sound of sense" and "sentence-sound" in Frost's words, are not lost in translation, and that the imagery of the original is properly shaped up. As to the translation of *ci*-poems, the English versions of those under a given tune name are so conducted that they consistently follow a tonal pattern and rhyme scheme of their own, in order that the reader might not be confused.

As it belongs in the research-oriented type, the translation of classics defies impetuosity, self-assurance and mass production out of shoddy workmanship. It would be dubiously stunning if a college teacher should annually churn out one or two books on the average and face the reader without feeling guilt. That's why I often remind myself of the paradox:

An ounce of gold is weightier than ten tons of rubbish.

By the way, it is noticed that certain published texts have been taken as "inter-textual reference" in translation or revision. (Bao Caixia, 2010: 158-161) Frankly speaking, inter-textual reference stands to reason only when the practice is restrained within reasonable limits. Without any evidence of originality, a slightly-altered variant to an alien translation does not justify the manipulator's authorship, otherwise a middle school student could do the job.

Could we presume that the cause in question entails conscience, precision, creativity, logical thinking, common sense and due reverence for cultural heritage, apart from an adequate bilingual and cross-cultural knowledge and a proper mastery of theories and skills? And is it necessary, I wonder, for us translators to conform to the ethics over translation that without manifesting in some way its predecessor as source or reference, any cloned or imitated version should be regarded as guilty of plagiary?

Well, the booklet has witnessed the brow-knitting pains and laugh-tickling gains in the long quest. I hope that it could in some way or other benefit literary devotees, textbook compilers, English or Chinese learners and teachers, cultural researchers, or those engaged in the careers involving oriental studies, corpus linguistics or international communication. As to its actual worth, I'm not in the position to pass judgement — the readers are.

Zhuo Zhenying
January 22, 2021